The Good Times Songbook

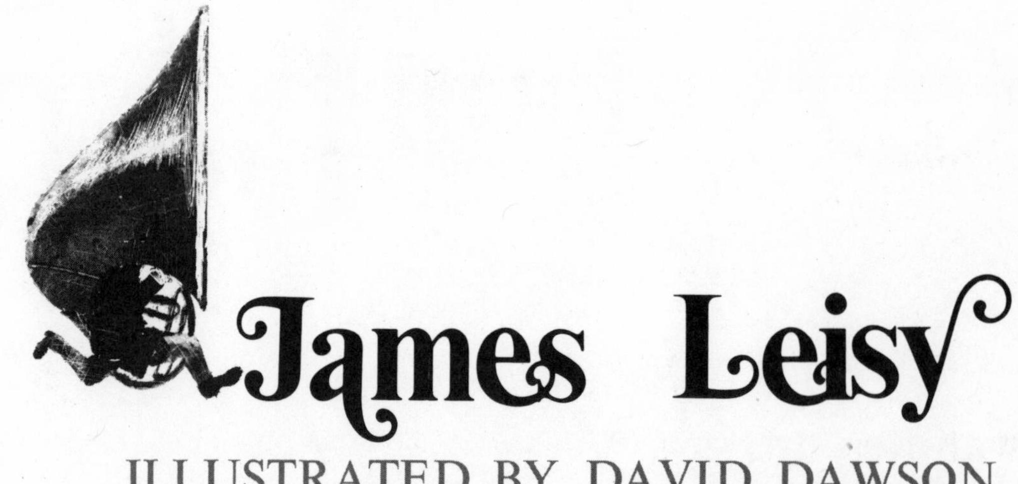
James Leisy
ILLUSTRATED BY DAVID DAWSON

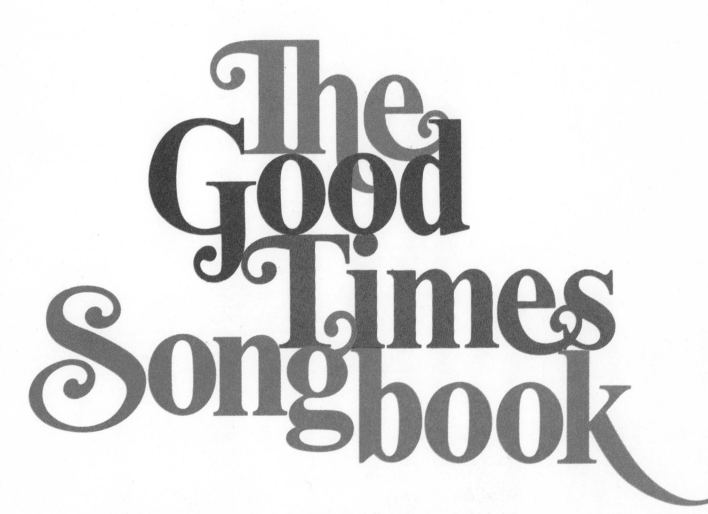

The Good Times Songbook

160 SONGS FOR INFORMAL SINGING

with Resources for Song Leaders, Accompanists, and Singers

ABINGDON PRESS NASHVILLE – NEW YORK

THE GOOD TIMES SONGBOOK

I am indebted to Hawthorn Books, Inc., publishers of my earlier book, *The Folk Song Abecedary,* for permission to reprint some material which appeared in that volume.

Library of Congress Cataloging in Publication Data

LEISY, JAMES F. comp.
The good times songbook.
1. Song-books. 2. Community music. I. Title.
M1977.C5L466 784 73-11248

ISBN 0-687-15573-8

MANUFACTURED BY THE PARTHENON PRESS, AT
NASHVILLE, TENNESSEE, UNITED STATES OF AMERICA

Preface

As a participant and leader of informal group singing, I've often wished somebody would put everything I needed together in one convenient package or system. Unfortunately, physical limitations make that impractical, but I hope *The Good Times Songbook* is a big step in the right direction. I've tried to create a complete, convenient package to serve the varied needs of song leaders, accompanists, and singers. Please bear with me while I, like a proud father, describe all the features of my offspring, and show what it can do for you.

I have included only those songs that have proved successful in a wide variety of informal singing situations, songs that people really enjoy singing. I've excluded those that require more individualistic interpretations or that enjoy only current popularity. Not every song in this collection is everybody's favorite, but everyone should find many favorites here. Furthermore, most of the songs have several facets to their personalities. The more you play around with them, the more interesting they become. They have been selected because of their multi-dimensional attributes for informal group singing.

A brief review of the program guide index in the back of the book will give you an idea of the variety of the songs. You'll find healthy helpings of those songs that work especially well with groups of amateur singers: spirituals, rhythmic gospel songs, swinging folk songs, nostalgic popular songs, Christmas carols, favorite hymns, cumulative songs, rounds, and so on. Whether you are singing with a group of three or four around a living room piano, two dozen folks around a campfire to the accompaniment of strumming guitars, or a hundred or more in a school or church or club auditorium, you should find more than enough variety to keep you occupied entertainingly for as long as you wish. All the songs are suitable for straight unison singing; but most of them are set up so you may do much more with them if you wish.

The Good Times Songbook includes the following features:

1. Complete vocal and accompanist's scores. The accompaniment scores are designed for anyone playing a keyboard instrument or a fretted string instrument, whether he reads music or plays by chord methods. I've tried to keep the arrangements simple but interesting, and stylistically appropriate—using jazz, folk, calypso, hymn, and even chamber-music styles as well as the customary swing-bass, oompah, and

arpeggio styles. The accompanist, however, should feel free to use these basic arrangements as a point of departure for his own improvisations.

2. Information about the source, meaning, idiom, mood, and other characteristics of the songs. This information should be useful to you in planning programs, introducing the songs to your singers, and interpreting and performing the songs effectively.
3. Advice concerning tempos, dynamics, performance techniques, and other matters related to making the performance of the songs more effective.
4. Information about significant lyrical, melodic, and harmonic subtleties that might otherwise be overlooked.
5. Definitions and explanations of unusual words and phrases in lyrics that might not be understood by today's singers.
6. Translations, explanations, and pronunciation guides for foreign language lyrics.
7. Programming suggestions and indexes of songs by programming categories.
8. Simple vocal arrangements and arrangement ideas for leaders who wish to go beyond unison singing. *All* the arrangements and ideas have been used successfully with typical groups of amateur singers ranging from those with no musical training to those who have musical training or experience. Informal singers don't want a music lesson, but they do enjoy adding special touches to their singing through a variety of techniques and special effects. Suggested arrangement ideas include simple harmony parts, descants, ostinatos, solos, calls and responses, imitations, sound effects, percussive accompaniments (handclapping, finger-snapping, foot-tapping, etc.), whistling and humming of choruses, and, in some instances, simple but extended part-singing.
9. Suggestions for changing, adapting, and varying some of the songs for specific purposes, needs, and events are made when appropriate.

As a leader of informal singing, you know that singers get out of a session what they put into it. I've tried to create a resource package that will make it convenient for you to lead singers as far as they are willing to be led. You may use the various features when they are appropriate, ignore them when they are not. You have all the ingredients you need to create your own special arrangement for the performance of each song, tailored by you to suit the talents of your singers and the needs and desires of the moment.

Available separately is an inexpensive singer's edition which contains melody lines and lyrics for all the songs. As in this book, the songs are numbered and arranged in alphabetical order, and pitched in keys that are comfortable for the average voice.

Contents

1

Ain't It a Shame?

Additional lyrics by J.F.L.

American Folk Song
Adapted by J.F.L.

Moderately fast
Clap (continue throughout)
F
Solo
F
Ain't it a shame to beat your
Vamp
B♭
F
All
(Melody in upper notes)
B♭
F
wife on Sun - day? Ain't it a shame? Ain't it a shame?
Solo
F
C
Ain't it a shame to beat your wife on Sun - day? Ain't it a shame?

All
(Melody in upper notes)
C
C7
All
F
F7
Ain't it a shame?
Ain't it a shame to beat your wife on Sun-day?
B♭
F
B♭
When you got Mon - day, Tues - day, Wednes-day;
Oh, ____ you got
F
B♭
F
B♭
F
D. S. 𝄋
Thurs - day, Fri - day, Sat-ur-day; Ain't it a shame? ____
D. S. 𝄋

2. Ain't it a shame to have to work on Sunday?
Ain't it a shame? (Ain't it a shame?)
Ain't it a shame to have to work on Sunday?
Ain't it a shame? (Ain't it a shame?)

Ain't it a shame to have to work on Sunday?
When you got Monday, Tuesday, Wednesday,
Oh, you got Thursday, Friday, Saturday,
Ain't it a shame?

Continue, as above:

3. Ain't it a shame to lie around on Sunday?
4. Ain't it a shame to stand in line on Sunday?
5. Ain't it a shame to eat chicken on Sunday?
6. Ain't it a shame to kiss the girls on Sunday?
7. Ain't it a shame to sing this song on Sunday?
8. Ain't it a shame to say ain't on Sunday?

PROGRAM GUIDE: *American folk song; humorous*

You can bring the audience alive with this rocking, revival-meeting type song. It's an American folk song that pokes fun at restrictive ideas about what should and should not be done on the Sabbath. Its deeper message is a protest against hypocrisy: If doing a certain thing is a bad idea on Sunday, what about the rest of the week?

You want to achieve a camp-meeting flavor and fervor in performance. The tempo should be moderately fast, easy and relaxed—not fast. Let the fervor and drive come from the rhythmic accents of the melody, the syncopation of the words. Handclapping is the easiest way to make it all happen as it should. Get everybody clapping on the first and third beat before you start singing, as indicated in the arrangement. If your group is not familiar with the song, have them clap the rhythm only while you sing the melody through once. For variety you may divide the men and women into two groups for the solo parts (if the subject of the song doesn't do that for you), as indicated on the vocal score. Reverse their roles with each chorus, appropriately (depending on the lyrics).

Things to watch for: The blue note (E^b) in measure 10 (counting from the double bar after the introduction). The stressed, sustained, and syncopated "Mon-" in measure 11. The stressed and sustained "Oh" in the thirteenth measure. Repeat the vamp, introduction, handclapping routine after each chorus to give everyone a breather—while you remind them what the next chorus is and who has the lead. But keep the rhythm (clapping and accompaniment) going while you talk; don't break the spell.

You can enhance the performance by thinking up "shames" by yourself (or by inventing them on the spot with the help of your audience, with a little coaching from you) that are especially significant to your group or circumstances. Who is known for what? What in particular is bugging everybody? What happened today or this week that's news, inconvenient, or funny? It's a shame to get religion, to tell the truth, to brush your teeth, and even to think of shame on Sunday when you have the rest of the week available. But watch out! Don't wear the song or the singers out. Four or five shames ought to be enough for any one session. Don't use them all at one time. Select.

In the arrangement simple harmonizations (the lower notes) have been indicated in the responses (measures 4 and 8 after the double bar). If you have some experienced harmonizers, encourage them to sing these parts.

2

All God's Children Got Shoes

American Negro Spiritual

Lightly
G
1. I got a shoe, you got a shoe, All God's chil-dren got shoes.
G7
C
G
D7
When I get to heav-en, gon-na put on my shoes, I'm gon-na tramp all o-ver God's
G
D7
G
heav-en.__ Heav-en,__ heav-en.__

G7
C
G
Ev-ery-bod-y talk-in' bout heav-en ain't a-go-in' there, Heav-en,—
D7
G
D7
G
heav-en,— Gon-na tramp all o-ver God's heav-en.—

2. I got a robe, you got a robe,
All God's children got a robe;
When I get to heaven, gonna put on my robe,
I'm gonna shout all over God's heaven.
Heaven, heaven;
Everybody talkin' 'bout heaven, ain't a-goin' there;
Heaven, heaven; Gonna tramp all over God's heaven.

Continue, as above:

3. I got a harp, you got a harp.
Gonna play all over God's heaven.

4. I got a crown, you got a crown.
Gonna sing all over God's heaven.

5. I got-a wings, you got-a wings.
Gonna fly all over God's heaven.

PROGRAM GUIDE: *American Negro spiritual*

Many American Negro sermons and religious songs drew inspiration from the Revelation of St. John the Divine. St. John's vivid imagery of the final judgment apparently supplied the symbols of salvation—harp, crown, robe, wings—for this popular spiritual. Whether or not Negroes consciously equated salvation with freedom, as is claimed by many folk-music scholars, the joy of freedom rings out in the theme and the lively mood. The theme coincides, at the least, with the hopes and expectations expressed as freedom approached for the Negroes:

> We knowed freedom was on us, but we didn't know what was to come with it. We thought we was going to get rich like the white folks. We thought we was going to be richer than the white folks, 'cause we was stronger and knowed how to work, and the whites didn't, and they didn't have us to work for them any more.

The song expresses a certainty that those who *live* as Christians will pass the tests of judgment, and it gives a warning for those who only *talk* like Christians.

Set a brisk, two-beats-to-the-measure pace, accompanied by handclapping and toe-tapping for a lively, joyous interpretation. There is no need to depart from a unison rendition, but you can add some very nice harmonic touches if you have several experienced harmonizers among the ladies. If so, encourage them to try these effects on the choruses (in measures 8, 9, 10, 13, and 14):

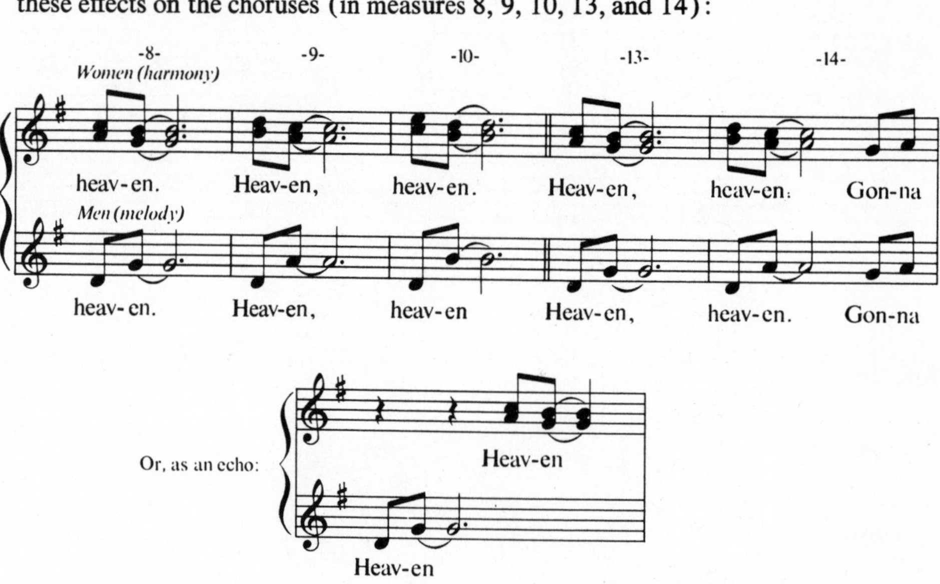
-8-
-9-
-10-
-13-
-14-
Women (harmony)
heav-en. Heav-en, heav-en. Heav-en, heav-en. Gon-na
Men (melody)
heav-en. Heav-en, heav-en Heav-en, heav-en. Gon-na

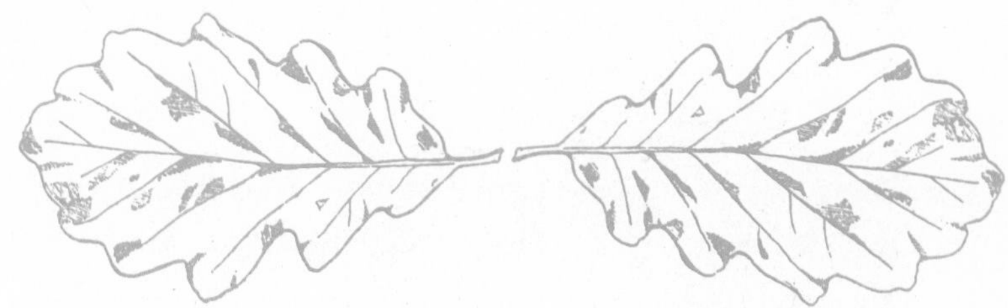
Or, as an echo:
Heav-en
Heav-en

3

Alouette

French-Canadian Folk Song

Brightly
(Melody in upper notes)
G
D7
G
A - lou-et - te, gen-tille A - lou-et - te, A - lou-et - te,
D7
G
Fine
Leader
G
All
D7
Je te plu-me-rai. Je te plu-me-rai la tête, Je te plu-me-rai la tête.
Fine
Leader
All
Leader
All
D.C.
D7
D7 C G D7
Et la tête, Et la tête. Et la tête, Et la tête. Oh,
D.C.

2. Alouette, gentille Alouette,
Alouette, je te plumerai.
Je te plumerai le bec,
Je te plumerai le bec.
Et le bec, et le bec,
Et la tête, et la tête,
Oh-h-h-h

3. Alouette, gentille Alouette,
Alouette, je te plumerai.
Je te plumerai le nez,
Je te plumerai le nez.
Et le nez, et le nez,
Et la tête, et la tête,
Et le bec, et le bec,
Oh-h-h-h

Continue, as above:

4. Le dos
5. Les pieds
6. Les pattes
7. Le cou

PROGRAM GUIDE: *French-Canadian folk song; cumulative; humorous*

This French-Canadian folk song describes the dressing (or, if you prefer, undressing) of a bird (the Canadian lark) for a feast. It's a grisly subject for happy singers to be concerned with, but it never seems to bother anyone. Perhaps the language barrier is a substantial aid in this respect. What we don't know won't hurt us. If your group is squeamish don't translate. Otherwise you might want to tell them, before or after, what they've done to our fine-feathered friend: *tête* is the head, *nez* the nose, *dos* the back, *pieds* the feet, *pattes* the claws, and *cou* the neck.

Use a brisk marching tempo. Encourage everyone to sing boisterously and urge those who can to supply natural harmony, or to follow the harmony notes cued below the melody in the vocal score for the first four measures. You may sing the leader's part yourself, or assign that part to half the group, letting the other half provide the response.

"Alouette" is a cumulative song. The accumulation takes place in the next to last measure, when all the anatomical parts are repeated in the order in which they were previously sung. When all the anatomy has been accounted for, a final chorus is repeated. Thus, the last chorus/verse/chorus routine goes like this:

Alouette, gentille Alouette,
Alouette, je te plumerai.
Je te plumerai le cou,
Je te plumerai le cou.
Et le cou, et le cou,
Et le tete, et la tete,
Et le bec, et le bec,
Et le nez, et le nez,
Et le dos, et le dos,
Et les pieds, et les pieds,
Et les pattes, et les pattes,
Et le cou, et le cou,
Oh . . .
Alouette, gentille Alouette,
Alouette, je te plumerai.

Here is a pronunciation guide:
Alouette: Ah-loo-weh-te(r)
Gentille: Zhah(n)-tee
Je te plumerai: Zhuh tuh pleu-me(r)-ray.
la tete: lah teht
Et: Ay (as in hay)
Le bec: luh behk
Le nez: luh nay (as in hay)
Le dos: luh do (as in oh)
Les pieds: peeay (or, P.A. as in P.A. system)
Les pattes: luh pat
Le cou: luh ku (or, coo, as in bill and coo)

4

Amazing Grace

John Newton | *Traditional, American*

Moderately slow

G G Em

A - maz - ing_ grace, how sweet the

Bm G G(+6)

sound, That saved a_ wretch like_ me!_____ I_

Bm Em G C Am Bm Em

once was_ lost, but_ now am_ found, Was blind, but_

1 - 4.
5.
Cmaj7
D
G
C
G
G
C
G
now I see. 2. 'Twas mine.

2. 'Twas grace that taught my heart to fear,
And grace my fears relieved;
How precious did that grace appear
The hour I first believed!

3. Through many dangers, toils, and snares,
I have already come;
'Tis grace has brought me safe thus far,
And grace will lead me home.

4. The Lord has promised good to me,
His word my hope secures;
He will my shield and portion be
As long as life endures.

5. The earth shall soon dissolve like snow;
The sun forbear to shine;
But God, who called me here below,
Will be forever mine.

PROGRAM GUIDE: *American folk hymn*

This folk hymn has been first in then out of fashion with urban churchgoers, depending on current attitudes toward what constitutes an appropriate cultural expression of their tastes. Its survival is probably due to the artistic merit of the modal tune and the sincerity of the message. The words were written in 1789 by John Newton. The song appeared in 1835, in William Walker's *Southern Harmony,* a popular shape-note hymnal (now available in reprint). Shape notes were once widely used as an aid to music reading. The shape of the note designated a particular pitch. Since both shape notes and shape-note singers are in short supply these days, your singers might appreciate a brief rehearsal if they are not familiar with "Amazing Grace." An easy and effective way to incorporate a rehearsal into the performance itself is to let your accompanist (guitar or piano or both) play the melody one time solo; then have the singers hum it softly; then begin singing the verses with accompaniment—all without pausing for discussion once you are underway. This arrangement can be so effective your singers may never let you do it differently thereafter. You may also add another soft humming chorus at the end. (If a singer cannot hear the accompaniment clearly he's humming too loud.) The tempo should be moderate to moderately slow, with accents on the first and third beat.

5

America

Samuel Francis Smith | *Traditional, European*

Moderately slow

F Dm Gm C F Dm Gm F C♯o7 Dm

1. My coun - try, 'tis of thee, Sweet land of lib - er - ty,

Gm F C F F Fmaj7 F6 F C7 F C7 C9 Gm7

Of thee I sing; Land where my fa - thers died, Land of the

C7 Dm7 C F B♭ B♭m F C7 F B♭ F C F

pil - grims' pride, From ev - ery moun - tain-side Let free-dom ring!

(C)

2. My native country, thee,
Land of the noble free;
Thy name I love:
I love thy rocks and rills,
Thy woods and templed hills;
My heart with rapture thrills,
Like that above.

3. Let music swell the breeze,
And ring from all the trees
Sweet freedom's song;
Let mortal tongues awake;
Let all that breathe partake;
Let rocks their silence break,
The sound prolong.

4. Our fathers' God, to thee,
Author of liberty,
To thee we sing.
Long may our land be bright
With freedom's holy light;
Protect us by thy might,
Great God, our King!

PROGRAM GUIDE: *Traditional American hymn; patriotic*

"America" is not our official national anthem, but it could truly be classified as our "national hymn." The words were written in 1831 by a young Baptist minister, Samuel Francis Smith (1808-95), who wrote many books and much religious verse. "America" was first performed publicly at a children's celebration of American independence at the Park Street Church in Boston that same year. The author had no hope or ambition of writing a national hymn at the time, and later apologized: "If I had anticipated the future of it, doubtless I would have taken more pains with it." The melody Smith chose for his words was a popular air that had also provided the tune for the British anthem "God Save the Queen (King)." The choice, despite our heritage, was only coincidental. Smith, unaware of the British anthem, borrowed the tune from a German song, "Heil Dir im Siegerkranz." The origin of the tune is obscure. An unlikely claim of authorship for the tune has been made in behalf of Henry Carey (1685?-1743), an English entertainer and songwriter. But the tune was used so widely throughout Europe, and with so many different texts, that it is more likely that Carey himself was simply another borrower of a good tune for one of his own songs.

One of the keys to the success of "America" lies in the point of view of the lyric—it is a personal statement. Oliver Wendell Holmes, a friend of Smith, believed the choice of *my* country instead of *our* country was a masterstroke that spelled the difference between mortality and immortality for the song. "Everyone who sings the song," he said, "at once feels a personal ownership in his native land. The hymn will last as long as the country."

Unison singing is recommended for informal participation. The mood of performance should be one of either quiet reverence or majestic pride. For example, the former style is appropriate for the closing of a sunrise or sunset religious service, whereas the latter is appropriate for an Independence Day celebration. For a short version, sing the first and last verse.

6

America, the Beautiful

Katharine Lee Bates *Samuel Augustus Ward*

Moderately fast and broadly

B♭ F7 B♭ D°7 F7

1. O beau - ti-ful for spa - cious skies, For am-ber waves of grain, For

B♭ F7 F°7 F C9 C7 F7

pur - ple moun-tain maj - es - ties A - bove the fruit - ed plain! A -

B♭ Cm7 F7 E♭ F7 B♭ B♭7

mer - i - ca! A - mer - i - ca! God shed his grace on thee, And

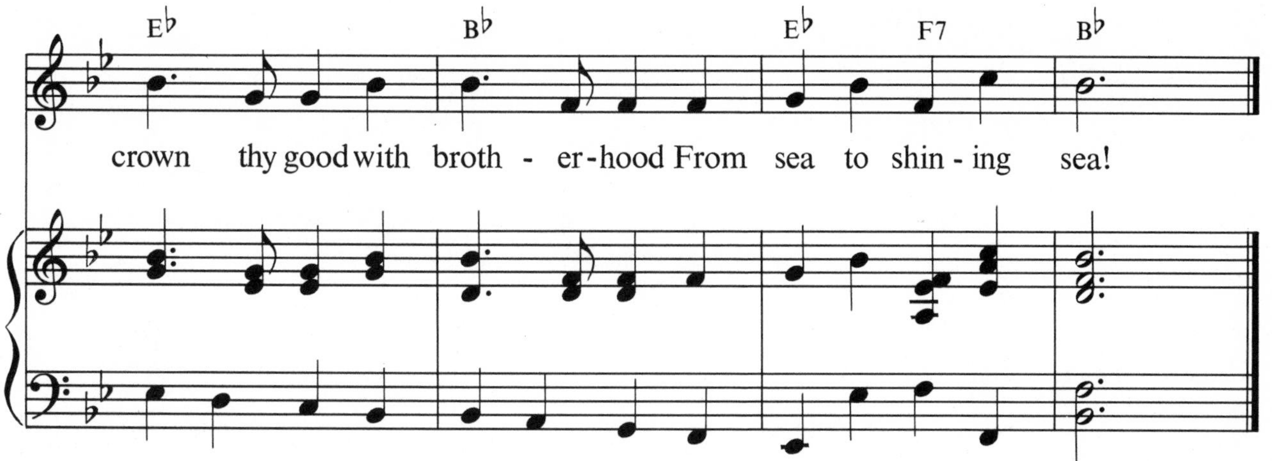
E♭
B♭
E♭
F7
B♭
crown thy good with broth - er-hood From sea to shin - ing sea!

2. O beautiful for pilgrim feet,
Whose stern, impassioned stress
A thoroughfare for freedom beat
Across the wilderness!
America! America!
God mend thine every flaw,
Confirm thy soul in self-control,
Thy liberty in law.

3. O beautiful for heroes proved
In liberating strife,
Who more than self their country loved,
And mercy more than life!
America! America!
May God thy gold refine,
Till all success be nobleness,
And every gain divine.

4. O beautiful for patriot dream
That sees beyond the years
Thine alabaster cities gleam
Undimmed by human tears!
America! America!
God shed his grace on thee,
And crown thy good with brotherhood
From sea to shining sea.

PROGRAM GUIDE: *Traditional American hymn; patriotic*

The magnificent panoramic sweep of America is displayed in this majestic tribute to our heritage. The rich lyric, flowing melody, and lush harmony couldn't be more perfectly mated. But though the words and music seem born for each other, the creator of neither intended it that way. Samuel Augustus Ward, a Newark music retailer, composed the tune in 1882 for the hymn "O Mother Dear, Jerusalem." Katharine Lee Bates, a Wellesley College English teacher, wrote the poem in 1893, inspired by the view from Pike's Peak in Colorado. After the poem appeared in the *Congregationalist* in 1895, it was revised, set to various tunes, and printed in many hymnals. By the 1920's the poem became permanently associated with Ward's melody.

I can't help wondering why we have not made this powerful and *singable* patriotic hymn our national anthem (a movement to do so in the 1920s failed), thereby earning the eternal gratitude of beleaguered amateur singers everywhere who have difficulty singing "The Star-Spangled Banner."

Not everyone agrees with my view on the wedding of this music with these words. There are those who feel the melody is dated, tied to the restricted style of its period.

The usual suggested tempo is *andante con moto,* moderately slow and even, with feeling. I prefer to sing it slightly faster, almost but not quite approaching the tempo of a stately march. I can never bring myself to stop short of four full verses but if you are really pressed for time, cut out verses 2 and 3.

Patriotic songs of this quality deserve to be sung much oftener than they are. Certainly this song should be programmed for patriotic holidays. But it's a shame to sing "America, the Beautiful" only on Sunday, when you've got Monday, Tuesday, Wednesday, Thursday, Friday, Saturday—ain't it a shame?

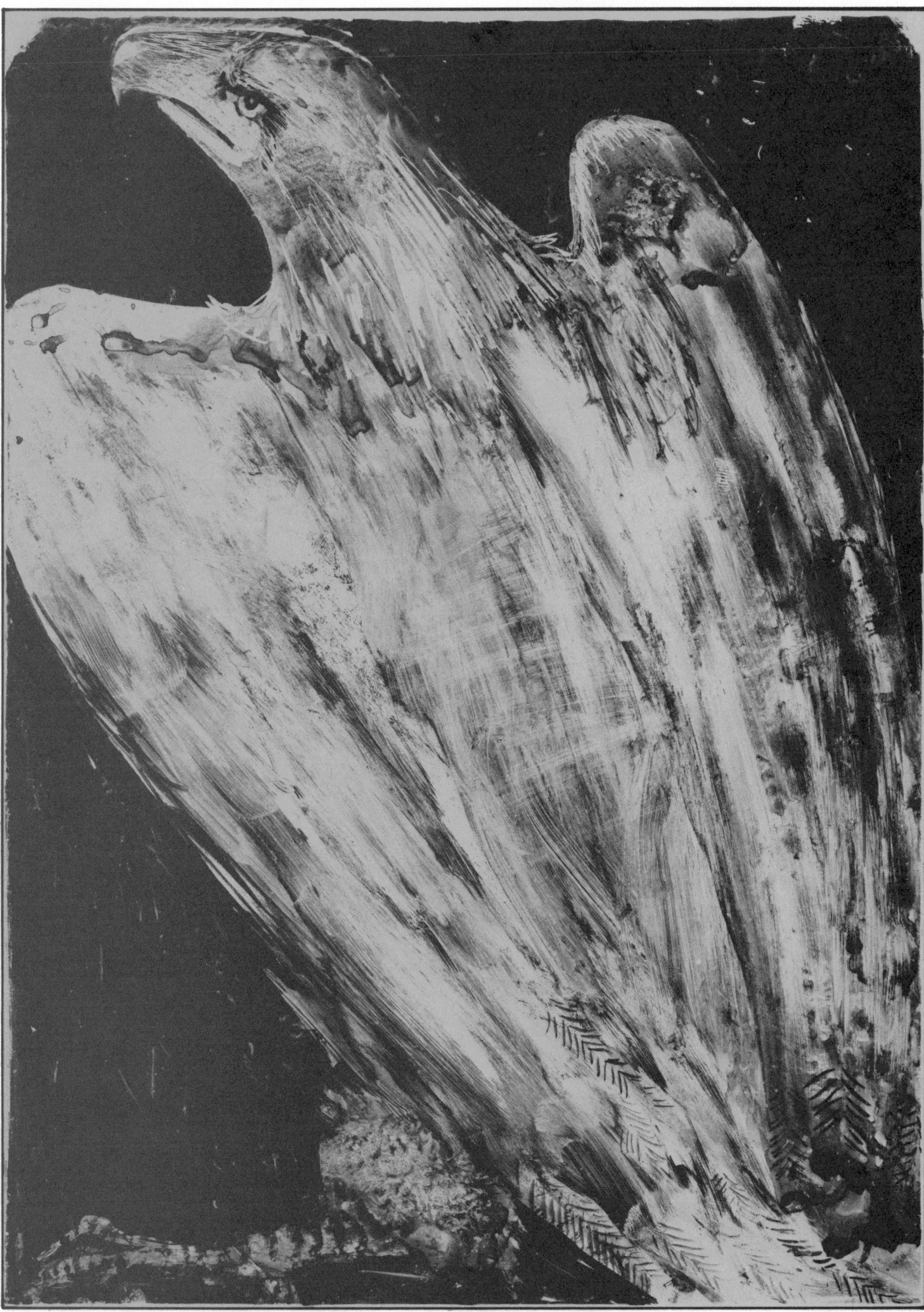

7

Angels, from the Realms of Glory

James Montgomery
Henry Smart
Moderately
B♭ Dm Gm F7 B♭ F7 Gm Dm E♭ Dm Gm F Cm-F7 B♭
1. An-gels, from the realms of glo - ry, Wing your flight o'er all the earth;
B♭ Dm Gm F7 B♭ F7 Gm D Gm D Gm F C7 F
Ye who sang cre - a - tion's sto - ry Now pro-claim Mes - si - ah's birth:
Refrain
F B♭ B♭9 E♭ Cm B♭ Cm Gm-Cm F(+4) F7 B♭
Come and wor-ship, Come and wor-ship, Wor-ship Christ the new-born King!

2. Shepherds, in the field abiding,
Watching o'er your flocks by night,
God with man is now residing;
Yonder shines the infant light: (*Refrain*)

3. Sages, leave your contemplations;
Brighter visions beam afar;
Seek the great Desire of nations;
Ye have seen his natal star: (*Refrain*)

4. Saints, before the altar bending,
Watching long in hope and fear,
Suddenly the Lord, descending,
In his temple shall appear: (*Refrain*)

PROGRAM GUIDE: *Traditional British hymn; Christmas*

This call to worship is a good opener for any worship service, and particularly during the Christmas season. Although the tempo is moderate, the tune is lively, with broad leaps in the melody, and may suffer if it drags, losing the mood of its message. The words were written by Scotsman James Montgomery (1771-1854), hymnwriter and editor of the *Iris,* a Sheffield, England newspaper, in which "Angels" first apeared December 24, 1816. The music was added later by Henry Smart (1813-1869), a well-known London organist and composer.

8

Au Clair de la Lune

Brightly
French Folk Song
F C7 F C7 F
1. Au clair de la lu - ne, Mon a - mi Pier - rot, Prê - te-moi ta
C7 F C7 F G
plu - me Pour é - crire un mot Ma chan-dell' est mor - te,
C7 F C7 F C7 F
Je n'ai plus de feu, Ou-vre-moi ta por - te Pour l'a-mour de Dieu!

2. Au clair de la lune
Pierrot répondit:
"Je n'ai pas de plume;
Je suis dans mon lit.
Va chez la voisine,
Je crois qu'elle y est,
Car dans sa cuisine
On bat le briquet."

3. Au clair de la lune
Pierrot se rendort.
Il rêve à la lune,
Son coeur bat bien fort,
Car toujours si bonne
Pur l'enfant tout blanc,
La lune lui donne
Son croissant d'argent.

PROGRAM GUIDE: *French folk song*

I speak French as well as the average Parisian speaks English, which is to say, not at all. But I enjoy pretending to sing French songs in French, and so do many other crazy singers. If you're one of us, have a go at it. According to my friend, David Earle (who is appalled by the way I handle any language, including French), this is what the story is about:

1. "My friend, Pierrot,
In this clear moonlight
Lend me your pen
To write a word.
My candle is dead,
I have no light.
Open the door,
For the love of God."

2. In the clear moonlight
Pierrot answered,
"I have no pen,
I am in bed.
Go to the neighbor's.
I know she is there
Because in the kitchen
Someone is starting a fire."

3. In the clear moonlight
Pierrot goes back to sleep.
He dreams of the moon and
His heart beats strongly
Because the good,
Pure white child
Of a moon gives to him
Its silver crescent.

And you always wondered, didn't you? Now, for pronunciation, here is how Dave says to do it. If you don't like his way, go find your own tutor.

1. Oh clare duh(r) la loonuh mo na-mē Pier-row
Preh-tuh-mwah tah ploo-muh, Poo-ray-cree ruh(n) mow.
Ma shan-dell eh mor-tuh, dzhuh nay plu duh fu(r).
Oo-vruh-mwah tah por-tuh, Poor lah-moor duh deeuh(r).

2. Oh clare duh(r) la loonuh, Pier-row ray-pon-dee.
Juh nay pah duh ploo-muh, juh swee dah(n) mo(n) lee.
Vah shay lah vwah-zee-nuh(r), dzhuh kwah-kell ee eh.
Kar dah(n) sah kwee-zee-nuh, o(n) ba luh bree-kay.

3. Oh clare duh(r) la loonuh, Pier-row suh ro(n)-door.
Eel reh vah lah loo-nuh, So(n) kur ba bie(n) for.
Kar too-joor see bun-nuh, pure lah(n)-fah(n) too bla(n).
Lah loo-nuh loo-ee dun-nuh, so(n) kwah-san dar-jah(n).

The secret to pronouncing French, of course, is to speak through your nose, put a ngya sound where you shouldn't and no sound where you should. It also helps to run your words together, except when they should be run apart. So, anyhow, enjoy yourself singing in pidgin French.

The song is from the early 1800s, though the tune may be older.

9

Auld Lang Syne

Traditional, Scottish

Moderately
F
C7
F
B♭
1. Should auld ac-quaint-ance be for-got And nev - er brought to mind? Should
F
C7
F
B♭
C9
C7
F
B♭
auld ac-quaint-ance be for-got, And days of auld lang syne? For
F
C7
B♭
F
B♭
auld lang syne, my friend, For auld lang syne; We'll

F
C7
F
B♭
C9
C7
F
take a cup of kind - ness yet, For auld___ lang___ syne.

2. And here's a hand, my trusty friend,
And give a hand of thine.
We'll take a cup of kindness yet
For auld lang syne.
For auld lang syne, my friend,
For auld lang syne.
We'll take a cup of kindness yet
For auld lang syne.

PROGRAM GUIDE: *Traditional Scottish song; New Year's Eve, brotherhood, parting*

New Year's festivities are incomplete without Robert Burns's tribute to old friendships and experiences. Because the titular phrase is traditional and familiar, most of us understand it more with our hearts than with our minds. By asking singers to define what *auld lang syne* means to them you may stir up some interesting, even touching, conversation and establish a memorable performance mood. The title from Scotland and Northern England, means literally *old long since* or *old long-ago* (days). The reference is to old times, especially times fondly remembered, or to an old or long friendship. "Auld Lang Syne" is an appropriate closing number for any group that comes together for the last time during some particular series of events, or for a group that gathers infrequently, or as a tribute to a member of a group who is leaving.

A couple of nice touches may be added to the performance, if a warm and cooperative spirit prevails, by asking everyone to hum a chorus softly between the first and last verses, while crossing arms and clasping hands with his neighbors. A moderate to moderately slow tempo is appropriate.

Robert Burns is believed to have added to or adapted the verses of a traditional song (rather than created the song) for one of his song collections. The tune is a traditional Scottish tune.

10

The Battle Hymn of the Republic

Julia Ward Howe *Attr. to William Steffe*

Majestically
F7 B♭
1. Mine eyes have seen the glo - ry of the com-ing of the Lord; He is
E♭ B♭ F7
tram-pling out the vin - tage where the grapes of wrath are stored; He hath
B♭
loosed the fate - ful light-ning of his ter - ri - ble swift sword; His

Cm
B♭
F7
B♭
truth is march - ing on.
Chorus
B♭
E♭
B♭
Glo - ry! glo - ry, hal - le - lu - jah! Glo - ry! glo - ry, hal - le - lu - jah!
B♭
Gm
Cm
B♭
F7
B♭
Glo - ry! glo - ry, hal - le - lu - jah! His truth is march-ing on.

2. I have seen him in the watchfires of a hundred circling camps;
They have builded him an altar in the evening dews and damps;
I can read his righteous sentence by the dim and flaring lamps;
His day is marching on.

3. I have read a fiery gospel writ in burnished rows of steel:
"As ye deal with my contemners, so with you my grace shall deal";
Let the Hero, born of woman, crush the serpent with his heel,
Since God is marching on.

4. He has sounded forth the trumpet that shall never call retreat;
He is sifting out the hearts of men before his judgment seat.
Oh, be swift, my soul, to answer him! Be jubilant, my feet!
Our God is marching on.

5. In the beauty of the lilies Christ was born across the sea,
With a glory in his bosom that transfigures you and me;
As he died to make men holy let us die to make men free,
While God is marching on.

PROGRAM GUIDE: *Traditional American song; patriotic*

Among the many anomalies of the war between the North and the South was the peculiar success of two of its most popular tunes. "Dixie," a minstrel tune written by a Northern entertainer, was sung by both sides, but emerged as a battle cry of the South. The North adopted a tune claimed by a Southern composer of Sunday school hymns. (Boyd Stutler, who has made a lifetime study of the tune, thinks the claim cannot be sustained.) The popular camp-meeting tune, attributed to William Steffe began, around 1856, asking: "Say, brothers, will you meet us? On Canaan's happy shore?" And answering: "Glory, glory, hallelujah, For ever, evermore." With a memorable tune and an easily parodied lyric pattern, *Canaan* was a natural for endless numbers of rewrites by anonymous lyricists. A glee club parody taunting a Massachusetts infantryman named John Brown swept the Union ranks after another John Brown was hanged in 1859 for his attack on Harper's Ferry. Julia Ward Howe, visiting Washington in 1861 with her husband, observed a skirmish near the city and heard the men go into battle singing "John Brown's Body." At the suggestion of the Rev. James Freeman Clark she wrote a new version, which appeared in the February 1862 issue of *Atlantic Monthly* and went on to become nationally popular.

Your singers may not be as notable as the Mormon Tabernacle Choir, but with a little coaching and coaxing they can feel almost as effective. The most obvious way to do this is to stress variation in dynamics and tempo. One possibility is to set an easy, marching tempo and start out *pianissimo.* Build the volume with each succeeding verse to a thundering climax in the fourth, perhaps also accelerating the tempo slightly with each new verse. Then, with *marching on* still ringing in your ears, bring everybody down, *piano subito* (suddenly soft), to a whisper for the last chorus. If you have a strong tenor or soprano in the group, turn him or her loose on a solo for the last verse while everyone else hums: then have everyone join the soloist on the last chorus.

There is an arty harmonic variation for the third measure from the end of the chorus. You may wish to use it sparingly (perhaps after the fourth or fifth verse only), if your singers and your accompanist are cooperative. Here is how it goes:

D
Gm
lu - jah! His

Julia Howe's poetic lyric sometimes loses a little in the translation by informal singers. Two words in particular are bothersome:

Trampling, in the first verse, has essentially the same meaning as tramping, but there is an important, subtle difference. While each word may be used to refer both to marching and to the process of treading on grapes, *trampling,* alone among its other meanings has the idea of *treading harshly and domineeringly. Trampling* is, perhaps, a slightly stronger word with greater dimension in meaning in the context of the song. More than making wine of the grapes of wrath, Julia Howe seems to have intended *stamping out* the wine (vintage) made of this particularly distasteful harvest of the grapes.

Contemners are people who treat or regard us with disdain, scorn, or contempt. They should not be confused with those who condemn, censure, or pronounce an unfavorable or adverse judgement on us. *Contemners* condemn, but *condemners* don't necessarily contemn. So the *contemners* in the third verse are not *condemners*.

Julia Howe might rest more comfortably if she knew singers today were still using her carefully chosen words instead of substituting words that are both less precise and less powerful. The singers, of course, probably won't care very much either way, and would rather get on with the singing.

In camping situations, or when the "Battle Hymn" has worn out its welcome, you might want to switch to the parody "Pink Pajamas" for comic relief.

PROGRAM GUIDE: *Traditional camp song; humorous*

1. I wear my pink pajamas in the summer when it's hot,
   I wear my flannel nighties in the winter when it's not,
   And sometimes in the springtime, and sometimes in the fall,
   I jump right in between the sheets with nothing on at all.

   Chorus:
   Glory, glory, what's it to you?
   Glory, glory, what's it to you?
   Glory, glory, what's it to you?
   If I jump right in between the sheets with nothing on at all.

   Continue, as above:

2. One grasshopper hopped right over another grasshopper's back (*4 times*).

   Chorus:
   They were only playing leapfrog, (*3 times*)
   As one grasshopper hopped right over another grasshopper's back.

3. One mosquito scratched another mosquito's 'squito-bite. (*4 times*)

   Chorus:
   They were only being friendly. (*3 times, then repeat line above*)

4. One flea-fly flew up the flue and another flea-fly flew down.

   Chorus:
   They were only playing flue fly.

5. One pink porpoise popped up the pole and another pink porpoise popped down.

   Chorus:
   Glory, glory, how peculiar!

11
A Bicycle Built for Two

Henry Dacre

Brightly
G
C
Dai - sy, Dai - sy, give me your an - swer,
G
D7
G
Em
do. I'm half cra - zy
A7
D7
all for the love of you. It won't be a styl - ish

G
C
G
D7
G
mar - riage, I can't af - ford a car - riage; But you'll look
D7
G
D7
G
D7
G
sweet up - on the seat of a bi - cy - cle built for two.

PROGRAM GUIDE: *Traditional American popular song*

Wouldn't it be ecologically more responsible to ride up to your wedding on a bicycle? Daisy didn't think so. Here's what she replied:

Henry, Henry, this is my answer true:
I'm not crazy over the likes of you.
If you can't afford a carriage,
Forget about the marriage;
I won't be jammed,
I won't be crammed
On a bicycle built for two.

But times change, and maybe Henry Dacre's tribute to the last bicycle craze will bring two-seater-cycle weddings back in style. Dacre, a professional song writer, brought his bicycle and the song with him from England to America in 1892.

The old-timers will appreciate it if you sing this lilting song in a straightforward singalong style.

12
Bill Bailey

Hughie Cannon

Moderately fast
F
"Won't you come home, Bill Bail-ey, Won't you come home?"
F♯o7
C7
She cries the whole night long.
C7
"I'll do the cook-ing, hon-ey, I'll pay the rent.

E7
F
I know I've done you wrong.
Re-mem-ber that
*
F7
rain-y eve-ning I drove you out, with noth-ing but a fine-tooth
Bb6
Bb
Bbm
F
F6
comb?
I know I'm to blame; Now, ain't that a
*
D7
G7
C7
F
shame? Bill Bail-ey, won't you please come home?"
*
Omit last time

Play all grace notes on the down beat.

PROGRAM GUIDE: *Traditional American popular song; humorous*

Hughie Cannon wrote "Bill Bailey" before you, or I were born, most likely back in 1902. It is not an answer to the expectations of women's liberators—or, is it? Anyhow, Cannon's masterpiece became one of the great dixieland jazz favorites, and that's the lively, robust mood in which it is best performed. If you have a jazzman (or woman) on the piano, don't forget to let him take a chorus of his own. And, of course, if anybody else has an instrument handy, let them join in. Maybe you can form a front line (cornet, clarinet, and trombone) from the group and give the rest of the singers a rest and a treat. I usually carry a kazoo in my pocket at singing sessions just for this kind of number. It takes at least three choruses to do this song justice, and there has to be an instrumental chorus, or something that approximates one, in the middle. If you don't carry a kazoo, wrap tissue paper around a comb and hum through it. If all else fails, for the jazz chorus ask the group to mimic their favorite instrument (cornet, clarinet, trombone, tuba, drums) using, instead of words, scat singing, "doots," "duhs," "oompahs," and whatever makes them feel funny. The shy ones can stamp their feet and clap their hands. Spoons and glasses are fine if you're near a dinner table and not afraid of breakage. Come on, now, let's see if we can't get Bailey back home!

13
Blow the Man Down

American Sea Chantey

Briskly
Call
C
Response
I'll sing you a song, a good song of the sea, To me way,
A7
Dm
G7
Call
G7
aye, blow the man down; And trust that you'll join in the
Response
F C G7 (+6) C
cho - rus with me, Give me some time to blow the man down.

2. 'Twas on board a Black Baller I first served my time,
And away, hey, blow the man down;
And on the Black Baller I wasted my prime.
Give me some time to blow the man down.

3. It's when a Black Baller's preparing for sea,
And away, aye, blow the man down;
You'd split your sides laughing at the sights you would see,
Give me some time to blow the man down.

4. With the tinkers and tailors and soldiers and all,
To me way, aye, blow the man down;
That ship as good seamen on board the Black Ball;
Give me some time to blow the man down.

5. It's when a Black Baller is clear of the land,
And away, hey, blow the man down;
Our boatswain (bosun) then gives us the word of command.
Give me some time to blow the man down.

6. It's larboard and starboard on the deck you will sprawl,
And away, aye, blow the man down;
For "Kicking" Jack Williams commands the Black Ball.
Give me some time to blow the man down.

7. "Lay aft!" is the cry "to the break of the poop!"
And away, hey, blow the man down;
"Or I'll help you along with the toe of my boot."
Give me some time to blow the man down.

8. Pay attention to orders, yes, you, one and all,
To me way, aye, blow the man down;
For see right above you there flies the Black Ball.
Give me some time to blow the man down.

9. It's when a Black Baller comes down to the dock,
And away, hey, blow the man down;
The lasses and lads to the pier-heads do flock.
Give me some time to blow the man down.

PROGRAM GUIDE: *American sea chantey*

Chanteys (pronounced "shanties") were the folk songs of seafaring men. The art of chanteying achieved its highest development in the early nineteenth century aboard American and British ships engaged in the vigorous, highly competitive merchant (or packet) trade that flourished on the high seas as the industrial revolution began to dominate the activity ashore. A thriving competitive environment that attracted men of vigor and action, combined with the relative isolation of life aboard ship, no doubt contributed much to the attention given to chanteying and to the elaboration and quality that evolved.

"Blow the Man Down" is one of the oldest, most famous, and most popular chanteys associated with the rugged packet ships. There are several versions of this work song, but none reflects the iron discipline and brutality of the hard life aboard these "red-hot blood ships" better than this one from the Black Ball Line, the first and most famous of the hard-driving lines.

The call-response form of the song, used frequently in all kinds of folk music, was particularly useful in work situations aboard ship. The solo lines were sung by the chanteyman (an ablebodied seaman with a talent for singing, remembering songs, and improvising), and the responses were sung by the crew as they worked. The chanteyman sang freely in his own individualized style and improvised both words and music with considerable variation from established patterns. He used unique embellishments, unusual stresses and holds, and special effects to add interest and color to his singing. The choruses were sung in unison to established melodic patterns. The chanteys were rarely accompanied instrumentally; sometimes, however, a fiddler or an accordionist would play along when he could be spared from the work itself for this luxury.

Innuendo and double entendre were very much a part of the chanteyman's art. While ostensibly singing about the work itself, his lead-in phrases were designed to provide an outlet for pent-up hostilities by the men in a bursting, blistering choral response. So it is with "Blow the Man Down," which refers simultaneously to *knocking* or *striking* down the object of the work itself and to whomever each seaman has in mind as a result of the chanteyman's inspiration.

An authentic mood combines sarcasm and wit in the solo calls with anger and pride in the choral response, a neat trick to accomplish with a contemporary crowd of landlubbers. How can it be done? Giving your singers a little background on the Black Ball Line may help. If you are good at raising hackles without losing your participants in the process, some mock-serious needling might contribute to the cause. Maybe a short encounter session could be focused on the question of virility in vocalizing. In any event, don't allow a pantywaist charade to masquerade for this rugged chanteyman's masterpiece. Do what you can to stir the troops up. Certainly, you or anybody else in the crowd who is an able improviser, can play around, melodically or lyrically, with the solo lines. Let 'em rip out and slash out and hit the target for real. Just imagine how you would feel wasting the prime of your life on a crummy ship with a motley crew and a bunch of egomaniacs running the show. There you are, rigging the ship for action; you've just smashed your thumb, and a bunch of sissies from town have come down to watch those tough sailors get underway. Sock it to 'em!

14
Buffalo Gals

Anonymous

Adapted from a tune by Cool White

Brightly

Verse

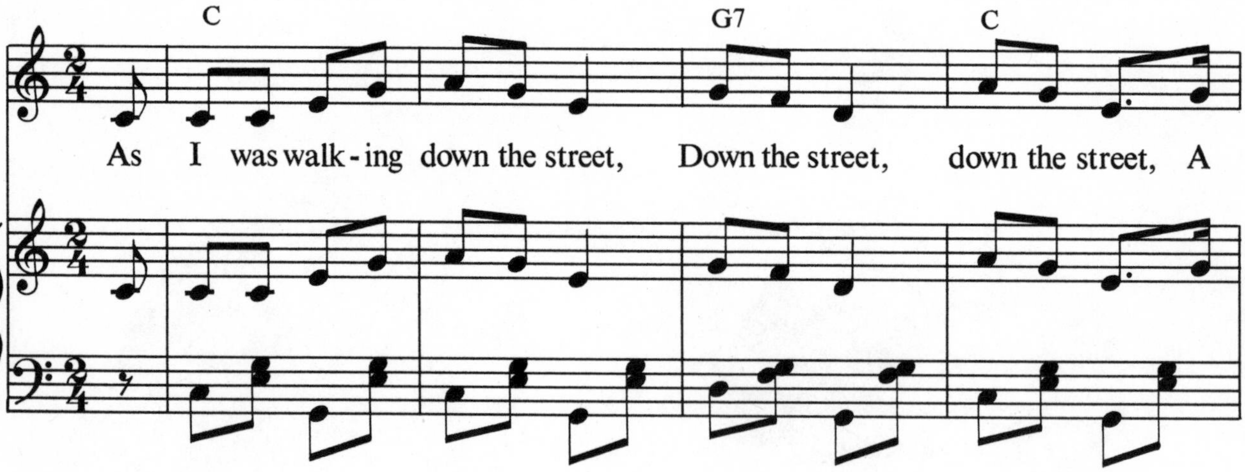

C G7 C

As I was walk - ing down the street, Down the street, down the street, A

C G7 C

pret - ty girl I chanced to meet, By the light of the sil - very moon. Oh,

Chorus

C G7 C

Buf-fa-lo gals, won't you come out to-night, Come out to-night, come out to-night? Oh,

C
G7
C
Buf-fa-lo gals, won't you come out to-night, And dance by the light of the moon?

2. I asked her if she'd stop and talk,
Stop and talk, stop and talk;
Her feet took up the whole sidewalk;
She was fair to view. (*Chorus*)

3. I asked her if she'd be my wife,
Be my wife, be my wife;
Then I'd be happy all my life,
If she'd marry me. (*Chorus*)

PROGRAM GUIDE: *Traditional American minstrel song; humorous*

Buffalo gals belong to the human zoo, as you probably have suspected, and reside in upstate New York. But they could be from Wichita or Mobile or Chicago or any other town of your choice. If you thought you heard Mr. Interlocutor talking to an end man when you examined the lyric, you were not mistaken. "Buffalo Gals" is a minstrel show tune from the 1800s. That's how it picked up the Buffalo tag. The performers traveled from town to town around the country making one-night stands, changing the name of the song to fit the town being played at the time. The original song, "Lubly Fan, Will You Cum Out Tonight?," on which this more contemporary version is based, was written by Cool White.

There is a little minstrel in us all. So why not unpack the popcorn and pass it around for everybody? It would be great if you could round up a couple of tambourines, a triangle, and some sticks to knock together, and form a rhythm band right on the spot with members of your group. Anyone who wants to clap hands or tap toes is also qualified for the band (clap the rhythm of the melody). Grab a bright tempo and sing out!

15
Clementine

Percy Montrose

Attr. to Percy Montrose

Brightly
F
C7
In a cav - ern, in a can - yon, Ex - ca - va - ting for a mine, Lived a
F
C7
F
min - er, for - ty - nin - er, And his daugh - ter, Clem-en - tine.

Chorus:

Oh my darling, oh my darling,
Oh my darling Clementine,
You are lost and gone forever,
Dreadful sorry, Clementine.

2. Light she was, and like a fairy,
And her shoes were number nine,
Herring boxes without topses,
Sandals were for Clementine.

3. Drove she ducklings to the water
Every morning just at nine,
Hit her foot against a splinter,
Fell into the foaming brine.

4. Ruby lips above the water,
Blowing bubbles soft and fine,
But, alas! I was no swimmer,
So I lost my Clementine.

5. In a churchyard near the canyon,
Where the myrtle doth entwine,
There grow roses and other posies,
Fertilized by Clementine.

6. In my dreams she still doth haunt me,
Robed in garments soaked with brine;
Though in life I used to hug her,
Now she's dead I draw the line.

7. Listen Boy Scouts, heed the warning
To this tragic tale of mine:
Artificial respiration
Could have saved my Clementine.

8. How I missed her, how I missed her,
How I missed my Clementine,
Till I kissed her little sister,
And forgot my Clementine.

PROGRAM GUIDE: *Traditional American popular song; camp, humorous*

Just as soon as you think you've laid Clementine to rest forever, somebody makes a request and you have to dig her back up again. Usually that happens on an outing of some kind. Clementine is rarely *in* inside. The idea is a relic of the days when the forty-niners descended on the West searching for gold during the great gold-rush at mid-nineteenth century, although the song itself was composed by Percy Montrose in 1863. Over the years Montrose's verses have been extended by imaginative singers (see verses 6 through 8). There isn't much you can do to breathe new life into Clementine. However, if you have several extroverts in the group you can freshen the song up a little by assigning each verse to a different soloist. On the other hand, if you are more concerned with getting the ordeal over and done with, you may shorten it by singing the chorus only twice, after the first and last verses. You may cut the song off after the fourth or fifth verse without losing any of the story. The tempo should be bright and spirited. However, if you are really entranced with Clementine, do the fifth verse and chorus very slowly and in a minor key, like this:

Fm
5. In a church-yard near the can - yon Where the myr - tle doth en -
C7
Fm
C7
Fm
twine; There grow ros - es and oth-er pos-ies Fer-til- ized by Clem-en - tine.

16
Come and Go with Me

American Negro Gospel Song

Moderately and rhythmically
F
B♭
Come and go with me to that land, Come and go with me to that
R. H.
L.H.
F
land, Come and go with me to that land where I am
C7
F
bound. Come and go with me to that

F7
B♭
F
land, Come and go with me to that land, Come and go
F
(Melody in lower notes)
C7
F
with me to that land where I am bound.

2. There ain't no bowing in that land,
   Ain't no bowing in that land,
   Ain't no bowing in that land where I am bound.
   There ain't no bowing in that land,
   Ain't no bowing in that land,
   Ain't no bowing in that land where I am bound.

   Continue, as above:

3. There ain't no kneeling in that land.

4. There ain't no poverty in that land.

5. There's love and brotherhood in that land.

6. There's peace and freedom in that land.

PROGRAM GUIDE: *American Negro gospel song; brotherhood*

This rhythmic Negro gospel tune is a sure winner with the swinging singers. It's easy to learn and a delight to sing at a relaxed but rhythmic tempo. Don't make the mistake of turning it into a shouter. It moves a lot better with a natural, even soft, but intense sound. Draw out each word and syllable to its full notational value, but keep the beat going steadily. You can add a very nice touch by assigning several people with a good sense of rhythm to clap out this pattern, again, relatively quietly:

1 2 3 4

If your rhythm section really gets the message let them feel free to improvise as the song grows on them. Select as many verses as you want to use, and repeat the first verse at the end as a chorus. I've provided a harmony cue in the last three measures of the vocal score.

17
Come, Follow

Traditional English Round

Brightly
1
Come, fol - low, fol - low, fol - low, fol - low, fol-low, fol-low me.
2
Whith-er shall I fol-low, fol - low, fol - low, whith-er shall I fol-low, fol-low thee?
3
To the green-wood, to the green-wood, to the green-wood, green-wood tree.

☐ Divide the group into three sections. Each section sings the entire round the agreed-upon number of times, beginning at point 1 when the preceding section reaches point 2. Thus the round begins and ends with one section singing alone: section 1 at the beginning and section 3 at the end.

PROGRAM GUIDE: *Traditional English round*

Turn back the pages of time a couple of centuries and place yourself in the drawing room of an old English manor. The ladies are seated, the gentlemen are standing, and everyone is in the mood for frivolity. Singing catches and rounds, even composing them, is a must among the social graces of all gentlemen and ladies. You must exhibit a pleasant voice, quick tongue, and a sharp wit. Bow to the ladies (ladies smile back fetchingly), hark to the briefly held tonic chord, played on the piano or harpsichord, and then begin. The room has been divided into three sections, and the first section will lead while the others follow in turn. If your ladies and gentlemen are sufficiently nimble you may wish to gradually accelerate the chase until all are breathlessly on the run. Now whither shall we follow?

18
The Crawdad Song

Anonymous
Verses 6, 7, 8, and 9 by J.F.L.

American Negro Folk Song

Moderately fast
F
You get a line and I'll get a pole, hon-ey.
C7
F
You get a line and I'll get a pole, babe.
You get a line and I'll get a pole;
B♭
F
C7
F
We'll go down to the craw-dad hole, hon-ey, ba - by mine.

2. Yonder is a man with a pack on his back, honey,
Yonder is a man with a pack on his back, babe,
Yonder is a man with a pack on his back,
Totin' all the crawdads he can pack,
Honey, baby mine.

Continue, as above:

3. A-settin' on the ice till my feet got hot,
A-watchin' that crawdad rack and trot.

4. Whatcha gonna do when the lake runs dry?
Sit on the bank and watch the crawdads die.

5. Whatcha gonna do when your man goes away?
Get me a better one very next day.

PROGRAM GUIDE: *American Negro folk song; humorous*

"The Crawdad Song" is as American as Saturday afternoon and fishing poles. It's a great outdoor song, and goes well inside when you need a lively tune to wake everyone up. For variety ask everybody to whistle through the tune after each of the verses you have selected to sing. Two or three verses should be enough for most purposes. Here are some additional verses (not shown in the singer's edition) in the event you need them:

Get up now you slept too late, honey,
Get up now you slept too late, babe,
Get up now you slept too late,
Crawdad man done passed your gate,
Honey, baby mine.

As above:

I heard the duck say to the drake,
There ain't no crawdads in this lake.

I sell crawdads three for a dime,
Your crawdads ain't as good as mine.

Crawdad, crawdad, better go to hole,
If I don't catch you, bless my soul.

19
Dear Lord and Father of Mankind

John Greenleaf Whittier — *Frederick Charles Maker*

Moderately slow
D D° D E7 A7 D Bm E7
Dear Lord and Fa - ther of man-kind, For - give our fool - ish
A D A7 D D+ G
ways; Re - clothe us in our right - ful mind, In
G B7 Em E7 A A7 D D7 G G°7 D
pur - er lives thy ser- vice find, In deep - er rev-erence, praise.

2. In simple trust like theirs who heard,
Beside the Syrian sea,
The gracious calling of the Lord,
Let us, like them, without a word,
Rise up and follow thee.

3. O Sabbath rest by Galilee,
O calm of hills above,
Where Jesus knelt to share with thee
The silence of eternity
Interpreted by love.

4. With that deep hush subduing all
Our words and works that drown
The tender whisper of thy call,
As noiseless let thy blessing fall
As fell thy manna down.

5. Drop thy still dews of quietness,
Till all our strivings cease;
Take from our souls the strain and stress,
And let our ordered lives confess,
The beauty of thy peace.

PROGRAM GUIDE: *Traditional American hymn*

This traditional hymn is a particularly good one to use when you need a song to serve as a prayer, or when you want a song with a philosophical theme. John Greenleaf Whittier (1807-92), a Quaker, was one of America's great poets. Many of his poems on religious themes have been used as texts for hymns. This text uses the concluding stanzas from Whittier's "The Brewing of Soma," which describes the East Indian custom of drinking intoxicating soma to commune with deity. Whittier suggests more natural ways of communicating with God. This tune was written in 1887, to serve as a musical setting for Whittier's lines, by Frederick Charles Maker (1844-1927), a Congregational organist from Bristol, England. Sing it quietly for maximum effectiveness.

20
Deck the Halls with Boughs of Holly

Traditional Welsh Carol

Brightly

F C7 F C7 Dm C F C7 F Gm F C F

Deck the halls with boughs of hol - ly, Fa la la la la, la la la la;

F C7 F C7 Dm C F C7 F Gm F C F

'Tis the sea - son to be jol - ly, Fa la la la la, la la la la.

C F C7 F B♭ F C F Am Dm C G7 C

Don we now our gay ap-par - el, Fa la la la la la la;

F C7 F C7 Dm C F B♭ F Gm F C7 F
Troll the an-cient Yule-tide car - ol, Fa la la la la, la la la la.

2. See the blazing yule before us,
   Fa la la la la, la la la la,
   Strike the harp and join the chorus,
   Fa la la la la, la la la la,
   Follow me in merry measure,
   Fa la la, la la la, la la la,
   While I tell of Yuletide treasure,
   Fa la la la la, la la la la.

3. Fast away the old year passes,
   Fa la la la la, la la la la,
   Hail the new, ye lads and lasses,
   Fa la la la la, la la la la,
   Sing we joyous all together,
   Fa la la, la la la, la la la,
   Heedless of the wind and weather,
   Fa la la la la, la la la la.

PROGRAM GUIDE: *Traditional Welsh Christmas carol*

The use of holly for Christmas had origins in both the Druidic practice of providing a protected winter home for the sylvan spirits, and the Roman Saturnalia of December 17-24. The Romans had long used holly wreaths or sprigs as a token of goodwill, and the extension of the custom to the Christmas holiday was natural. According to a German legend, holly formed Christ's crown of thorns and the berries, originally yellow, were stained with his blood. In many countries, a sprig of holly in the house was thought to repel lightning and to make animals docile. A large body of folklore grew up in Europe about the merits of holly—the proper time to cut it, bring it into the house, take it down, and dispose of it—and much of that tradition was carried to the New World. Singers seem to naturally gravitate to the brisk, lively tempo called for in this traditional Welsh Christmas carol of unknown origin.

21

Do, Lord, Remember Me

Optional verses by J.F.L.

American Negro Gospel Song

Moderately fast
G
G7
Do, Lord, oh do, Lord, oh do re-mem-ber me.
C
G
Do, Lord, oh do, Lord, oh do re-mem-ber me.
G
Do, Lord, oh do, Lord, oh do re-mem-ber me.

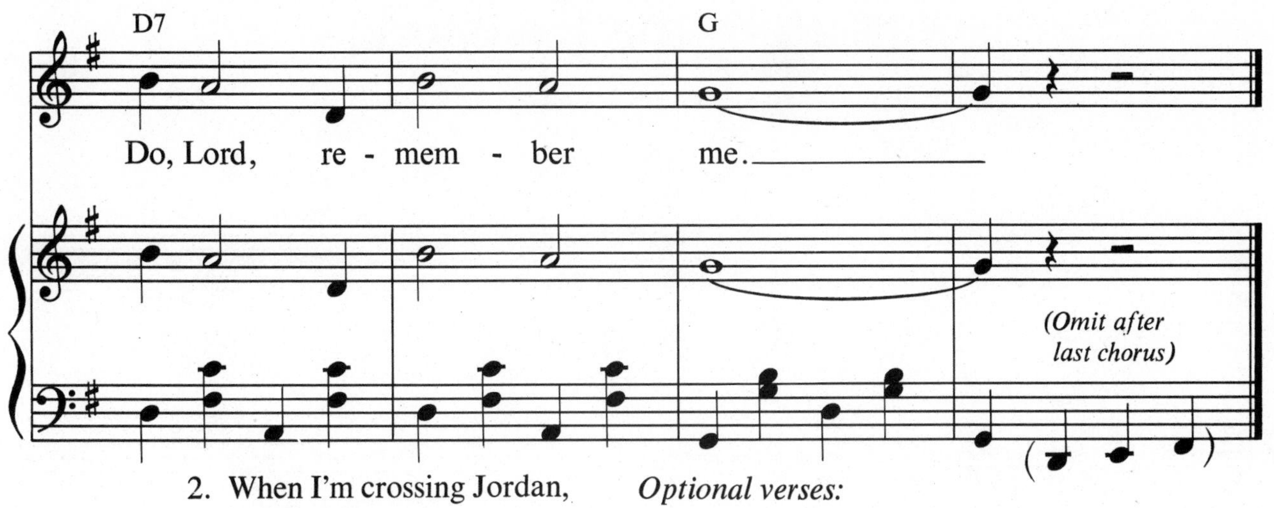

D7
G
Do, Lord, re - mem - ber me.
(Omit after last chorus)

2. When I'm crossing Jordan,
   Do remember me.
   When I'm crossing Jordan,
   Do remember me.
   When I'm crossing Jordan,
   Do remember me.
   Do, Lord, remember me.

   Continue, as above:

3. When I've got no friends at all.
4. When I'm bound in trouble.
5. When I'm goin' from door to door.

Optional verses:

When I wander from the path.

When I get to heaven, Lord.

When I'm scared and lonely, Lord.

When the day of judgment comes.

Paul and Silas bound in jail.

One did sing while the other did pray.

PROGRAM GUIDE: *American Negro gospel song*

"Do Lord" is another great gospel spiritual that cries out for do-it-yourself percussion. Why not form a rhythm band of three sections, with finger-snappers, hand-clappers, and foot-tappers? Here's a score for them:

Beat	1	2	3	4	1	2	3	4	1	2	3	4	1	2	3	4
Finger Snappers	x	𝄽	x	𝄽	x	𝄽	x	𝄽	x.	𝄾	𝄽	𝄽	𝄽	𝄽	𝄽	𝄽
Hand Clappers	𝄽	x	𝄽	x	𝄽	x	𝄽	x	𝄽	𝄾 x	x	x	x	𝄽	𝄽	𝄽
Foot Tappers	x	𝄽	x	𝄽	x	𝄽	x	𝄽	x.	𝄾	𝄽	𝄽	𝄽	x	x	x

By repeating that same four-measure pattern four times you'll have a complete accompaniment for each verse. Tell the rhythm section to forget about singing responsibilities; they should concentrate on what they are doing. The singers may be divided into two groups for the call and response in the verses. Or have several good soloists take turns leading the calls. A bright happy tempo is appropriate, but don't go so fast you make it tough for your newly formed rhythm section. And, by all means, give the rhythm section a good rehearsal. It's all part of the act. The first verse is often repeated as a chorus.

22

Down by the Riverside

American Negro Spiritual

Moderately fast

Verse

G Em D7 G *Clap*

1. Gon-na lay down my sword and shield Down by the

D7 G D7 *Clap* G *Clap*

riv - er - side, Down by the riv - er - side, Down by the

D7 G Em D7 G *Clap*

riv- er - side. Gon-na lay down my sword and shield, Down by the

(Melody in lower notes)
D7 G D7 G
riv - er - side, Down by the riv - er - side.
Chorus
G D7 G7 C Am G D7
I ain't gon-na stud-y war no more, Ain't gon-na stud-y war no
G D7 Em D7 C D7 G D7(+13) G7 D7 G7
more, Ain't gon-na stud-y war no more. I ain't gon-na
C Am G D7 G D7 Em
stud-y war no more, Ain't gon-na stud-y war no more. Ain't gon-na

(Melody in lower notes)
1.
Last verse
D7
G
G
stud-y
war no
more.
2. Gon-na
more.

2. Gonna join hands with everyone,
Down by the riverside,
Down by the riverside,
Down by the riverside,
Gonna join hands with everyone,
Down by the riverside,
Down by the riverside.

Continue, as above:

3. Gonna put on my long white robe.
4. Gonna put on my starry crown.
5. Gonna put on my golden shoes.
6. Gonna ride on a milk-white horse.
7. Gonna talk with the Prince of Peace.

PROGRAM GUIDE: *American Negro spiritual*

Here's another lively Negro spiritual that became a jazz favorite of dixieland bands. There are several things you can do to enhance the performance with amateur singers. The easiest effect to get is to have everybody clap and/or tap out those accented beats that precede the "down by the riverside" phrases, as indicated in the cues on the vocal score. If you can locate a few natural basses among your singers, you can add them to the arrangement by asking them to sing those accented bass notes found in the piano score in the bottom line. You may also wish to add a few self-controlled foot-stompers if the above is not enough. Use all the natural harmony you can get, but if you are not getting any at all, at least end on a flourish by teaching the simple harmonization indicated in the upper notes at the end of each verse and chorus.

23
Down in the Valley

American Folk Song

Moderately slow
F
1. Down in the val - ley, the val - ley so low,
Hear the wind blow, love, hear the wind blow.
legato
C7
Late in the eve - ning, hear the wind blow.
(Melody in lower notes)
F
last time

2. If you don't love me, then love who you please,
Throw your arms 'round me, give my heart ease.
Give my heart ease, dear, give my heart ease,
Throw your arms 'round me, give my heart ease.

3. Roses love sunshine, violets love dew;
Angels in heaven know I love you.
Know I love you, dear, know I love you,
Angels in heaven know I love you.

4. Build me a castle forty feet high,
So I can see him as he goes by.
As he goes by, dear, as he goes by,
So I can see him as he goes by.

5. Writing this letter, containing three lines,
Answer my question, "Will you be mine?"
"Will you be mine, dear, will you be mine?"
Answer my question, "Will you be mine?"

Repeat first verse.

PROGRAM GUIDE: *American folk song; romantic, camp song*

This southern mountain song of unrequited love is a part of the standard repertoire for group singing, especially in camps. Either you like it or you don't—many don't. Those who do like the song like it, I think, for the opportunity to do some elemental, country harmonizing, rather than for the unrequited love aspect. "Unrequited," by the way, is a descriptive term used by folk music buffs to describe songs in which the girl or boy is giving love and getting none in return. *The Random House Dictionary of the English Language* says that *requited* means "to give or do in return" and of course the prefix simply reverses the meaning. You may want to toss the term around among singers (who could care less) to impress them.

Here are some things you can do for the harmonizers. You may provide the highest return for the least effort by simply letting them do as they please. Next easiest thing to do is to encourage some of the ladies to pick up those harmony notes (the upper ones) in the last two measures of the vocal score. If you have a large number of enthusiasts on your hands (and they want some guidance), here is a two-part version, with extended measures thrown in, which you can throw at them:

Down in the val - ley, the val-ley so low,
Late in the eve - ning, hear the wind blow.

If the two-part version makes a hero of you, see if you can enhance your reputation still more by introducing a multi-part arrangement. Here is how it goes. You sing the first verse as it is written in the singer's edition, including the harmony notes at the end. For the second verse you teach everybody this simple arrangement which starts with three parts and ends with five:

2. If you don't love me, then love who you please,
Give my heart ease, dear, oh, give my heart ease,
2. If you don't love me, then love who you please, who you please.
Give my heart ease, dear, oh, give my heart ease, my heart ease.
(Solo voice)
(Give my heart ease.)
Throw your arms 'round me, give my heart ease.
(Solo voice)
(Give my heart ease.)
Throw your arms 'round me, give my heart ease.
(won't you)

After that you may go back to the first-verse score for verses three and four, and then return to the second verse score for the fifth verse and a repeat of the first verse. Or, you may simply alternate the two different scorings any way you want to. This arrangement has worked well for me with small groups of eager amateur singers who want to invest a little time learning to do more than the ordinary. Good luck!

24
The Doxology

Thomas Ken (I)
William Kethe (II)

Attr. to Louis Bourgeois

I
G D Em Bm Em D G D Em C G D G
Praise God, from whom all bless-ings flow; Praise him, all crea-tures here be-low; Praise
D G D G C D7 G G Em D Am G D7 G C G
him a- bove, ye heaven-ly host; Praise Fa-ther, Son, and Ho - ly Ghost. A - men.
II
G D Em Bm Em D G
All peo - ple that on earth do dwell, Sing

D Em C G D Em D G D G C D
to the Lord with cheer-ful voice. Him serve with mirth, his praise forth
G Em D Am G D G
tell, Come, ye be - fore him and re - joice.

PROGRAM GUIDE: *Traditional Anglo-American hymn*

Doxology is defined as a hymn or form of words containing an ascription of praise to God. The word comes from a Greek word meaning honor or glory. There are many versions of "Doxology," or "Old 100th," differing in the words, pacing, melody, and harmonization of the music.

The most commonly used tune was composed or collected by Louis Bourgeois, the music editor of Calvin's *Genevan Psalters,* and may have been based on the French chanson "There Is None Here Without His Fair One." As a religious song it first appeared in 1551 using Psalm 134 for a text. The English Puritans changed to a text by William Kethe based on Psalm 100:

All people that on earth do dwell
Sing to the Lord with cheerful voyce;
Him serve with mirth, his praise forth tell,
Come ye before him and rejoice.

The "Old 100th" version (named for the psalm) was sung in a spirited fashion and became very popular with our forefathers for its "lively and jocund tune." The current fashion is usually much more sedate. The words in version I in the singer's edition were written in 1692 by British Bishop Thomas Ken. "Doxology" is often used as a grace or benediction by informal singers, in addition to its obvious appropriateness for worship services.

So you will be more fully equipped for demands for special versions of "Doxology," what follows is a mini-encyclopedia of the versions I was able to locate and/or obtain permission to use (there are also several excellent copyrighted contemporary music stylings available):

William Kethe's full text:

All people that on earth do dwell,
Sing to the Lord with cheerful voice:
Him serve with mirth, his praise forthtell,
Come ye before him and rejoice.

Know that the Lord is God indeed;
Without our aid he did us make;
We are his flock, he doth us feed,
And for his sheep he doth us take.

O enter then his gates with praise,
Approach with joy his courts unto;
Praise, laud, and bless his name always,
For it is seemly so to do.

For why? the Lord our God is good,
His mercy is forever sure:
His truth at all times firmly stood,
And shall from age to age endure.

A text by Isaac Watts:

From all that dwell below the skies,
Let the Creator's praise arise;
Let the Redeemer's name be sung
Through ev'ry land, by ev'ry tongue.

Eternal are thy mercies, Lord;
Eternal truth attends thy word
Thy praise shall sound from shore to shore,
Till sun shall rise and set no more.

A text by Charles H. Lyttle:

Praise God, the Love we all may share;
Praise God, the Beauty everywhere;
Praise God, the Hope of Good to be;
Praise God, the Truth that makes us free.

Here are two more pacings and harmonizations of the melody, and the Tallis Canon:

III
G G D Em Bm Em D G D Em C G D
Em D G Am G C D7 Em D G A7 D C G D G
IV
G D C D G D G D G C G D G
D G D G C D G D G D C G D G
V Thomas Tallis' four-part round
1 2
Praise God, from whom all bless-ings flow; Praise him, all crea-tures here be-low;
3 4
Praise him a-bove, ye heaven-ly host; Praise Fa-ther, Son, and Ho-ly Ghost.

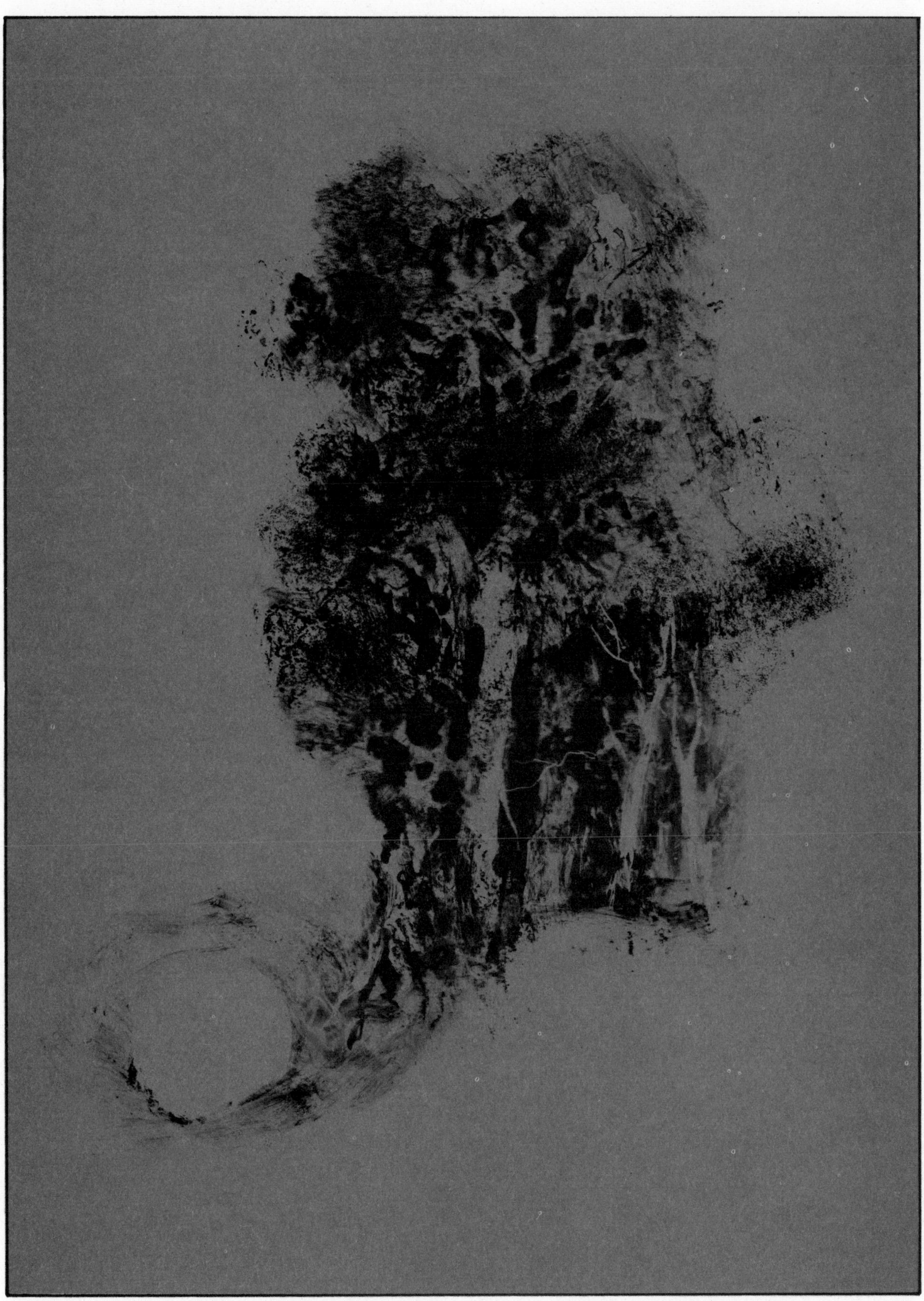

25
Every Time I Feel the Spirit

American Negro Spiritual

Brightly
Chorus
G
D
Ev - ery time I feel the spir - it Mov - ing in my heart,
D7
G
I will pray. Yes, ev - ery time I feel the
D
Fine
spir - it Mov - ing in my heart, I will pray.
Fine

Bass (slowly, ad lib.) D

1. Up - on the moun - tain, ___ when my Lord spoke, ___

slowly

Em G G7 D *a tempo* *D.C.*

___ Out of his mouth came ___ fire and smoke. ___

D.C.

a tempo

2. I looked around me;
It looked so fine;
I asked the Lord
If it was mine.

Chorus

3. There ain't but one train
On this here track.
It runs to Heaven,
And it don't run back.

Chorus

PROGRAM GUIDE: *American Negro spiritual*

Warn your singers about the change of clef at the beginning of the verse: I've arranged this popular spiritual for bass solos, or male voices only, on each verse. You don't have to do it this way, of course. But, why not, unless your singers are all female? The chorus should be sung brightly, but not too fast. I've suggested that the bass solos be sung slowly and *at liberty* (with improvised, irregular rhythm) for contrast. Emphasize the syncopation in the chorus and, by all means, encourage the use of natural harmony. You can add to the effectiveness by changing the dynamics as you go along. For example, you might produce a very effective last chorus by singing it in almost a whisper, and at a very slow tempo. For percussion, you might set up a rhythm section of hand clappers using this pattern (repeated, to complete chorus):

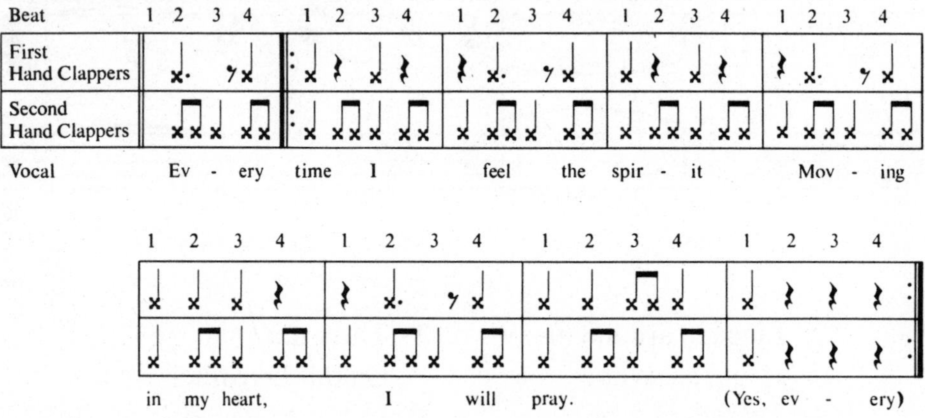
Beat
1 2 3 4 1 2 3 4 1 2 3 4 1 2 3 4 1 2 3 4
First Hand Clappers
Second Hand Clappers
Vocal
Ev - ery time I feel the spir - it Mov - ing
1 2 3 4 1 2 3 4 1 2 3 4 1 2 3 4
in my heart, I will pray. (Yes, ev - ery)

If you do the last chorus at a slow tempo, remember to cut the rhythm section off when you get there.

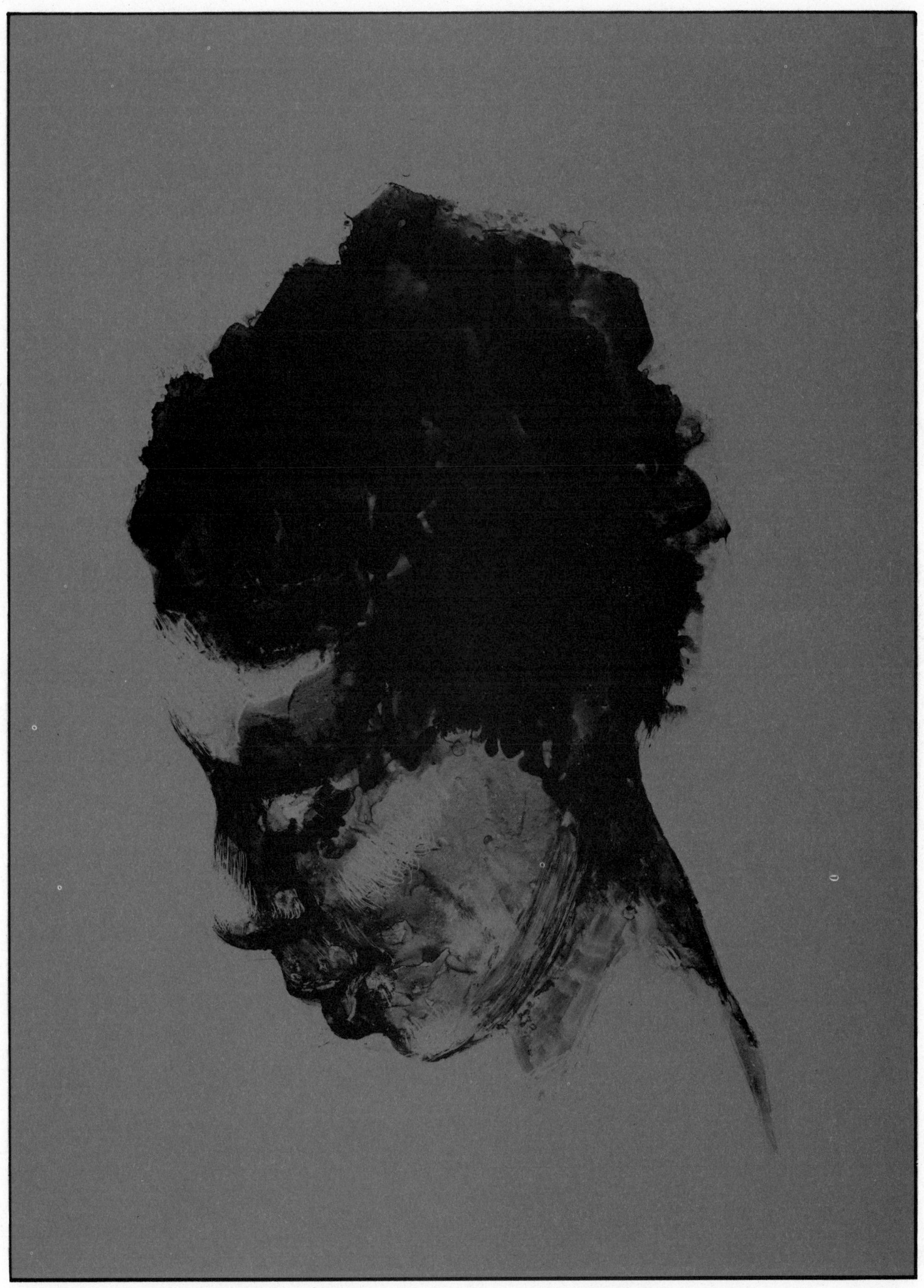

26
Everybody Loves Saturday Night

West African Folk Song

Moderately (Calypso)
(Melody in upper notes)
G
D7
Em
D7
G
Ev - ery-bod - y loves Sat-ur-day night,
G
D7
Em
D7
Ev - ery-bod - y loves Sat-ur-day
G
night,
Ev - ery-bod - y,

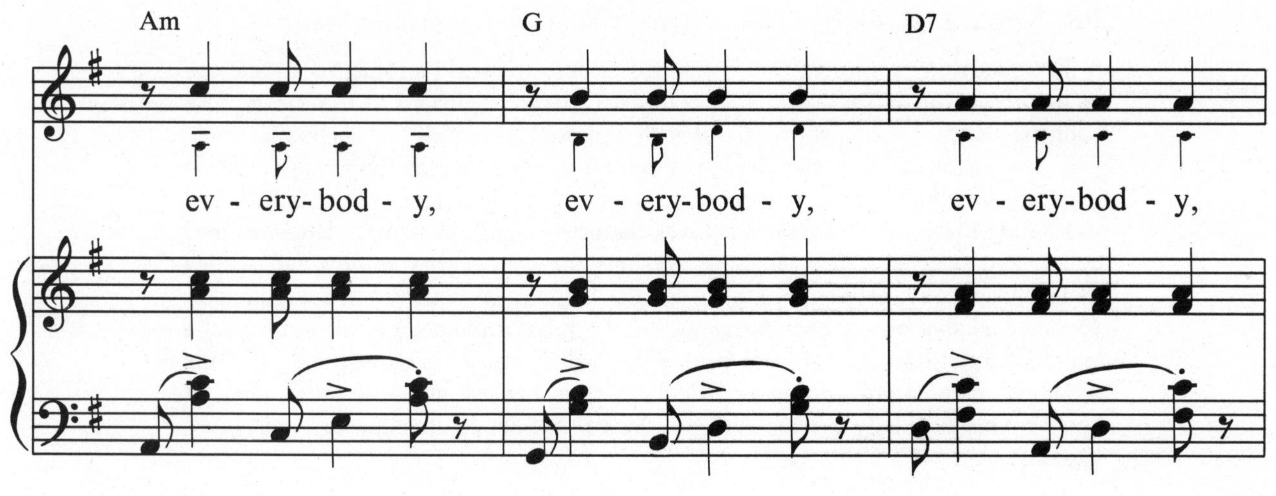
Am
G
D7
ev - ery- bod - y,
ev - ery- bod - y,
ev - ery- bod - y,

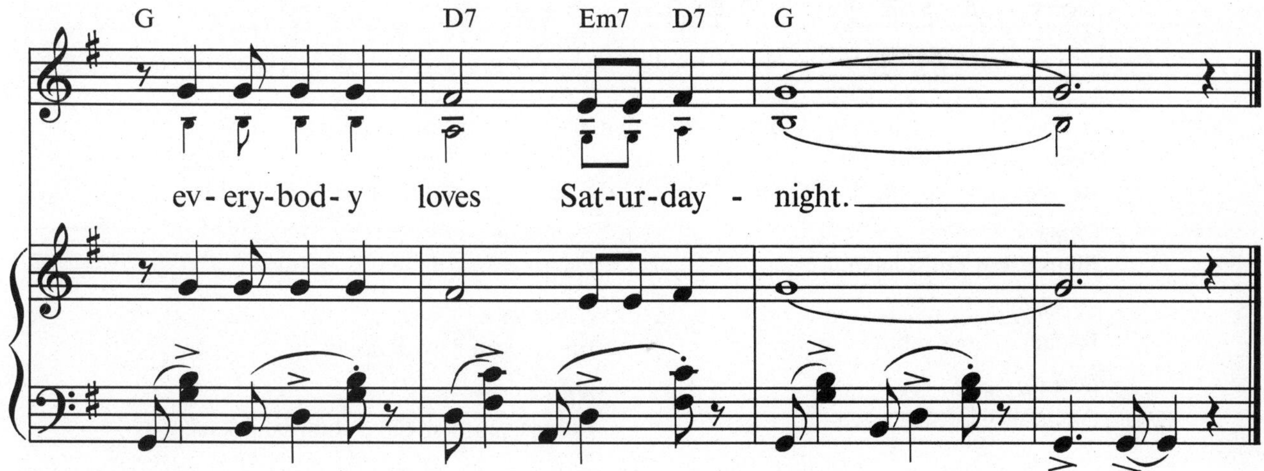
G
D7
Em7
D7
G
ev - ery- bod- y
loves
Sat- ur- day -
night.

Selected verses, spelled phonetically:

French:

Too luh moanduh em Sahmehdee swahr.
Too luh moanduh em Sahmehdee swahr.
Too luh moanduh, too luh moanduh,
Too luh moanduh, too luh moanduh,
Too luh moanduh em Sahmehdee swahr.

Continue, as above:

German:

Yaydermahn leept Sahmstak Nahkt.

Greek:

Ohlee ahgahpoon toe Sahvahtoh Vrathee.

Italian:

Ohnyounoh amah Sahbahtoh nohtteh.

Norwegian:

Hehler vehrden elsker lurdahgskvel.

Russian:

Fsyeh lyubyat soobawtnyee vyeacher.

PROGRAM GUIDE: *West African folk song; brotherhood*

Everybody loves to sing this combined tribute to world brotherhood and one of the best nights of the week. It is believed to have originated in a West African country, Sierra Leone, when the British imposed a curfew six nights a week. The free night on Saturday had a special meaning for the population. When the song was imported to this country, singers took to it immediately and began translating the phrase "Everybody loves Saturday night" into every language they could. I've selected a few language versions for the singer's edition and spelled them phonetically. Don't hesitate to use the linguists in your group for guidance. I've used a calypso-styled arrangement, set at a relaxed tempo. I've also indicated a simple harmonization that can be learned easily as a counter-melody by the ambitious men in your group (it will be a little low for most of the ladies). If you have insistent lady harmonizers, put them in the act on the repeated *everybody*, like this:

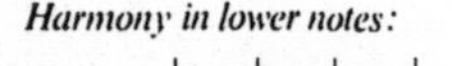
Harmony in lower notes:

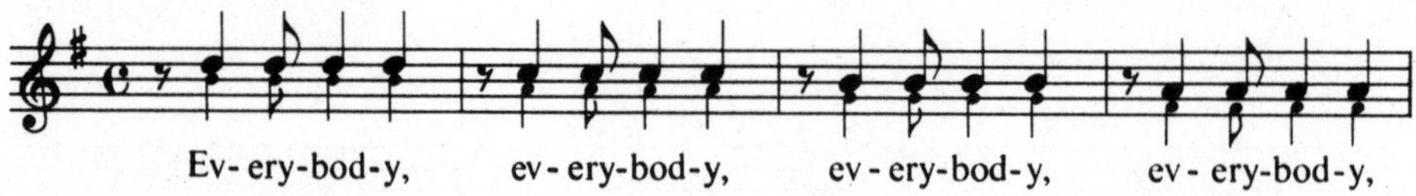
Ev- ery-bod-y, ev - ery-bod-y, ev - ery-bod-y, ev - ery-bod-y,

Someday we'll have a definitive collection of verses in all languages. You can help. Collect them from your singers and compile them yourself, or send them to me care of the publisher. Here is the present state of my collection:

Chinese:
Phon.: Ren ren si huan li pai lu.

Czech:
Kazhdi ma rad sabotu vietcher.

Danish:
Alle elsker Lordag asten.

French:
Tout le monde Samedi soir.
Phon.: Too luh moanduh em Sahmehdee swahr.

German:
Jedermann liebt Samstag Nacht.
Phon.: Yaydermahn leept Sahmstak Nahkt.

Greek:
Ολοι ἁ γαποῦν τὸ Σάββατο Βράδι
Phon.: Ohlee ahgahpoon toe Sahvahtoh Vrathee.

Italian:
Ognuno ama Sabato notte.
Ohnyounoh amah Sahbahtoh nohtteh.

Japanese:
Da re demo do yo bi gasuki.

Nigerian:
Bobo waro fero Satodeh.

Norwegian:
Hehler vehrden elsker luhrdahgskvel.

Russian:
Fsyeh lyubyat soobawtnyee vyeacher.
or:
Vsiem nravitsa subbota vietcherom.

Spanish:
El Sábado ama todo el mundo.
Phon.:

Sudanese:
Mofe moni s'mo ho gbeke.
Phon.: Maw fay monee s'maw haw bekay.

Yiddish:
Jeder eyne hot lieb Shabas ba nacht.

I cannot vouch for the accuracy of any of these. I only pass them on to you the way I have received them myself from well-intentioned singers. Use them with care, and find out for yourself.

27

Ezekiel Saw the Wheel

American Negro Spiritual

Lively
Chorus
Solo
F
Response
(Melody in upper notes)
F
C7
F
Solo
E - ze-kiel saw the wheel, 'way up in the mid-dle of the air. E -
Response
F
F
C7
F
Solo
ze-kiel saw the wheel, 'way in the mid-dle of the air; And the
Response
F
F
C7
F C7 F
Solo
lit-tle wheel run by faith, and the big wheel run by the grace of God, A

Solo
Response
F
F
C7
F
Fine
wheel in a wheel (wheel in a wheel) 'way in the mid-dle of the air.
Fine
Verse
Solo
Response
Solo
F
F
C7
F
Some go to church for to sing and shout, 'way in the mid-dle of the air. Be -
Response
F
F
C7
F
D.C.
fore six months they's shout-ed out. 'way in the mid-dle of the air.
D.C.

2. Let me tell you what a hypocrite'll do,
'Way in the middle of the air,
He'll talk about me and he'll talk about you,
'Way in the middle of the air.

Chorus

Continue, as above:

3. Don't pray for things that you don't need,
The Lord don't like no sin and greed.

4. There's one thing sure that you can't do,
You can't serve God and Satan, too.

5. One of these days about twelve o'clock,
This old world's gonna reel and rock.

PROGRAM GUIDE: *American Negro spiritual*

It's really easy to make a production number out of this lively spiritual, with or without a sprinkling of trained singers. First, decide who is going to sing the solos, or divide the group into leaders and responders. Put your harmonizers, if you have any, in the responder group. And if you don't, try to create them on the spot. The harmony part is easily learned by anyone with an ear for music.

Another effective way to perform the chorus is to have the men sing the leader calls and the melody on the responses. Teach the ladies the harmony part for the responses. Then put the two together. If you then add soloists for the calls in the verse, you have an instant (well, not quite) choral group. If they come anywhere near your expectations take them on a tour. The routine is chorus, verse, chorus, verse, chorus, etc., ending, of course, on the chorus.

28

Fairest Lord Jesus

Anonymous

Silesian Folk Tune

Moderately

D A7 D A7 D G

Fair - est Lord Je - sus, Rul - er of all na - ture, O thou of

D A7 D A7 D A7 D G D A7

God and man the Son; Thee will I cher - ish,

D D7 G D A7 D

Thee will I hon - or, Thou, my soul's glo - ry, joy, and crown.

2. Fair are the meadows,
Fairer still the woodlands,
Robed in the blooming
Garb of spring;
Jesus is fairer,
Jesus is purer,
Who makes the woeful
heart to sing.

3. Fair is the sunshine,
Fairer still the moonlight,
And all the twinkling
starry host.
Jesus shines brighter,
Jesus shines purer,
Than all the angels
heaven can boast.

PROGRAM GUIDE: *Traditional European hymn*

This hymn dates back to the seventeenth century. Sing it softly. It is particularly effective for outdoor and camp programs in the evening. Legend has it that German crusaders sang this song on the way to Jerusalem. The song first appeared in *Münster Gesangbuch* in 1677. The words are by an unknown author. The music is a Silesian folk melody.

29
The First Nowell

Traditional English Carol

Moderately
D Bm A7 D G D
The first Now-ell, the angel did say, Was to
D Em6 D G A7 D A7 D A7 D Bm
cer-tain poor shep-herds in fields as they lay; In fields where
A7 D G D G D Em6 D G A7
they lay keep-ing their sheep On a cold win-ter's night that

Refrain
D A7 D A7 D Bm F♯m D G
was — so deep. Now - ell, — Now - ell, Now - ell, Now -
D A Bm Dmaj7 G D G A7 D A7 D
ell, Born is the King — of Is - ra - el.

2. They looked up and saw a star
Shining in the East, beyond them far;
And to the earth it gave great light,
And so it continued both day and night.

Refrain

3. This star drew nigh to the Northwest,
O'er Bethlehem it took its rest,
And there it did both stop and stay
Right o'er the place where Jesus lay.

Refrain

4. Then entered in those wisemen three,
Full rev'rently on bended knee,
And offered there in his presence,
Their gold and myrrh and frankincense.

Refrain

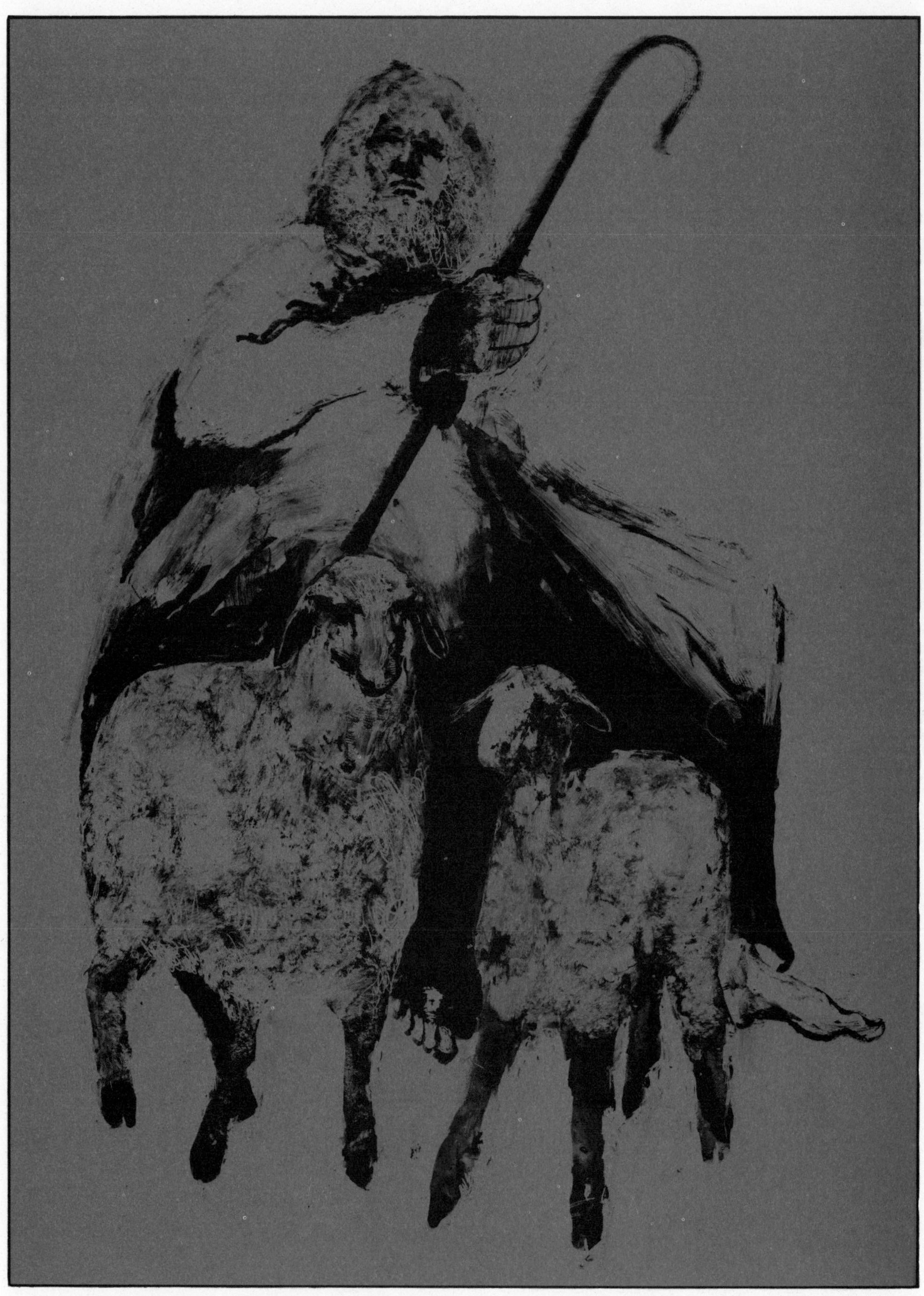

PROGRAM GUIDE: *Traditional English Christmas carol*

Noël, or *nowell,* means "Christmas carol" (or even the Christmas season itself). The term is thought by some scholars to be derived from the Latin word for birthday, *natalis.* The French *noëls* are story or ballad carols, believed to have originated with the troubadours. The troubadours were medieval lyric poets who flourished principally in southern France from the eleventh to thirteenth centuries, writing songs and poems mostly about courtly romance. "The First Nowell" is neither French nor the first *noël,* but an English ballad carol, which may explain why it is often spelled differently. I've heard various theories on this point, but none that sounds as though it has a corner on the truth. All of this is a long way of saying that "The first Nowell," being a ballad carol, tells a story: The story of Christmas and of how the first nowell allegedly came into being. The tempo usually indicated is *moderato.* A little contrast in dynamics enhances the performance. Try singing the verses softly, the choruses louder, swelling to a magnificent *crescendo* on the fourth *nowell,* followed by a *diminuendo* in the last four measures, perhaps tapering off to a whisper by the last measure.

30
For the Beauty of the Earth

Folliot Sandford Pierpoint *Conrad Kocher*

Moderately
G D7 G D7 G C G C D7 G C D D7 G
For the beau- ty of the earth, For the glo - ry of the skies,
G D7 G D7 G C G C D7 G C D D7 G
For the love which from our birth, O - ver and a - round us lies;
G D7 G D7 G C D7 G C G D7 G
Lord of all, to Thee we raise This our hymn of grate-ful praise.

2. For the wonder of each hour
Of the day and of the night,
Hill and vale, and tree and flow'r,
Sun and moon, and stars of light;
Lord of all, to thee we raise
This our hymn of grateful praise.

3. For the joy of human love,
Brother, sister, parent, child,
Friends on earth, and friends above,
For all gentle thoughts and mild;
Lord of all, to thee we raise
This our hymn of grateful praise.

PROGRAM GUIDE: *Traditional English hymn*

This nature hymn, written in 1864, was originally intended for Anglican communion services in 1864. The text was written by Folliott Sandford Pierpoint (1835-1917), an English classicist and poet. His idea came from a letter written by Pliny the Younger to the Roman Emperor Trajan. In the letter, Pliny referred to an early Christian gathering where they repeated in turn "a hymn to Christ as a god." In Pierpoint's original version the refrain began "Christ, our God, to thee we raise." This is the altered and abridged version that is widely sung today. The original text had eight stanzas. The music was composed by Conrad Kocher (1786-1872), director of music for the collegiate church in Stuttgart, Germany. Because of its message the hymn is particularly useful for outdoor and camp programs.

31
The Four Marys

British Ballad

Moderately

D G D A7 G D A7 D

Last night there were_ four Ma - rys, To - night there'll be but three.___ There was Ma - ry Bea - ton and Ma - ry Sea - ton, And Ma - ry Car - mi - chael and me.___

2. Oh, often have I dressed my queen
And put on her braw silk gown;
But all the thanks I've got tonight
Is to be hanged in Edinburgh town.

3. Full often have I dressed my queen;
Put gold upon her hair;
But I have got for my reward
The gallows to be my share.

4. They'll tie a kerchief around my eyes
That I may not see to dee;
And they'll never tell my father or mother,
But that I'm across the sea.

5. Last night there were four Maries,
Tonight there'll be but three;
There was Mary Beaton and Mary Seaton,
And Mary Carmichael and me.

PROGRAM GUIDE: *British ballad*

Word's gane to the kitchen,
And word's gane to the ha,
That Marie Hamilton gangs wi bairn
To the hichest Stewart of a'.

So begins one of the most popular and beautiful of the old Scottish ballads. Long before soap operas were invented the ballad medium was used to entertain us during the long dreary stretches of the day or night. "The Four Marys" tells the story of a legendary scandal at the court of Mary Stuart—Mary, Queen of Scots. There are so many Marys in the song and in its historical scene that it is difficult to keep them all straight. Mary Stuart had four ladies in waiting: Mary Seaton, Mary Beaton, Mary Fleming, and Mary Livingston. The four Maries, as they were popularly known in France, were chosen to accompany her when she went to France as a little girl of five or six. These four girls, who were about her own age and who came from "honorable houses," remained with Mary Stuart while she was in France and returned to Scotland with her thirteen years later, in 1561. Despite the fact that they have been woven into the ballad, there is no record to indicate that any of these Marys was involved in a specific situation that would provide a basis for the story of this ballad. The Mary Carmichael and Mary Hamilton of the ballad appear from nowhere, although historians have located a Mary Hamilton who was a Scottish maid of honor at Peter the Great's court and was beheaded for infanticide (the crime in this ballad) in 1719. Surrounding Mary Stuart and her court there was considerable gossip, rumor, and criticism of romantic and political intrigues. This atmosphere in itself was sufficient to provide the basis for ballad and legend. Stories of illegitimate births occurring to members of her court and to the queen herself circulated widely at the time. Until research and scholarship turn up a better answer, if they ever do, we will have to assume the ballad emerged from this background of popular rumor and legend, with the customary confusions and distortions that accompany the folk processes of oral circulation. This short version of the ballad enables you to get through the song in less time than it would take you to explain the story. There are longer versions that run in excess of twenty verses. The melody flows very nicely at a slow one-beat-to-the-measure pace, or a relatively fast three beats to the measure. *Braw* (verse 2, line 2) means *"fine-looking,"* or *"splendid."* It can also mean "gaudy."

32
The Fox

British Ballad

Moderately fast
F
The fox went out on a chil - ly night, Prayed for the moon to
C7 F B♭ F C7
give him light, For he'd man-y a mile to go that night Be - fore he reached the
F C7 F B♭
town - o, the town - o, the town - o, He'd man-y a mile to

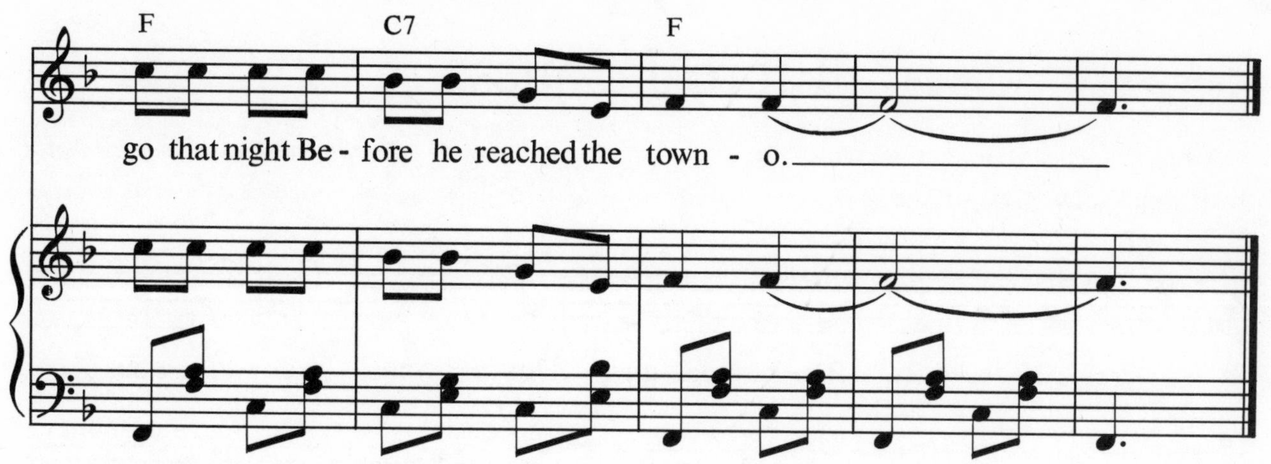
F
C7
F
go that night Be - fore he reached the town - o.

2. He ran till he came to a great big pen
Where the ducks and the geese were put therein,
"A couple of you will grease my chin
Before I leave this town-o,

This town-o, this town-o,
A couple of you will grease my chin
Before I leave this town-o.

Continue, as above:

3. He grabbed the gray goose by the neck,
Throwed a duck across his back;
He didn't mind their quack, quack, quack,
And their legs all dangling down-o (*etc.*)

4. The old mother Flipper-Flopper jumped out of bed,
Out of the window she cocked her head,
Crying, "John, John, the gray goose is gone,
And the fox is on the town-o" (*etc.*)

5. Then John, he went to the top of the hill,
Blowed his horn both loud and shrill;
The fox, he said, "I better flee with my kill
Or they'll soon be on my trail-o" (*etc.*)

6. He ran till he came to his cozy den;
There were the little ones, eight, nine, ten.
They said, "Daddy, better go back again,
For it must be a mighty fine town-o" (*etc.*)

7. Then the fox and his wife without any strife
Cut up the goose with a fork and knife;
They never had such a supper in their life,
And the little ones chewed on the bones-o (*etc.*)

PROGRAM GUIDE: *British ballad; humorous*

The unknown writer's clever lyric is just as fresh today as it must have been way back when it was written. It's a great story, and tackling the tickling, tongue-tripping lyric is a joy. It's not fair to cut out any of the verses—you'll miss some of the story. Beware! From time to time the timing of the words may throw you if you are not well rehearsed. The song works well with singers of all ages and on almost any conceivable occasion when you need something light to brighten the program.

33
Frère Jacques

Traditional French Round, Adapted

Moderately fast
1
2
Frè - re Jac-ques, frè - re Jac-ques, Dor-mez-vous? dor-mez-vous?
3
4
Son-nez les ma- ti - nes, son-nez les ma- ti - nes, Din, din, don; din, din, don.

Divide the group into four sections. Each section sings the entire round the agreed-upon number of times, beginning at point 1 when the preceding section reaches point 2. Thus the round begins and ends with one section singing alone: Section 1 at the beginning and Section 4 at the end.

English version:
Are you sleeping, are you sleeping,
Brother John, brother John?
Morning bells are ringing, morning bells are ringing,
Ding dong, ding, ding, dong, ding.

Spanish version:
Fray Felipe, Fray Felipe,
Duermus tu, duermus tu?
Toca la campana, toca la campana,
Tan, tan, tan; tan, tan, tan.

German version:
Onkel Jakob, Onkel Jakob,
Schlafst du noch, schlafst du noch,
Ringe an der Glocke, ringe an der Glocke,
Bim bam, bom; bim, bam, bom.

PROGRAM GUIDE: *Traditional French round*

Rounds provide the easiest way possible to do part-singing with amateur singers. And "Frère Jacques" is one of the best known rounds in America. So here it is in four languages. Take your pick or use them all. You can sound like a meeting at United Nations headquarters by instructing each of your four groups to sing in a different language. Why not sing it through once in the familiar way, then combine.

34
Froggie Went A-Courting

British Ballad

Brightly
F
B♭ F
(Ah hah)
B♭ F
(Ah hah)
Frog-gie went a-court-ing and he did ride, A - hum, a - hum.
F
B♭
Frog-gie went a-court-ing and he did ride, A sword and pis - tol
F
B♭ F C7
(Ah hah)
F
by his side, A - hum, a - hum.

2. He rode up to Miss Mousie's door,
A-hum, a-hum,
He rode up to Miss Mousie's door,
Where he had often been before.
A-hum, a-hum.

3. He said: "Miss Mouse, are you within?"
A-hum, a-hum,
He said: "Miss Mouse, are you within?"
"Just lift the latch and do come in"
A-hum, a-hum.

Continue, as above:

4. He took Miss Mousie on his knee,
And said: "Miss Mouse, will you marry me?"

5. "Without my Uncle Rat's consent,
I would not marry the President."

6. Now, Uncle Rat, when he came home,
Said: "Who's been here since I've been gone?"

7. "A very fine gentleman has been here,
He wishes me to be his dear."

8. Then Uncle Rat laughed and shook his sides,
To think his niece would be a bride.

9. Then Uncle Rat, he went to town
To buy his niece a wedding gown.

10. Where will the wedding breakfast be?
Way down yonder in a hollow tree.

11. What will the wedding breakfast be?
Two green beans and a black-eyed pea.

12. The first to come was the bumble bee.
He danced a jig with Miss Mousie.

13. The next to come was Mister Drake,
He ate up all of the wedding cake.

14. They all went sailing on the lake,
And they all were swallowed by a big black snake.

15. So, that's the end of one, two, three,
The rat, the frog, and Miss Mousie.

16. There's bread and cheese upon the shelf.
If you want anymore just sing it yourself.

PROGRAM GUIDE: *British ballad; humorous*

How did a young mouse like this one ever get mixed up with a stupid frog masquerading as one of the three "mousketeers"? Furthermore, why would singers like yours want to get mixed up with this silly little soap opera anyhow? The answer: to see what happens. Will Miss Mouse marry Mister Frog? Will Uncle Rat give his consent? What will the wedding breakfast be? Who will be there? And (to the accompaniment of minor chords rolled on the piano), what happens when the big black snake drops in on the festivities? Sing it and find out. If you lose your audience with the courting frog you may be the first to do so since the late 1500s when the ballad of "a most strange Wedding of the Frog and the Mouse" was licensed to Edward White (a song collector) at Stationers' Hall in London.

I've set you up (see vocal score) for a simple little arrangement to try when your singers know the song very well. The routine could go like this:

Ladies: Froggie went a-courting and he did ride.

Men: A-hum.

Ladies: Ah hah.

Men: A-hum.

Ladies: Ah hah.

All: Froggie went a-courting and he did ride,
A sword and pistol by his side.

Men: A-hum.

Ladies: Ah hah.

Men: A-hum.

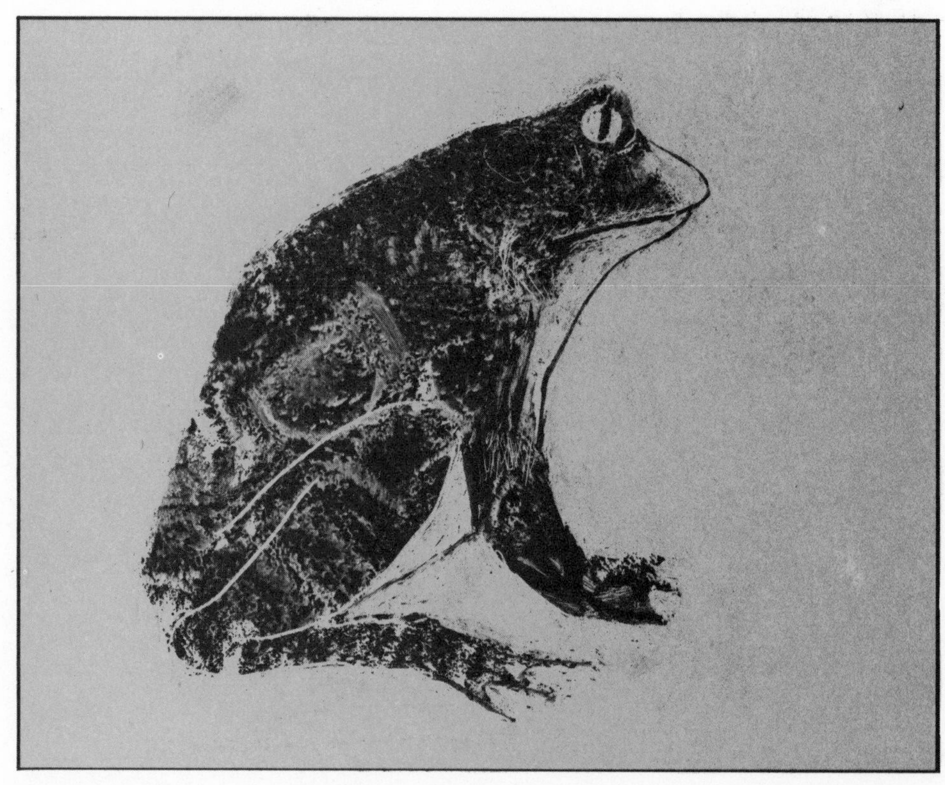

If your singers take to this idea you can introduce another feature that will add still more variety. In subsequent verses the "ah hah" can be changed to follow the story, like this:

Verse	First time	Second time	Third time
2.	Knock knock	knock knock	ah hah.
3.	Come in	come in	ah hah.
4.	Wowee	why me?	ah hah.
5.	My unk's	consent	ah hah.
6.	Ah hah	oh ho	ah hah.
7.	Ah hah	oh yes	ah hah.
8.	Ha ha	ho ho	ha ha.
9.	To town	downtown	a gown.
10.	Ah hah	oh yes	ah hah.
11.	You'll see	it's free	ah hah.
12.	Buzz buzz	buzz buzz	ah hah.
13.	Quack quack	quack quack	ah hah.
14.	Oh ho	oh ho	oh no.
15.	Yes one	two-three	uh huh.
16.	So what?	so what?	the end.

These cues are not indicated in the singer's edition because they would only be confusing to anyone not following the arrangement. If, or when, you decide to use the arrangement, you may ask the singers to write the cues in their books underneath each extra verse.

You may want to assign these vocal cues to a selected group of male and female singers who are particularly skilled at this sort of thing, and let the main body of your singers concentrate on singing just the verses themselves. Whatever you do, use a bright tempo—it's a long story.

35

Go Down, Moses

American Negro Spiritual

Slowly and majestically

Leader (boldly) — *Response (softly)* — *Leader*

Em B7 Em B7 Em

When Is-rael was in E-gypt's land, Let my peo-ple go. Op-

Response (a little louder)

Em B7 Em B7 Em

pressed so hard they could not stand, Let my peo-ple go.

All (boldly) — *cresc.* — *ff* — *(melody in upper notes)*

Em Am Em

Go down, Mo-ses, 'Way down in E-gypt's land;

softly
Em
D
B7
Em
Tell old Pha - raoh, Let my peo - ple go.

2. Thus saith the Lord, bold Moses said:
   Let my people go.
   If not I smite your firstborn dead.
   Let my people go.

   Chorus

   Continue, as above:

3. No more shall they in bondage toil,
   Let them come out with Egypt's spoil.

4. Oh, Moses, the cloud shall cleave the way,
   A fire by night, a shade by day.

5. Your foes shall not before you stand,
   And you'll possess fair Canaan's land.

PROGRAM GUIDE: *American Negro spiritual*

"Go Down, Moses" is one of the most powerful and beautiful of the many anthem-like spirituals from the highly varied Negro religious music tradition. It deserves a powerful performance—which you can arrange with very little difficulty by varying the dynamics (as noted on the vocal score) and the voices used. If you have an experienced bass or baritone in your group, turn the leader calls over to him. Otherwise, use only the male voices for the calls and all voices combined for the responses, encouraging harmony on the responses among those who can and will supply it. In any event, try for that harmony part in measures 11 and 12 (it's easy to learn). With the dynamics carefully applied (see score) you may create a magnificent, awesome performance.

36

Go Tell Aunt Rhody

American Folk Song

Moderately fast
D
A7
D
Go tell Aunt Rho - dy, Go tell Aunt Rho - dy,
A7
D
Go tell Aunt Rho - dy The old gray goose is dead.

2. The one she's been savin',
   The one she's been savin',
   The one she's been savin'
   To make a feather bed.

   Continue, as above:

3. She died in the millpond,
   Standin' on her head.

4. The goslins are cryin',
   Because their mommy's dead.

5. Go tell Aunt Rhody,
   The old gray goose is dead.

PROGRAM GUIDE: *American folk song; humorous*

Almost everybody's aunt has been or will be the recipient of the bad news about the old gray goose. So don't feel you are stuck with Rhody. You can hold some sort of contest, if you like, to select a favorite aunt from your audience to use in place of Aunt Rhody. Whether you do it as a surprise or as a planned variation, you can have some fun with your singers by switching the D major chords to D minor chords in, say, the third and fourth verses. Your accompanist will have to collaborate on the plot, of course, or you will never get there. All she or he has to do is flat the F sharps in the piano score and change the D chords to Dm chords in the guitar symbols. Sing Rhody brightly or everyone will think it is a sad song.

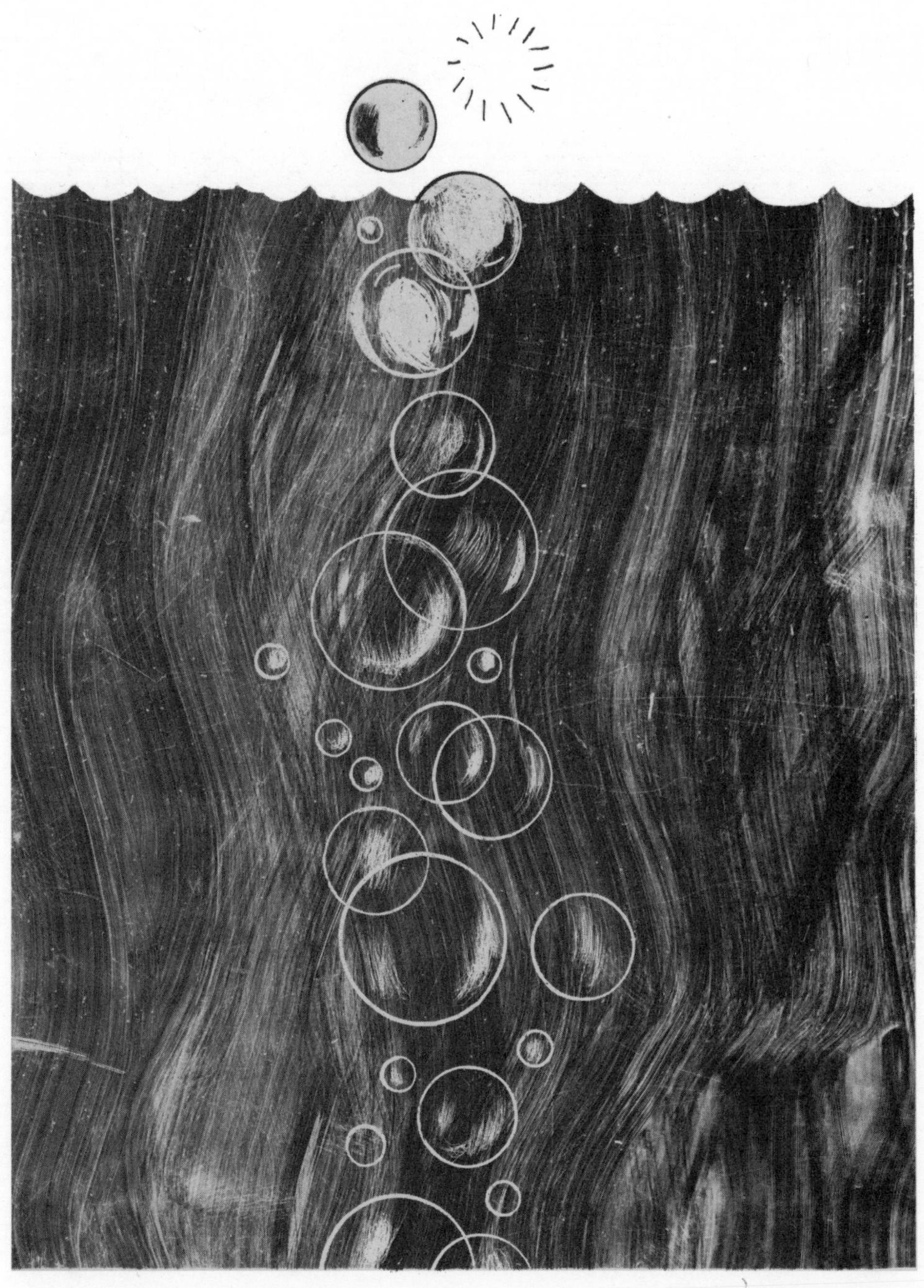

37

Go, Tell It on the Mountain

American Negro Spiritual

Moderately
Chorus
Echo (in small upper notes)
Tell it on the moun-tain
F C7 F B♭ F
Go, tell it on the moun - tain, O-ver the hills and ev - ery-where,
simile
Echo
Tell it on the moun-tain
F B♭ F C7 F
Fine
Go, tell it on the moun - tain, That Je - sus Christ is a - born.
Fine
Verse
F C7 F C7 F
Oh, when I was a sin-ner, I prayed both night and day; I

F
G7
C7
D.C.
asked the Lord to help me, And he showed me the way.
D.C.

2. When I was a seeker,
I sought both night and day;
I asked my Lord to help me,
And he taught me to pray.

Chorus

3. He made me a watchman
Upon the city wall;
And if I am a Christian,
I am the least of all.

Chorus

4. It was in a lowly manger
That Jesus Christ was born;
The Lord sent down an angel
That bright and glorious morn.

Chorus

PROGRAM GUIDE: *American Negro spiritual; Christmas*

This popular spiritual is especially appropriate for Christmas singing. Though it is a fine spiritual to use anytime and is very effective when sung outdoors. You may wish to assign soloists for each of the verses. Otherwise, the verses may be traded back and forth between the men and women for variety. I've indicated an echo repeat of the initial motive in the second and sixth measures which you may wish to assign to selected male or female voices. The tempo can be moderate, about halfway between fast and slow. The mood and style are joyful and stately. Quiet or bold dynamics, or a mixture of the two, are effective. Try the chorus at *forte* and the verses at *piano,* then the last chorus at almost a whisper. The routine is chorus, verse, chorus, verse, chorus, etc.

38

God Rest You Merry, Gentlemen

Traditional English Carol
Arr. by John Stainer

Moderately fast
Dm A Dm Am B♭ F B♭ A Dm Gm
1. God rest you mer - ry, gen - tle - men, Let noth - ing you dis -
2. From God our heav'n - ly Fa - ther A bless - ed an - gel
A Dm Dm A Dm Am B♭ F B♭ A Dm Gm
may, Re - mem - ber Christ our Sav - ior, Was born on Christ - mas
came; And un - to cer - tain shep - herds Brought tid - ings of the
A D Gm C F B♭ F B♭ F A7 Dm G7 C F
Day; To save us all from Sa - tan's pow'r When we were gone a -
same; How that in Beth - le - hem was born The Son of God by

Refrain
C C7 Dm C F B♭ F C7 Dm A Dm G7
stray.
name.
O— tid - ings of com - fort and joy, com-fort and
C Dm C7 F B♭ F B♭ F C7 Dm A Dm
joy; O— tid - ings of com - fort and joy.

3. "Fear not, then," said the angel,
   Let nothing you affright,
   This day is born a savior
   Of a pure virgin bright,
   To free all those who trust in him
   From satan's power and might."

   Refrain

4. Now to the Lord sing praises,
   All you within this place,
   And with true love and brotherhood
   Each other now embrace;
   This holy tide of Christmas
   All others doth deface.

   Refrain

PROGRAM GUIDE: *Traditional English Christmas carol*

The writers of this popular Christmas carol are unknown. But it dates back at least to 1833 when it was published in a popular collection. The minor mode and the joyful text make interesting companions. This arrangement was made by John Stainer (see "What Child Is This?" number 154). However, I have transcribed the arrangement one whole step lower to accommodate average voice ranges.

39

Goin' Down the Road Feeling Bad

American Folk Song

Lively
D
D7
I'm go-in' down the road feel-in' bad, Lord, I'm
G
D
D7
go-in' down the road feel-in' bad. I'm
G
D
go-in' down the road feel-in' bad, Lord, Lord, And I

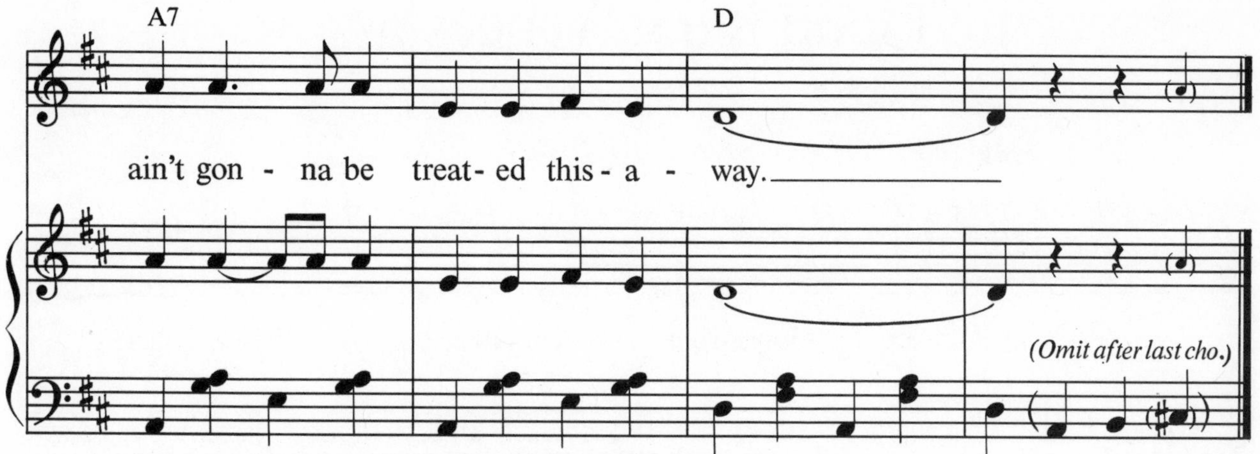
A7
D
ain't gon - na be treat- ed this - a - way.
(Omit after last cho.)

2. I'm goin' where the climate suits my clothes,
   I'm goin' where the climate suits my clothes,
   I'm goin' where the climate suits my clothes, Lord, Lord,
   And I ain't gonna be treated this a-way.

Continue, as above:

3. I'm a-lookin' for a job with honest pay.
4. These two-dollar shoes hurt my feet.
5. But ten-dollar shoes fit 'em neat.
6. I'm down in the jailhouse on my knees.
7. I'm leaving and I'm never coming back.

PROGRAM GUIDE: *American folk song; humorous*

The hoboes of the 1930s probably created most of the verses for this happy/sad song of the open road. But new verses are being added all the time, made up right out of life's experiences. Maybe something happened to you or one of your singers that should be interpolated when you perform. For example:

Such-and-such place's food tastes like paste.
Doohickey's water tastes like turpentine.
So-and-so's stupid songs make you sick.
I couldn't sleep a wink all night long.

It's also nice if you can tie two verses together (see verses four and five above). "Road" is what is known as a *protest song* among folk song devotees and, as such, it provides a handy format for this kind of creative songmaking with campers and others with a little time on their hands. Don't discourage anyone from adding a hillbilly falsetto harmony part on top of the melody:

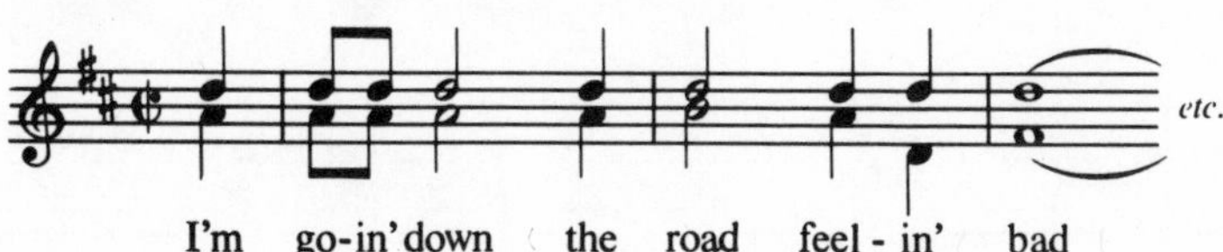
etc.
I'm go-in' down the road feel - in' bad

40
Good King Wenceslas

John M. Neale *Traditional, European*

Moderately brisk

G Em D G C D C G C D7 G

Good King Wen-ces - las looked out On the Feast of Ste - phen,

G Em D G C D C G C D7 G

When the snow lay round a - bout, Deep and crisp, and e - ven:

G C G D7 G D7 Em C G C D7 G

Bright- ly shone the moon that night, Though the frost was cru - el,

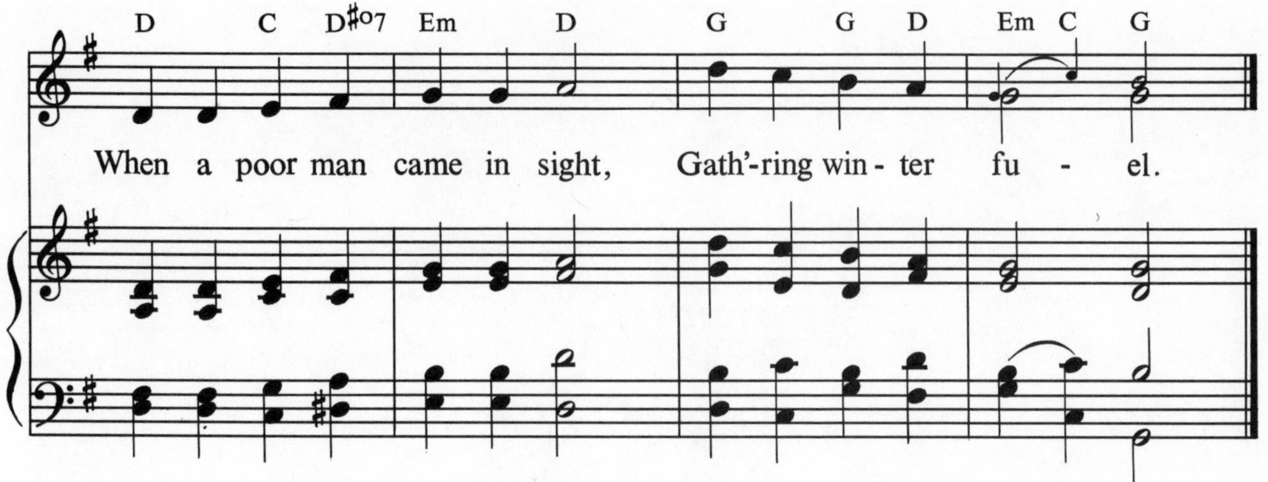
D C D♯o7 Em D G G D Em C G
When a poor man came in sight, Gath'-ring win - ter fu - el.

2. "Hither, Page, and stand by me,
If thou knows't it; telling,
Yonder peasant, who is he?
Where and what his dwelling?"
"Sire, he lives a good league hence,
Underneath the mountain;
Right against the forest fence,
By Saint Agnes' fountain."

3. "Bring me flesh, and bring me wine,
Bring me pine logs hither;
Thou and I will see him dine,
When we bear them thither."
Page and monarch forth they went,
Forth they went together;
Through the rude wind's wild lament,
And the bitter weather.

4. "Sire, the night is darker now,
And the wind blows stronger;
Fails my heart, I know not how,
I can go no longer."
"Mark my footsteps, my good page,
Tread thou in them boldly:
Thou shalt find the winter's rage,
Freeze thy blood less coldly."

5. In his master's steps he trod,
Where the snow lay dinted;
Heat was in the very sod
Which the Saint had printed.
Therefore, Christian men, be sure,
Wealth or rank possessing,
Ye who now will bless the poor,
Shall yourselves find blessing.

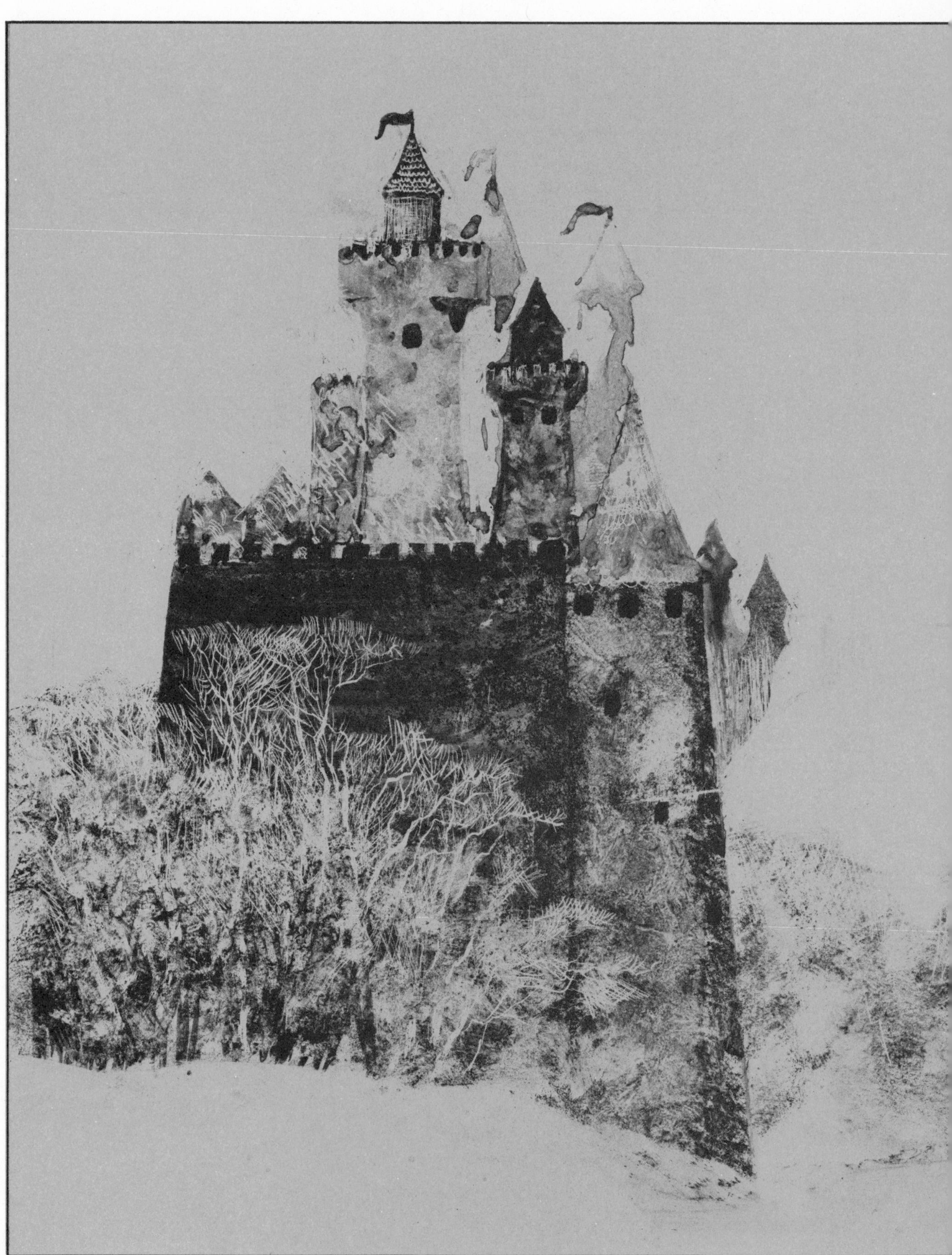

PROGRAM GUIDE: *Traditional English Christmas carol*

Dr. John M. Neale wrote the words to this popular carol in 1863 to celebrate the Feast of Stephen (December 26), basing the story on an old Bohemian legend about King Wenceslaus. Literary critics dismiss Neale's effort as doggerel, but carolers don't appear to be a bit concerned. I can't help but feel the critics have a point; the story does seem a bit slow and labored. Also, I feel sorry for the freezing page who is pressed into a forced march because of Wenceslaus' sudden inspiration to "do good" for *one* poor man. Why didn't the King throw a feast at the castle for *all* the poor folk, and give the page a night off and a raise in pay? Or, better still, why did he not turn the castle into a poor folk's home? Oh well, you can't blame Neale for the flaws in the legend, or for the desire of the folk to perpetuate a nearsighted legend. Neale used a fine tune from the fifteenth century as a setting for his words.

A moderately brisk tempo is appropriate, particularly if you want to hurry through the whole story. However, I don't think it matters much if you decide to cut out a couple of verses. We never do find out whether the king, and his now "boldly" treading page got to the poor man's home with the feast. Presumably they did, but Neale doesn't say. According to my dictionary a league is about three miles. That's a long way to carry the wine, flesh, and pinelogs at a bold pace. Who is carrying all that stuff? The page? If so, no wonder he was complaining. Three miles there; three miles back! But I'm sure what really counts is the thought, and I shouldn't be raising all these questions about the good king (I wonder what bad kings were like).

41
Good News

Moderately fast and rhythmic

American Negro Spiritual

Women
G6
Good news!
Char-i-ot's a-com-in', Good
Men
Talk a-bout your good news! Char-i-ot's a-com-in',
R.H.
L.H.
D7
G6
news! Char-i-ot's a-com-in', Good news!
Sing a-bout the news: The Char-i-ot's a-com-in'. Shout a-bout your good news!
C
G6
D7
G
Fine
Char-i-ot's a com-in', And I don't want it to leave me be - hind.
Fine
Char-i-ot's a com-in', And I don't want it to leave me be - hind.
Fine

G6
There's a long white robe in heav-en I know,
There's a
C G6 D7 G6
There's a long white robe in
long white robe in heav-en I know, There's a long white robe in
C G D7 G
D. S.
heav-en I know, And I don't want it to leave me be - hind. (Good)
heav-en I know, And I don't want it to leave me be - hind.
D. S.

Continue, as above:

2. There's a long white robe in heaven I know.
3. There's a starry crown in heaven I know.
4. There's a golden harp in heaven I know.
5. It's a better place than this world I know.

PROGRAM GUIDE: *American Negro spiritual*

Good News! Gospel rock (well, almost)—and it's easy! It only looks hard when you see it all at once. But that's not the way to do it, all at once. You take things one at a time. There are only three vocal parts to "Good News" and each one is a singable melody all its own. First you divide the ladies into high voices and low voices and teach them their songs one at a time. Then send them off to practice by themselves, or give them a rest, while you teach the men their songs. Five or ten minutes later you put all the voices together and you have an incredibly exciting sound—and everybody wonders how you did it with a bunch of no-talents like them. Next thing you know they'll want you to build a repertoire and take them on the road.

Keep the tempo relaxed, there will be plenty of rhythmic action without rushing it. The routine is chorus, verse, chorus, verse, chorus, etc. Good luck!

42
The Gospel Train

American Negro Spiritual

Moderately fast and lively

Verse

G
The gos-pel train is com-ing; I hear it just at hand; I
C
G
G
D7
G
Chorus
hear the wheels a - mov-ing and rum-bling thro' the land. Get on
C
G
board, lit-tle chil-dren; Get on board, lit-tle chil-dren; Get on

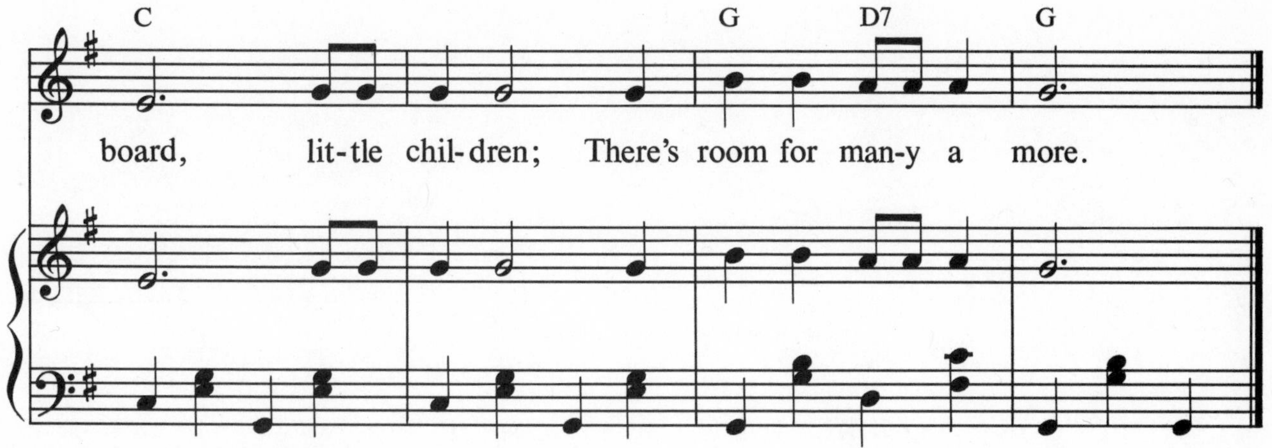
C
G
D7
G
board, lit-tle chil-dren; There's room for man-y a more.

2. I hear the bell and whistle,
A-comin' 'round the curve;
She's playing all her steam and power
And straining every nerve.

3. No signal for another train
To follow on the line,
Oh, sinner, you're forever lost
If once you're left behind.

4. She's coming to the station,
Oh, sinner, don't be vain,
But come and get your ticket,
And be ready for the train.

5. The fare is cheap and all can go,
The rich and poor are there,
No second-class on board the train,
No difference in the fare.

6. We soon shall reach the station,
Oh, how we then will sing,
With all the heavenly army,
We'll make the welkin ring.

PROGRAM GUIDE: *American Negro spiritual*

This familiar, lively spiritual is frequently sung without much imagination or variation. William C. Handy, whose early association with blues earned him the title "father of the blues," tells us that in minstrel days (many people don't realize there were Negro minstrels also) "Gospel Train" was "ragged" with hand-clapping, offbeat rhythm, syncopation, and gestures. By ragging it yourself you may be able to recreate the spontaneity that leads everyone to the improvisations Handy was talking about. You can't order it to be done very successfully, but you can encourage it, and show the way.

Start by getting everyone to clap on or off the beat. Then fix up that repetitive chorus. Here's the way Handy remembered singing it:

Get on board, little children,
Get on board, big children,
Get on board, all the children,
There's room for many a-more.

Syncopate those new "children" phrases and you'll be getting there. Here is some more variation, this time from the Bahamas:

Get on board, you swearers,
Get on board, rum drinkers,
Get on board, backsliders,
There's room for many a-more.

Maybe you should select soloists for the verses. Any volunteers? Or divide the singers into groups, each with the responsibility for a different verse. Before you make the "welkin" ring in the sixth verse, you're entitled to know what the welkin is: *the sky, the vault of heaven.* The routine is verse, chorus, verse, chorus, etc. Some singers like to repeat the chorus before going on to each new verse. What's your pleasure?

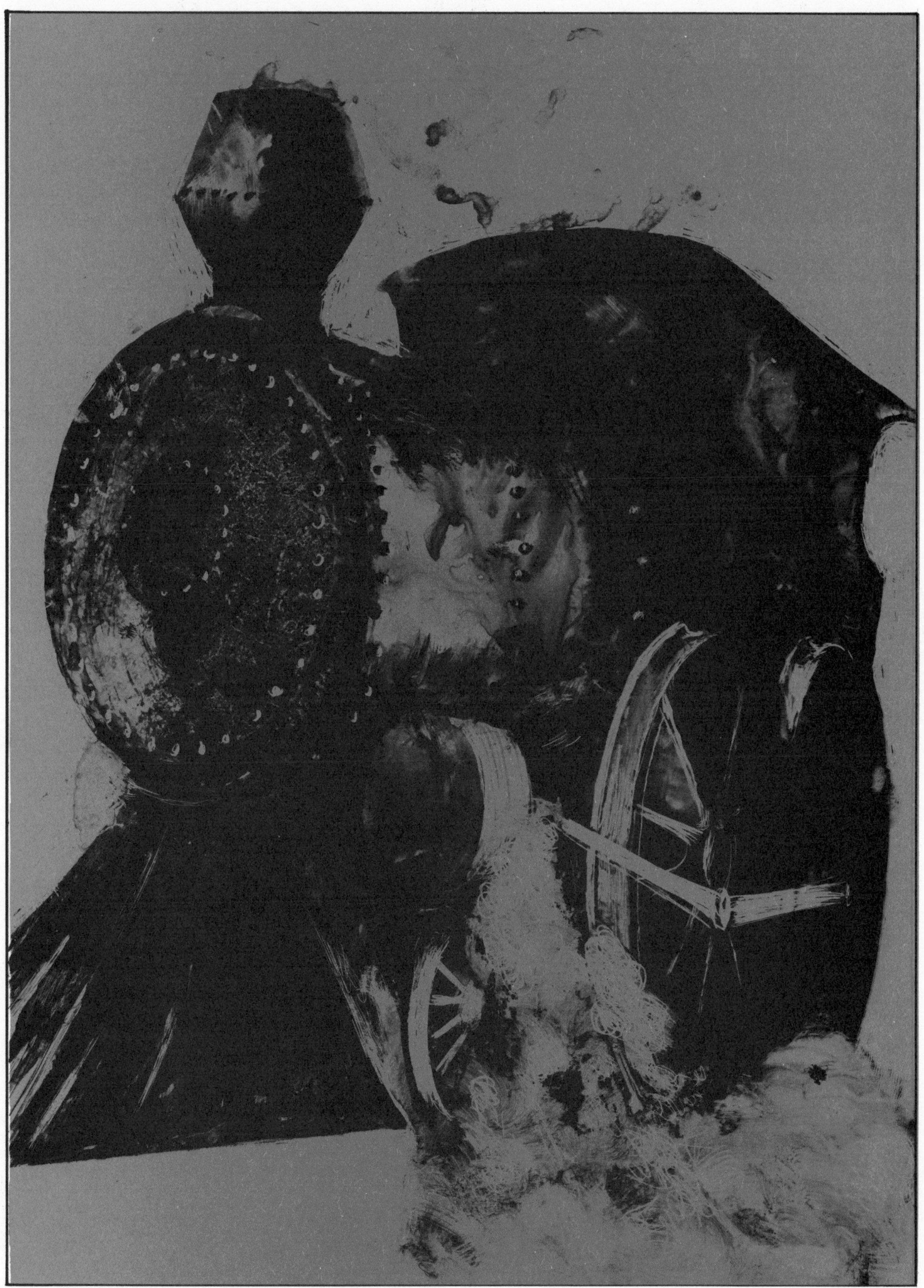

43

The Great Meat Pie

British Folk Song

Majestically

C G C Dm G7 C

The great meat pie was a ti- dy size, And it took a week to make it, A

C G C Dm G7 C

day to car-ry it to the shop, And just a week to bake it. And

Am G Am E7 Am G7

if you'd seen it, I'll be bound, Your won-der you'd scarce gov - ern. They were

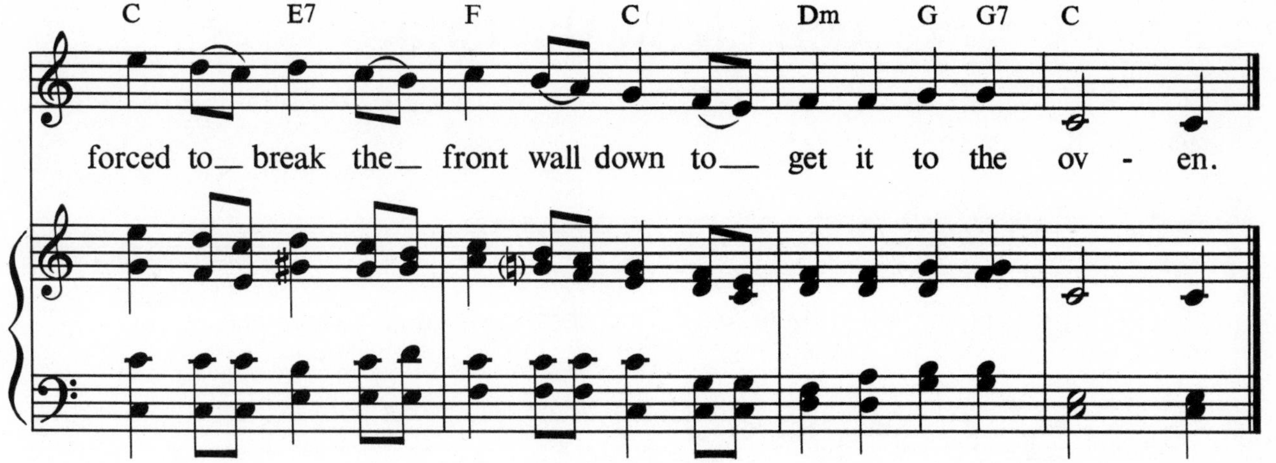
C
E7
F
C
Dm
G
G7
C
forced to_ break the_ front wall down to_ get it to the ov - en.

2. It took full thirty sacks of flour,
It's a fact now that I utter,
Three hundred pails of water, too,
And a hundred tubs of butter.
The crust was nearly seven feet thick,
You couldn't easily bruise it,
And the rolling pin was such a size
It took ten men to use it.

3. There were twenty-five spareribs of pork,
I'm sure I'm not mistaken,
With two and thirty hams from York,
And twenty sides of bacon.
The pie was made by fifty cooks,
And all of them first raters,
And then they filled up all the nooks
With a ton of kidney 'taters.

PROGRAM GUIDE: *Traditional British pseudo-hymn; humorous*

Let us pause, ladies and gentlemen (pause), in solemn reverence to pay tribute to England's finest contribution to the sustenance and succor of the world. Known by many, feared by all, the great meat pie is an institution, and one that we can depend upon in these times of change, stress, and strain. Meat pie makers everywhere rejoice in the sure knowledge that, no matter what worlds may tumble and crumble around us, the Great Meat Pie shall never fall. So now let us stand and raise our voices, singing in a proud and stately manner the noble anthem we all love so well. And if our voices waver as we soar to the precipice of those high and mighty tones at the climax, I say, Let them ring proudly in their wavering! For a man or a woman who can sing *without* emotion—at a time like this—is no man, or woman, and certainly not a friend of meat pies.

44

Green Grow the Lilacs

Irish-American Folk Song

Moderately
G G7 C G
Oh, green grow the li - lacs and so does the rue. How sad's been the
A7 D7 G G7
day since I part- ed from you. But at our next meet - ing our
(Melody in lower notes)
C G C G D7 G
love we'll re - new, We'll change the green li - lacs for the red, white, and blue.

2. I once had a sweetheart but now I have none;
He's gone off and left me to live here alone.
He's gone off and left me contented to be;
He must love another girl better than me.

3. I passed my love's window both early and late,
The look that he gave me it made my heart ache.
The look that he gave me was painful to see,
For he loves another one better than me.

4. I wrote my love letters in red rosy lines,
He sent me an answer all twisted in twines,
Saying, "Keep your love letters and I will keep mine.
Just you write to your love and I'll write to mine."

5. On top of the mountain where green lilacs grow,
And over the valley where the still waters flow,
I met my true love and he proved to be true.
We changed the green lilacs for the Red, White, and Blue.

PROGRAM GUIDE: *Irish-American folk song; romantic*

A true folk poet's hand may be found in this popular song. But you have to look beyond the words as they are now sung to find his, or her, subtle touch. Some folk music scholars believe the first line was originally written, "Oh, green grows the *laurel* and so does the rue," and the last line: "We'll change the green *laurel* for the *marjoram* blue." Marjoram is a blue plant. In folk ballad symbolism the *laurel* represents virginity, *rue* the opposite, and blue is the color of *fidelity*. The symbolism indicates, then, that the girl is giving up maidenhood for a true love. Some scholars add that marjoram is also a symbol of fertility, thus broadening the symbolism. When Irish immigrants brought this lovely song with them to America they quite understandably changed marjoram blue to red, white, and blue, losing the symbolism in the process. If you wish, you may restore it by changing the words back. Because "Green Grow the Lilacs" was very popular with Irish-American troops during the 1846 war with Mexico it has been suggested that the first two words of the title provided the basis for the Mexican word *gringo,* which means foreigner or American from the United States. But that may be just folklore. The tune is Irish and should be sung with a lilt. Harmony notes are indicated in the last three measures for your adventurers, but feel free to encourage harmony throughout.

45

Green Grow the Rushes

English Folk Song

Moderately fast
(Guitar tacet)
Solo
C G7 C
Response
(Guitar tacet)
Solo
1. I sing you one O, Green grow the rush-es O. What is your one O?
C G7 C
Response
Solo
F
G7
C
Green grow the rush-es O. One is one and all a- lone And ev-er-more shall be so.
R.H.
L.H.
(Guitar tacet)
Solo
C G7 C
Response
(Guitar tacet)
Solo
2. I sing you two O, Green grow the rush-es O. What is your two O?

C G7 C
Response
Green grow the rush-es O.
C F D7 G7
Solo
Two for the lil-y-white boys Cloth-ed all in green O.
C F G7 C
All
One is one and all a-lone And ev-er-more shall be so.
(Guitar tacet)
Solo
3. I sing you three O.
C G7 C
Response
Green grow the rush-es O.
(Guitar tacet)
Solo
What is your three O?
C G7 C
Response
Green grow the rush-es O.
C G7 C G7
Solo
Three, three, the riv - als,
C F D7 G7
(All, or as directed)
Two for the lil-y-white boys Cloth-ed all in green O.

C F G7 C
All
(Guitar tacet)
Solo
One is one and all a-lone And ev-er more shall be so. 4. I sing you four O.
C G7 C
Response
(Guitar tacet)
Solo
C G7 C
Response
Green grow the rush-es O. What is your four O? Green grow the rush-es O.
G7 C C G7 C G7 C F
Solo
(All, or as directed)
Four for the gos-pel mak-ers, Three, three the riv - als, Two for the lil-y-white boys
D7 G7 C F G7 C
All
Cloth-ed all in green O, One is one and all a-lone And ev-er-more shall be so.

(Guitar tacet) Solo — C G7 C Response — (Guitar tacet) Solo

5-12. I sing you five O, Green grow the rush-es O. What is your five O?
I sing you six O, Green grow the rush-es O. What is your six O?
I sing you seven O, Green grow the rush-es O. What is your seven O?
etc. etc.

C G7 C Response

Green grow the rush-es O.

Guitar (see note * and ** below)
Solo (ad lib.)

For verses 5, 7, 8, 9, 11, 12.

5. Five for the symbols at your door.
7. Seven for the seven stars in the sky.
8. Eight for the April rainers.
9. Nine for the nine bright shiners.
11. Eleven for the eleven who went to heaven.
12. Twelve for the twelve apostles.

*Use sustained C Chord throughout if preferred

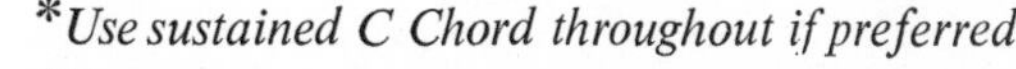

**If guitar uses the chord changes, they are: C F B♭9 C

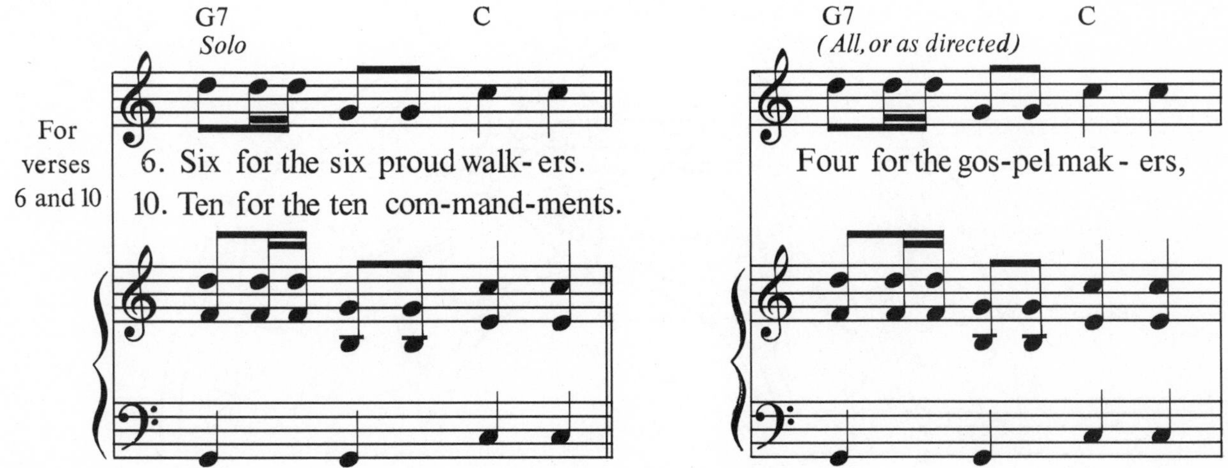

G7
Solo
C
For verses 6 and 10
6. Six for the six proud walk-ers.
10. Ten for the ten com-mand-ments.
G7
(All, or as directed)
C
Four for the gos-pel mak - ers,

C G7 C G7 C F
Three, three, the riv - als, Two for the lil-y-white boys

D7 G7 C F G7 C
All
Cloth-ed all in green O. One is one and all a-lone And ev-er-more shall be so.

PROGRAM GUIDE: *Traditional English folk song; cumulative*

"Green Grow the Rushes" provides a *tour de force* for lovers of cumulative singing. If you have a very small or unambitious group of singers you may wish to have everybody sing all the parts all the way through. With a large group of enthusiastic singers you can make a spectacular production by designating up to twenty-four soloists, two for each verse. Here is the routine:

1. First soloist: I'll sing you one O.
   All: Green grow the rushes O.
   Second soloist: What is your one O.
   All: Green grow the rushes O.
   First soloist: One is one and all alone
   And evermore shall be so.

2. Third soloist: I'll sing you two O.
   All: Green grow the rushes O.
   Fourth soloist: What is your two O?
   All: Green grow the rushes O.
   Third soloist: Two for the lily white boys
   Cloth-ed all in green O.
   All: One is one and all alone
   And evermore shall be so.

3. Fifth soloist: I'll sing you three O.
   All: Green grow the rushes O.
   Sixth soloist: What is your three O?
   All: Green grow the rushes O.
   Fifth soloist: Three, three, the rivals.
   Third soloist: Two for the lily white boys
   Cloth-ed all in green O.
   All: One is one and all alone
   And evermore shall be so.

Continue, as above, to the final accumulation, which is:

12. Twenty-third soloist: I'll sing you twelve O.
   All: Green grow the rushes O.
   Twenty-fourth soloist: What is your twelve O?
   All: Green grow the rushes O.
   Twenty-third soloist: Twelve for the twelve apostles.
   Twenty-first soloist: Eleven for the eleven who went to heaven.
   Nineteenth soloist: Ten for the ten commandments.
   Seventeenth soloist: Nine for the nine bright shiners.
   Fifteenth soloist: Eight for the April Rainers.

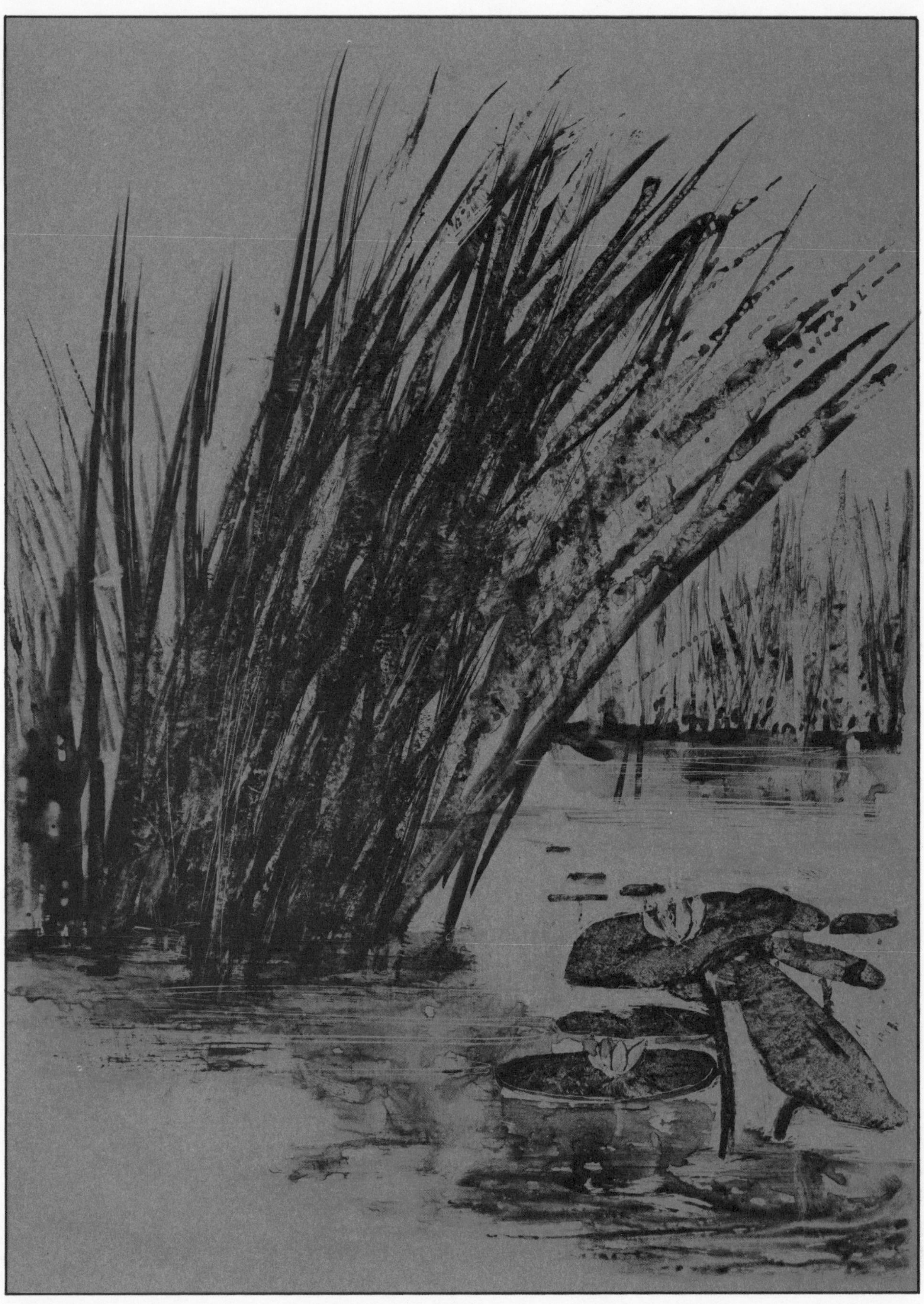

Thirteenth soloist: Seven for the seven stars in the sky.
Eleventh soloist: Six for the six proud walkers.
Ninth soloist: Five for the symbols at your door.
Seventh soloist: Four for the gospel makers.
Fifth soloist: Three, three the rivals.
Third soloist: Two for the lily white boys
Cloth-ed all in green O.
All: One is one and all alone
And evermore shall be so.

Speed up the tempo as you progress, and award a prize to the soloist who doesn't goof. (A free invitation to sing "Green Grow the Rushes" in a sidewalk group in front of Carnegie Hall on the Monday night of his or her choice would be appropriate.) Of course you may cut down on the confusion (and the fun) by using only twelve soloists. Each can respond to his own question, or you can respond, or the group can respond, or you can appoint some one person as a responder. Further, you may cut down the number of soloists, say to only two, by doubling up. If only two are being used, let one take the even numbered verses, the other take the odd.

"Rushes" is a fine musical exercise for restless campers. It may be too long and arduous, however, for indoor singers and apathetic groups.

Folk song scholars have traced the theme of this popular song to extremely antique antecedents coming from an original in Hebrew—specifically, a chant in the service for the second night of the Passover:

Who knoweth thirteen?
I, saith Israel, know thirteen:
Thirteen divine attributes,
Twelve tribes,
Eleven stars,
Ten Commandments,
Nine months before child birth,
Eight days before circumcision,
Seven days in the week,
Six books of the Mishnah,
Five books of the law,
Four matrons,
Three patriarchs,
Two tables of Covenant,
But one is God alone,
Which is over heaven and earth.

Other titles by which the song is known to singers include "The Twelve Prophets," "The Carol of the Twelve Numbers," and "The Ten Commandments."

46
Greensleeves

Traditional English Folk Song

Moderately slow (in two)
Em
D
C
B7
A - las! my love,_you do me wrong_To cast me off_ dis-cour-teous-ly; And
Em
D
C
B7
Em
I have lov - ed you so long_De - light - ing in_ your com - pa - ny.
G
D
Em
B7
Green - sleeves_was all my joy,___ Green - sleeves_was my de-light.

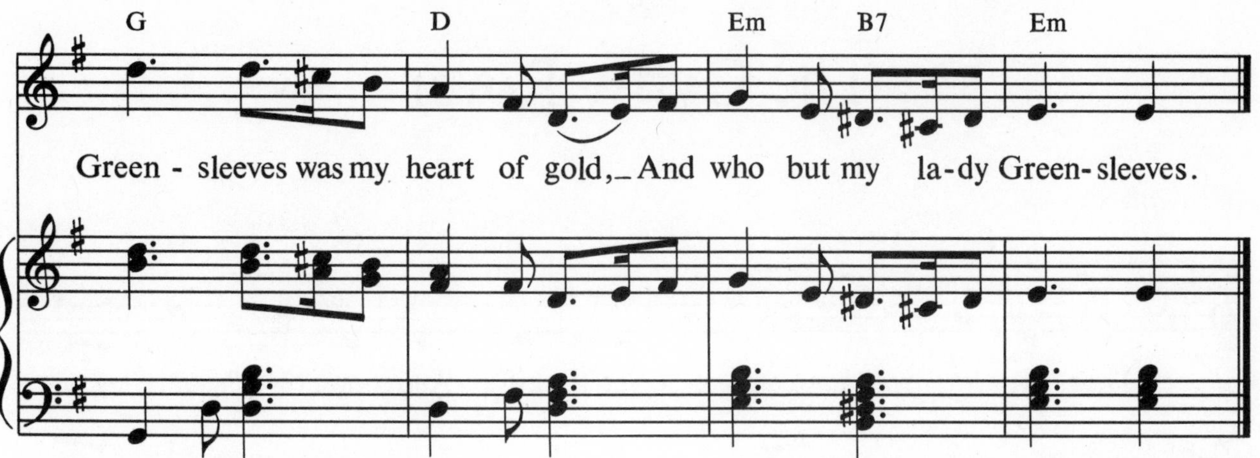
G
D
Em
B7
Em
Green - sleeves was my heart of gold,_And who but my la-dy Green-sleeves.

2. I have been ready at your hand,
   To grant whatever you would crave;
   I have waged both life and land,
   Your love and good-will for to have.

3. If you intend thus to disdain,
   It does the more enrapture me,
   And even so, I still remain
   A lover in captivity.

4. My men were clothed all in green,
   And they did ever wait on thee;
   All this was gallant to be seen;
   And yet thou wouldst not love me.

5. Thou couldst desire no earthly thing
   But still thou hadst it readily.
   Thy music still to play and sing;
   And yet thou wouldst not love me.

6. Well, I will pray to God on high,
   That thou my constancy mayst see,
   And that yet once before I die,
   Thou wilt vouchsafe to love me.

7. Ah, Greensleeves, now farewell, adieu,
   To God I pray to prosper thee,
   For I am still thy lover true,
   Come once again and love me.

PROGRAM GUIDE: *Traditional English folk song; romantic*

"Greensleeves" has one of the most durable melodies in folk music. During the almost four centuries of its known life, the melody has had texts fitted to it to please the man in the street, the drawing room set, opera-goers, the clergy, and twentieth-century teenagers. The texts have been bawdy, religious, political, social, literary, mundane, and temporal, but the melody has never failed to survive. The texts most frequently sung today are entitled "Greensleeves" and "What Child Is This?" (see number 154). The lyric to "Greensleeves" is tolerated by adults and ignored by children. In *The Ballad Mongers: Rise of the Modern Folk Song,* Oscar Brand suggests a method for communicating the text to children:

> Just tell the children that they are to raise their elbows on the word "greensleeves" as if they were wearing sleeves of that color. It'll be great fun . . .
>
> You can tell them to put their right palms to their foreheads on the word "alas." On "you do me wrong," they must point an accusing finger at the head in front of theirs. On the phrase "to cast me off" they are to simulate throwing a bundle into the aisle. When they sing "For I," let them touch hand to breast sadly. This helps with the beat since it makes a wonderfully resounding "thwack." When they sing "you so long," the accusing finger is again indicated. And "delighting in your company" deserves a joyful throwing up of hands to the accompaniment of a wide-mouthed phony smile.
>
> The preceding exercise may forever sour the observing adults on "Greensleeves," but it will delight juvenile Audiences.*

* (Funk and Wagnalls, 1962.)

47

The Gypsy Rover

Irish Ballad

Brightly

G D7 G D7 G D7

The gyp - sy rov - er came o - ver the hill, And down thro' the val - ley so

G D7 G D7 Bm Em

shad - y. He whis-tled and he sang till the green woods rang And he

Bm Am G C G D7 G D7

won the heart of a la - dy. Ah dee doo, ah dee

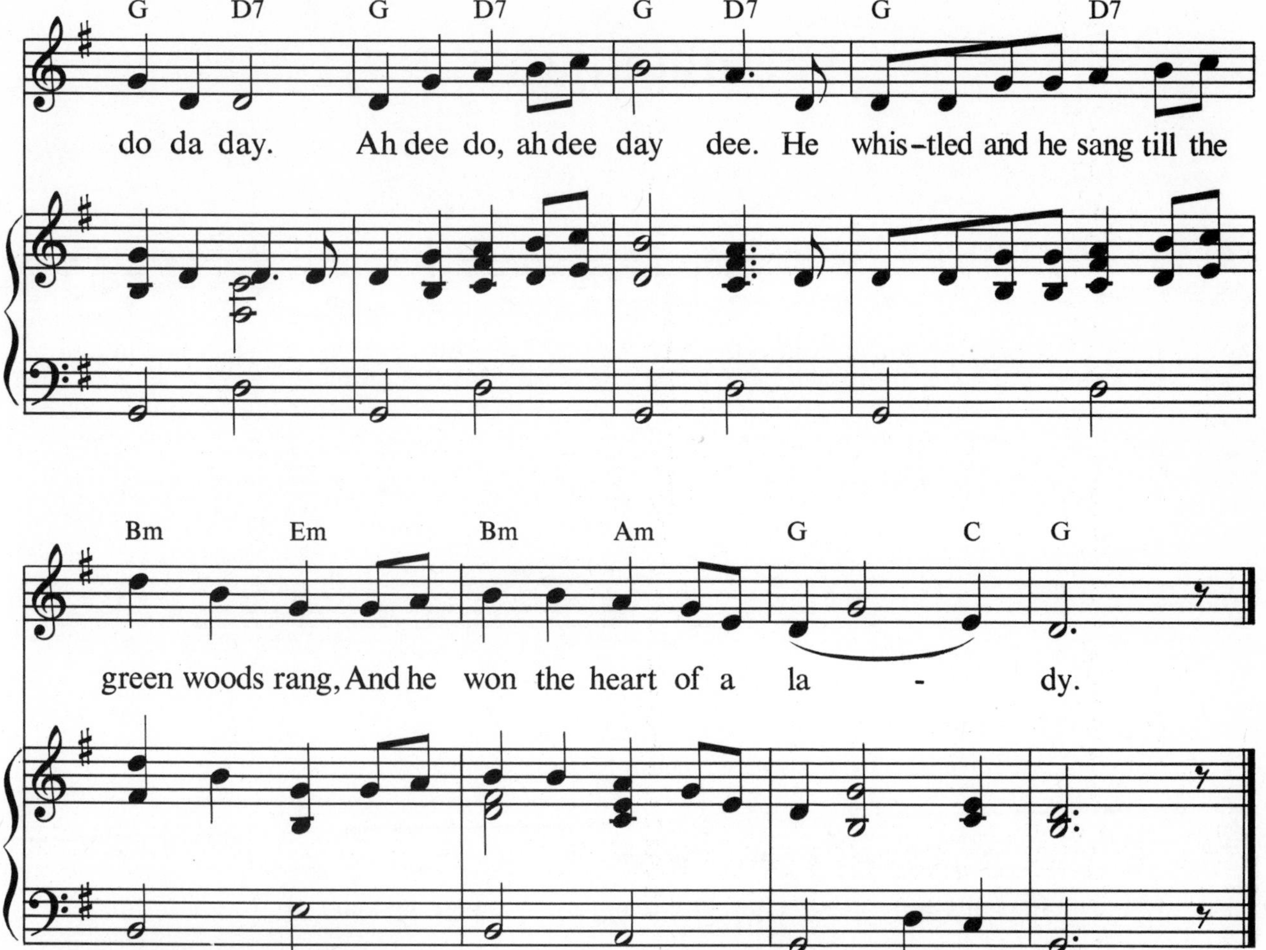

G D7 G D7 G D7 G D7
do da day. Ah dee do, ah dee day dee. He whis-tled and he sang till the
Bm Em Bm Am G C G
green woods rang, And he won the heart of a la - dy.

2. She left her father's castle gate;
She left her own true lover;
She left her servants and her estate
To follow the gypsy rover.

3. Her father saddled his fastest steed
And roamed the valley all over.
He sought his daughter at great speed,
And the whistling gypsy rover.

4. He came at last to a mansion fine
Down by the River Clayde;
And there was music and there was wine
For the gypsy and his lady.

5. "He's no gypsy, my father," said she,
"He's lord of freelands all over;
And I will stay till my dying day
With my whistling gypsy rover."

PROGRAM GUIDE: *Irish ballad; romantic*

"The Gypsy Laddie" is one of the great British ballads that come down to us in many different forms and variations. You probably know two popular versions of it: "Gypsy Davey" and "The Wraggle Taggle Gypsies." They all tell pretty much the same story: A young maiden leaves her comfortable home and wealthy family to run away with a handsome gypsy. Gypsies were widely persecuted at the likely time of the origin of this ballad (1500s). They were formally expelled from Scotland by an act of Parliament in 1609. "The Gypsy Rover" version of the ballad comes from Ireland and has the most lyrical tune of them all. You may add a nice touch by asking everyone to whistle every other chorus, or by asking the men to whistle while the ladies sing. Use a bright, lilting tempo.

48
Hallelujah

Palestinian Folk Song

Very fast
Gm
Dm Gm
Hal-le-lu-jah, hal-le-lu-jah, hal-le-lu-jah, hal-le-lu! Hal-le-lu-jah,
hal-le-lu-jah, hal-le-lu-jah, hal-le-lu! Hal-le-lu-jah, hal-le-lu!
Hal-le-lu-jah, hal-le-lu! Hal-le-lu-jah, hal-le-lu-jah, hal-le-lu-jah, hal-le-lu!

PROGRAM GUIDE: *Palestinian folk song*

You absolutely cannot miss with this spirited, rhythmic Palestinian chant—even the monotones have a chance to excel. And, once learned, nobody forgets the lyric. Clapping and foot stamping can be used for percussive effects; one stamp per measure and, mostly, four claps per measure, like this:

Note: Two times (i.e. repeat this first pattern, then go on)

Hand Clappers	: ♫ ♫	♫ ♫	♫ ♫	♫ ♩ :
Foot Stampers	: ♪ 𝄾 𝄽	♪ 𝄾 𝄽	♪ 𝄾 𝄽	♪ 𝄾 𝄽 :
Singers	: Hal - le - lu - jah	hal - le - lu - jah	hal - le - lu - jah	hal - le - lu! :
Beat	1 2	1 2	1 2	1 2

Hand Clappers	♫ ♫	♫ ♩	♫ ♫	♫ ♩
Foot Stampers	♪ 𝄾 𝄽	♪ 𝄾 𝄽	♪ 𝄾 𝄽	♪ 𝄾 𝄽
Singers	Hal - le - lu - jah	hal - le - lu!	Hal - le - lu - jah	hal - le - lu!
Beat	1 2	1 2	1 2	1 2

Hand Clappers	♫ ♫	♫ ♫	♫ ♫	♫ ♩
Foot Stampers	♪ 𝄾 𝄽	♪ 𝄾 𝄽	♪ 𝄾 𝄽	♪ 𝄾 𝄽
Singers	Hal - le - lu - jah	hal - le - lu - jah	hal - le - lu - jah	hal - le - lu!
Beat	1 2	1 2	1 2	1 2

If your singers want to turn it into a contest, keep repeating the song and accelerating the tempo until everyone is exhausted.

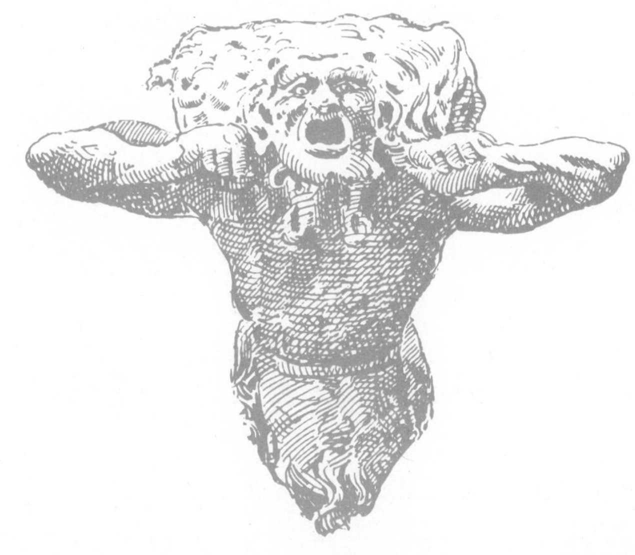

49

Hark! the Herald Angels Sing

Charles Wesley
Alt. by George Whitefield

Felix Mendelssohn
Adapted by William H. Cummings

Moderately slow and joyfully

G D G D G D C G D G

Hark! the her - ald an- gels sing,__ "Glo- ry to the new-born King;

G D Em A7 Bm D Gmaj7 A7 D

Peace on earth, and mer - cy mild,__ God and sin - ners rec - on- ciled!"

G D7 G D G D7 G D

Joy- ful, all ye na- tions, rise,__ Join the tri- umph of the skies;__

C
Am E7 Am
D7
G
D7 G
With th'an-gel - ic host pro-claim, "Christ is__ born in Beth-le-hem!"
Refrain
C
Am E Am
D
G
D7 G
Hark! the her-ald an-gels sing, "Glo - ry__ to the new-born King!"

2. Christ, by highest heav'n adored;
Christ, the everlasting Lord!
Late in time behold him come,
Offspring of the virgin's womb.
Veiled in flesh the Godhead see;
Hail th'Incarnate Deity,
Pleased as man with men to dwell,
Jesus, our Emmanuel. (*Refrain*)

3. Hail! the heaven-born Prince of Peace!
Hail the Sun of Righteousness!
Light and life to all he brings,
Risen with healing in his wings,
Mild he lays his glory by,
Born that man no more may die,
Born to raise the sons of earth,
Born to give them second birth. (*Refrain*)

PROGRAM GUIDE: *Traditional English Christmas hymn*

A long and drawn-out collaboration produced this popular Christmas hymn. First, Charles Wesley wrote a text in 1739 about the Incarnation, beginning:

Hark, how all the welkin rings,
Glory to the King of kings.

Then a friend and associate of Wesley, George Whitefield, altered the lines to their present form. Wesley's original four-line stanzas were rearranged into ten-line stanzas by William Cummings, the Waltham Abbey organist, in 1850. Cummings then set the words to a chorus from Mendelssohn's cantata *Festgesang,* which was written in 1840 to celebrate the invention of printing.

The suggested tempo is *andante con moto,* moderately slow and even, with feeling, but don't let it drag.

50
Heaven Is So High

American Negro Gospel Song

Medium bounce
F
1st cue:
high
C7
2nd cue:
low
Heav-en is so high, you can't get o-ver it, So low you
F
3rd cue:
wide
(Melody in lower notes)
can't get un-der it, So wide you can't get a-round it; You
C7
F
Fine
Verse
Solo
F
must come in at the door. You might as well just make
Fine

Response
C7
F
Solo
up your mind. You must come in at the door. Broth-er,

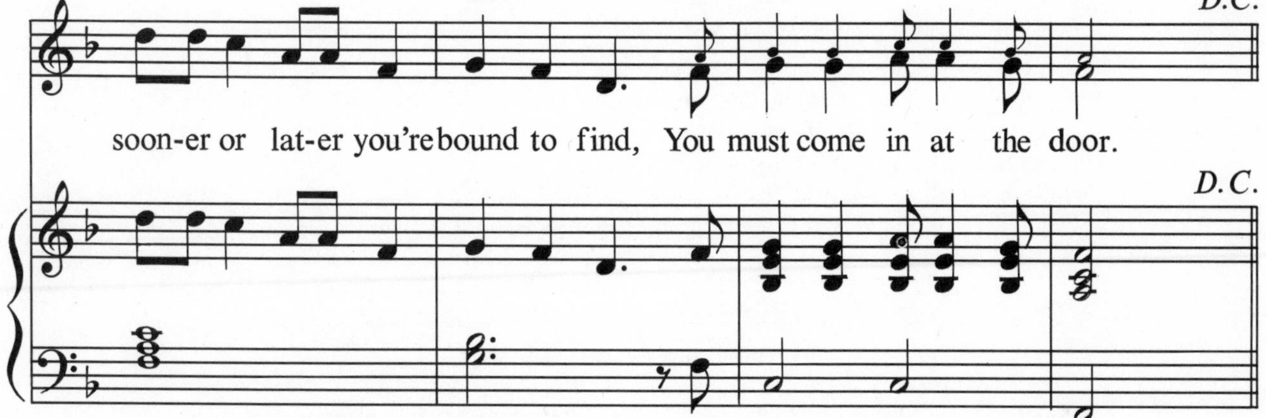
Response
Gm
C7
F
D.C.
soon-er or lat-er you're bound to find, You must come in at the door.
D.C.

2. There's only one path that takes you there,
It leads right up to the door;
It's narrow and straight, but it's free from care,
You must come in at the door.

3. If you get there before I do,
You must come in at the door,
Don't worry or wait, I'm coming, too,
You must come in at the door.

4. You'll find it's always open wide,
You must come in at the door;
So, brother, don't stop till you're inside;
You must come in at the door.

PROGRAM GUIDE: *American Negro gospel song*

Here is another great handclapping gospel song. I've indicated several ideas on the vocal score that can make your performance really swing. All you really need are two experienced harmonizers among the ladies and one good strong bass among the men to pull off those cues in the chorus. The ladies do the first and third cues and supply the harmony above the melody line indicated in the last two measures (also, as indicated, in the verses). The bass sings the second cue in the chorus and supplies this bass line in the last two measures (with a pickup up):

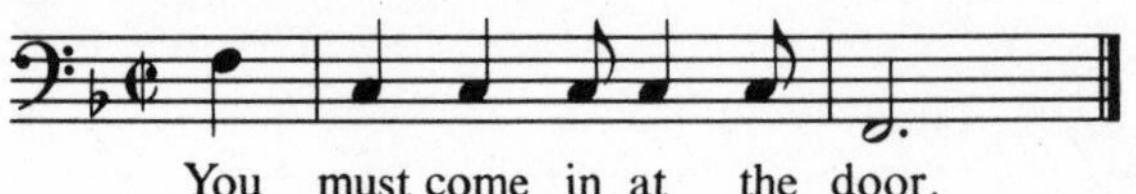
You must come in at the door.

Ask your harmonizers to attack those three cues sharply and clearly, and right on the downbeat. Find somebody who feels left out at this point to sing the solo lines in the verse (Note: Tell men to sing an octave lower). If several people feel left out, let them take turns or team up. Use a good medium bounce jazz tempo for best results. You may add handclapping if you wish—but with the above, there may be enough going on already. The routine is chorus, verse, chorus, verse, chorus, etc., ending with last chorus.

51

Here We Come A-wassailing

Traditional British Carol
Moderately fast
Verse
E♭ B♭7 E♭ B♭7 E♭ B♭7 E♭ B♭
Here we come a - was - sail - ing A - mong the leaves so green,
A♭ E♭ B♭ B♭7 E♭ Fm E♭ B♭7 E♭ B♭7
Here we come a - wan - d'ring, So fair to be seen;
Refrain
E♭ B♭7 E♭ A♭ B♭9 E♭ B♭7 E♭ B♭ E♭ F7
Love and joy come to you, And to you your was - sail

B♭ E♭ A♭6 B♭m C7 Fm E♭ B♭7 E♭ B♭7 E♭ Cm
too, And God bless you, and send_ you a hap - py New
Fm E♭ A♭ B♭ C7 Fm E♭ B♭7 E♭
Year, And God send you a hap - py New_ Year.

2. We are not daily beggars
That beg from door to door;
But we are neighbors' children,
Whom you have seen before. (*Refrain*)

3. God bless the master of this house,
Likewise the mistress, too;
And all the little children,
That round the table go. (*Refrain*)

4. And all your kin and kinfolk
That dwell both far and near,
We wish a Merry Christmas
And Happy New Year. (*Refrain*)

PROGRAM GUIDE: *Traditional British Christmas carol*

This popular nineteenth-century carol from Yorkshire explains the special practices of begging with song at Christmastime. Notice the time change from 6/8 to 4/4 between verse and chorus. Two different songs may have been put together to make this one, but they fit well despite the differences in structure. *Wassail* is both a toast and the ingredient used for toasting, and *wassailing* puts it all together in a gestalt of Christmas season merriment, singing, and other festivities. The traditional tempo is *allegretto moderato:* light, graceful, and moderately fast. It's a fine song to use when you go caroling.

52

He's Got the Whole World in His Hands

Add.lyrics J.F.L.

American Negro Spiritual

Moderately and rhythmically
D
G
D
He's got the whole world in His hands He's got the
A7
G
D
whole world, in His hands, He's got the whole world
G
D
A7
D
in His hands, He's got the whole world in His hands.

2. He's got the little bitty babies in his hands,
He's got the little bitty babies in his hands,
He's got the little bitty babies in his hands,
He's got the whole world in his hands.

3. He's got you and me, brother, in his hands,
He's got you and me, sister, in his hands,
He's got you and me, brother, in his hands,
He's got the whole world in his hands.

4. He's got the gamblin' man in his hands,
He's got the gamblin' man in his hands,
He's got the gamblin' man in his hands,
He's got the whole world in his hands.

Additional verses, as above:

Drinkin' man

Worldly sinners

Cheaters and liars

Rich and poor

Meek and humble

PROGRAM GUIDE: *American Negro spiritual*

As with "Gospel Train," you can enliven the proceedings by varying the words of this lively, medium-tempo, handclapping spiritual. Try this:

He's got the little bitty children in his hands,
He's got the grown-up children in his hands,
He's got all the children in his hands,
He's got the whole world in his hands.

This is a good unison number, but feel free to encourage natural harmony—and solos, if anyone feels the spirit. I've listed some additional verses in the singer's edition so that you will have a greater variety from which to select. The possibilities, of course, are endless, and you may want to invent some of your own, appropriate to the time or situation or group. Here are some more ideas to spark your thinking:

The President
Liberated women
Drunken driver
Hollywood actor (starlet)
Jazz musician
Amateur singers

You might also set up a handclapping rhythm section following this pattern:

53

Hey! Ho! Nobody Home

Traditional English Round

Briskly
1
Hey! ho! No - bod - y home.
2
Meat or drink or mon - ey have I none.
3
Yet will I be mer - ry, mer - ry, mer - ry, mer - ry.

□ Divide the group into three sections. Each section sings the entire round the agreed-upon number of times, beginning at point 1 when the preceding section reaches point 2. Thus the round begins and ends with one section singing alone: section 1 at the beginning and section 3 at the end.

PROGRAM GUIDE: *Traditional English round; Christmas*

"Hey! Ho! Nobody Home" is a rather unique kind of round for the Christmas singing season: Carolers sing it as they walk away from an empty house, having drawn a blank with their offering of "We Wish You a Merry Christmas." I doubt that the round was invented for this purpose, but it could have been. Door-to-door singing was once a widely practiced form of begging, an extension of the minstrel idea (from class to mass) by the man on the street. Of course, this three-part round may be sung anytime or anywhere you want a brisk round of practice with the medium.

54
Hey Lollee

Verses: J.F.L.

West Indian Folk Song
Adapted by J.F.L.

Moderately fast calypso
Chorus
C
G7
Hey Lol-lee, lol - lee, lol-lee, Hey Lol-lee, lol - lee lo.
Calypso style
G7
C
Fine
Hey Lol-lee, lol - lee, lol-lee, Hey lol-lee, lol-lee lo.
Fine
Verse
Call
C
Response
G7
Call
1. This is a cra-zy kind of song, Hey lol-lee, lol - lee lo. You

G7
Response
C
D.C.
make it up as you go a - long,
Hey Lol - lee, lol - lee lo.
D.C.

2. When calypso singers sing this song,
Hey lollee, lollee lo.
It sometimes lasts the whole day long,
Hey lollee, lollee lo.

3. First you invent a simple line,
Hey lollee, lollee lo,
Then another one to rhyme,
Hey lollee, lollee lo.

PROGRAM GUIDE: *West Indian folk song (adapted); humorous*

Ah, calypso! Now we'll find out how creative your singers are. To do justice to "Hey Lollee," all of you must put your thinking caps on and make up your own song. I've written only three verses for the singer's edition, just enough to explain to your singers what is happening and, perhaps, to whet their appetites for more. You can take it from there and condition them a little more. You can make up your own verses, or use these to get started:

While you catch on I'll sing a verse,
Hey lollee, lollee lo,
Then you do one that's even worse,
Hey lollee, lollee lo.

I know a girl named Emily (*use any name that rhymes*)
Hey lollee, lollee lo,
She sings "Hey Lollee" in just one key,
Hey lollee, lollee lo.

Tonight we've chosen another key.
Hey lollee, lollee lo.
You won't be hearing from Emily.
Hey lollee, lollee lo.

Pick the name of a man or woman from your audience that ends in an *ee* sound if you can (e.g. Arthur B., Betty C., Reebeckee [Rebecca]). Don't hesitate to distort the name to make it work, and to sock it to her or him as done in the above, or in the following:

She (he) sings "Hey Lollee" day and night.
Hey lollee, lollee lo.
It never seems to come out right.
Hey lollee, lollee lo.

Or pick on someone else like this:

I know a man named Mister Jones,
Hey lollee, lollee lo.
When he sings, everybody groans,
Hey lollee, lollee lo.

One of the most natural ways to use calypso is to needle whomever you can, wherever and whenever the opportunity arises. Unlike the masters of calypso, you probably will want to concentrate only on those people whose feelings won't or can't be hurt, or at least to be reasonably gentle about your digs.

Also, you don't have to worry about meter (or even rhyme). Just squeeze the words in as best you can, and don't hesitate to mix them up:

The singer you fast the getter it's tough,
Hey lollee, lollee lo,
To line up makes that you won't muff,
Hey lollee, lollee lo.

You have to be prepared to supply verses yourself when everybody else runs out of ideas. Or you can plant, in advance, several appropriate verses with shills in your audience. Keep the song going as long as everybody is having fun. But when it has worn out its welcome, quit. Here's a verse to close on:

Let's put this song back on the shelf.
Hey lollee, lollee lo,
If you want anymore you can sing it yourself,
Hey lollee, lollee lo.

The chorus, of course, is always sung by everyone. The response, after each invented line is also sung by everyone. A chorus after every verse is a good idea. It gives you some time to get the next verse and victim ready. The routine is chorus, verse, chorus, verse, chorus, etc., ending with a final chorus.

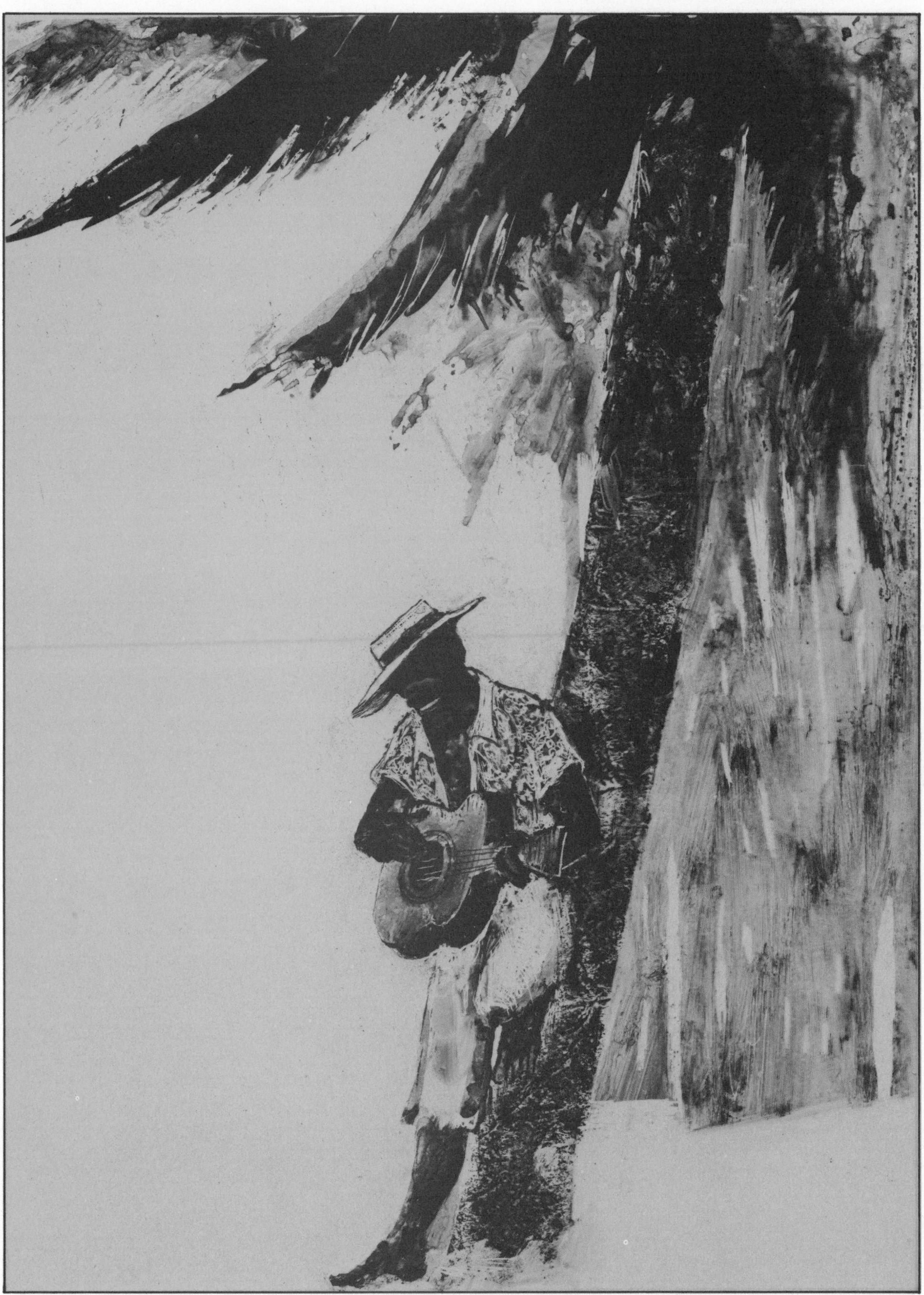

55

The Hokey Pokey

American Folk Song

Moderately and rhythmically
G
You put your right foot in, You put your right foot out, You put your
D7
right foot in And shake it all a-bout. And then you do the hok-ey pok-ey and you
A7
D7
G
turn your-self a-bout; And that's what it's all a - bout. Hey!

2. You put your left foot in,
   You put your left foot out,
   You put your left foot in
   And shake it all about,
   And then you do the hokey pokey
   And you turn yourself about;
   And that's what it's all about.

Continue, as above:

3. Right hand.
4. Left hand.
5. Right shoulder.
6. Left shoulder.
7. Right hip.
8. Left hip.
9. Whole self.

PROGRAM GUIDE: *American folk song; action song*

"The Hokey Pokey" is one of the few action songs that children of all ages up to a hundred seem to enjoy. As always, you must know your audience, but the chances are pretty good they'll go for this one—under the right, relaxed conditions. Depending on the circumstances, you may perform with everyone moving in place (where they are), in a circle, or even in a conga line. The tempo should be moderate but rhythmic. If you sing it too fast somebody may get injured. The actions speak for themselves. Do what comes naturally. You can shorten the routine easily by cutting out some of the anatomy. You may also lengthen it by adding parts of the anatomy to wiggle about (e.g. elbows, fingers, ears).

56
Holy, Holy, Holy

Reginald Heber *John Bacchus Dykes*

Broadly
Eb Cm Bb7 Eb Ebmaj7 Ab Bb9 Ab Fm6 Eb Bb Eb Bb
Ho-ly, ho-ly, ho - ly! Lord God al - might - y! Ear - ly in the
Cm F7 Bb Eb Bb F7 Bb Bb7 Eb Cm Bb Bb7 Eb Ebmaj7
morn - ing our song shall rise to thee; Ho-ly, ho-ly, ho - ly,
Ab Bb9 Ab Fm6 Eb Cm Ab Eb Eb7 Ab Eb Eb7 Ab Fm Bb7 Eb
mer - ci-ful and might - y; God in three per-sons, bless-ed Trin - i - ty.

2. Holy, holy, holy! All the saints adore thee,
Casting down their golden crowns around the glassy sea;
Cherubim and seraphim falling down before thee,
Which wert, and art, and evermore shalt be.

3. Holy, holy, holy! Though the darkness hide thee,
Though the eye of sinful man thy glory may not see;
Only thou art holy; there is none beside thee,
Perfect in power, in love, and purity.

4. Holy, holy, holy! Lord God Almighty!
All thy works shall praise thy name in earth and sky and sea;
Holy, holy, holy! merciful and mighty;
God in three persons, blessed Trinity!

PROGRAM GUIDE: *Traditional English hymn*

The music was composed for *Hymns Ancient and Modern,* published in 1861, by John Bacchus Dykes (1823-76), precentor of Durham Cathedral and a founder of the University Musical Society at Cambridge. During his lifetime Dykes wrote about 300 hymn tunes. The text was written by Reginald Heber (1783-1826), an Anglican clergyman and hymnwriter who became bishop of Calcutta before his death. "Holy, Holy, Holy!" was written when Heber was vicar of Hodnet (1807-23), but was published after his death, as were all his hymns. This hymn was among the very first hymns to celebrate the concept of a triune God. The hymn is also sung in churches that oppose this doctrine. However, they substitute the last line of the second stanza for the last line of the first and fourth stanzas. *Cherubim* and *seraphim* are those childlike celestial beings (angels) you've seen so often. The seraphim are the highest order and the cherubim the second highest.

57
I Am a Pilgrim

American Gospel Song

Moderately
D7
G
I am a pil - grim, and a stran - ger,
C
G
Trav-eling through this wea-ri-some land.
G7
C
I got a home in that yon-der cit - y, Oh

G
D7
G
Lord, and it's not made,
not made by hand.

2. I got a mother, a sister, and a brother,
   Who have gone to that sweet land.
   I'm determined to go and see them, good Lord,
   All over on that distant shore.

3. As I go down to that river of Jordan,
   Just to bathe my weary soul,
   If I could touch but the hem of his garment, good Lord,
   Well, I believe it would make me whole.

PROGRAM GUIDE: *American gospel song*

This swinging gospel favorite requires some attention to details to bring out its better qualities. The blue notes, discordant harmonies, slurs, and syncopations make the song what it is, and much is lost if they are not observed. And yet, it will not work out well unless the singers are relaxed and natural. There is an apocryphal story about the jazz musician who was asked, "How do you learn to play jazz?" "If you have to ask, you can't," was his answer. The same idea applies to "Pilgrim," either you feel it or you don't. I've tried to convey the feeling in the vocal score and the piano arrangement. But neither has to be nor should be followed strictly as written. Much more varied but natural syncopation should emerge in your performance. In the final analysis, the success of "Pilgrim" will depend on how comfortable you and your singers feel with it. If it doesn't feel right, pass it up. The tempo is a moderate, medium bounce. You may wish to experiment with various on-beat and off-beat handclapping accompaniments. Ask four or five singers to form a rhythm section and try:

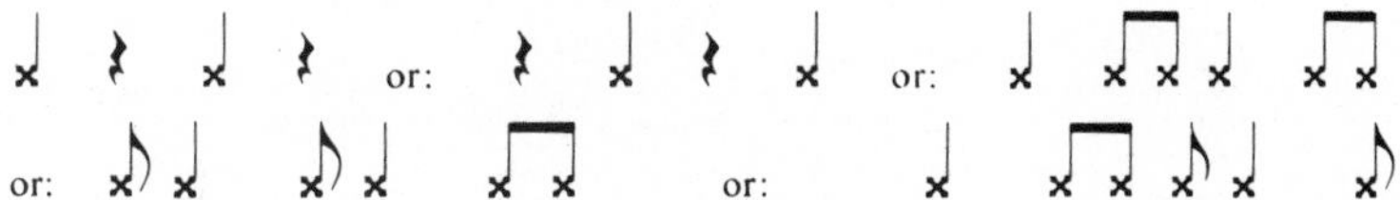
or:
or:
or:
or:

This southern gospel song was rather extensively adapted from a very popular Italian (yes, Italian) song of the 1800s. The only discernible relationship today is in the words.

58
I Couldn't Hear Nobody Pray

American Negro Spiritual

Moderately slow
D
G
I could-n't hear no-bod-y pray; Oh, I could-n't hear no-bod-y
D
G
D
G
D
G
pray. Oh, way down yon-der by_ my-self, Oh, I could-n't hear no-bod-y
D
G
D
pray (all a-lone),_ could-n't hear no-bod-y pray (kneel-ing down),_

D G D
could-n't hear no-bod - y pray, I could-n't hear no-bod - y
G D
pray, Oh, I could-n't hear no-bod - y pray, Oh,
G D G D G D
way down yon-der by_my - self, Oh, I could-n't hear no-bod- y pray.

PROGRAM GUIDE: *American Negro spiritual*

This is a good spiritual to choose when you are looking for variety. The format is a little different than most others. It calls for a quiet, subdued performance at a moderately slow tempo. You can assign the response lines in the middle part of the song to the ladies or to a male or female soloist.

59

I Heard the Bells on Christmas Day

Henry Wadsworth Longfellow *J. Baptiste Calkin*

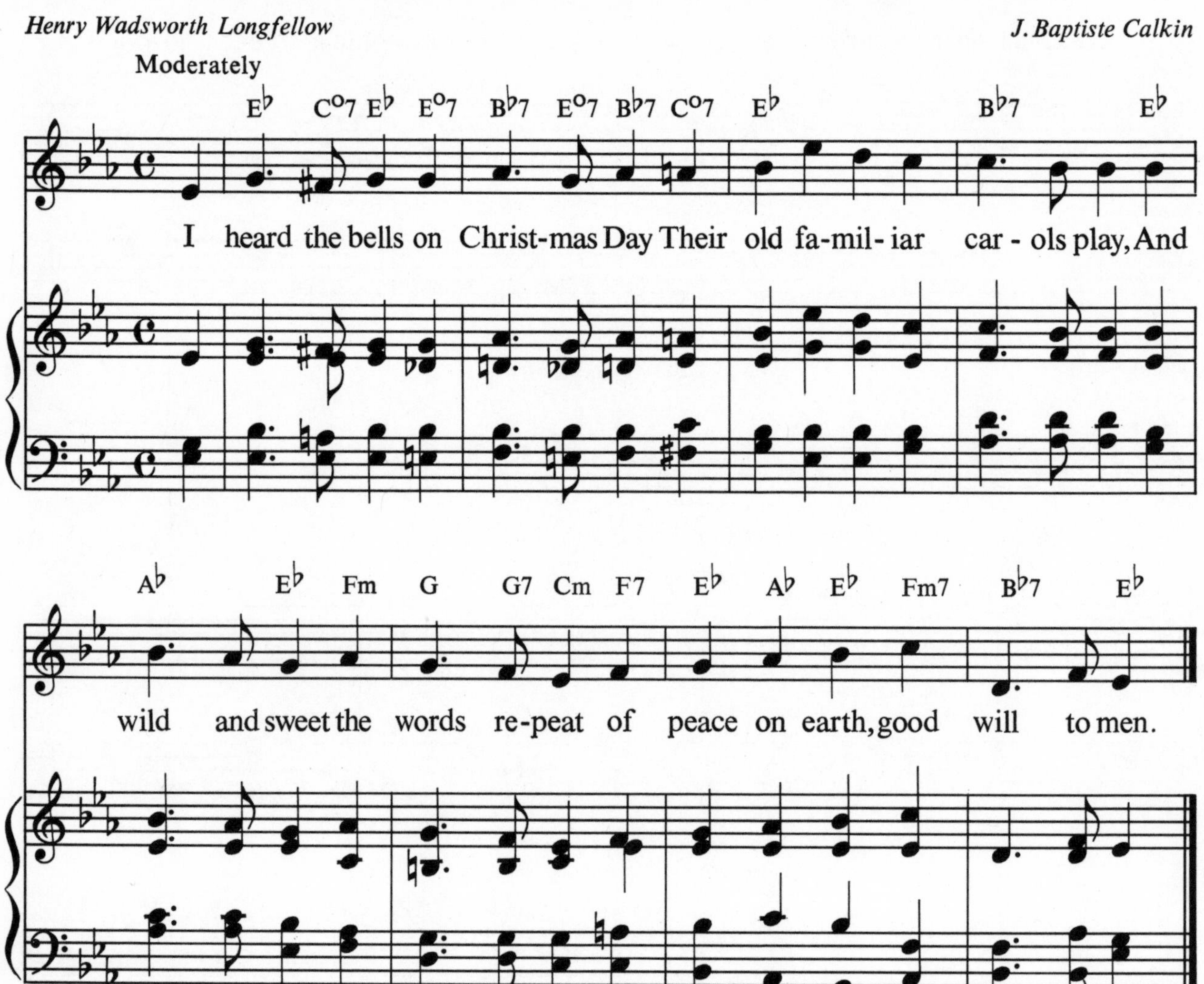
Moderately
E♭ C°7 E♭ E°7 B♭7 E°7 B♭7 C°7 E♭ B♭7 E♭
I heard the bells on Christ-mas Day Their old fa-mil-iar car-ols play, And
A♭ E♭ Fm G G7 Cm F7 E♭ A♭ E♭ Fm7 B♭7 E♭
wild and sweet the words re-peat of peace on earth, good will to men.

2. I thought how, as the day had come,
   The belfries of all Christendom
   Had rolled along th' unbroken song
   Of peace on earth, good will to men.

3. And in despair I bow'd my head:
   "There is no peace on earth," I said,
   "For hate is strong, and mocks the song
   Of peace on earth, good will to men."

4. Then pealed the bells more loud and deep:
   "God is not dead, nor doth he sleep;
   The wrong shall fail, the right prevail,
   With peace on earth, good will to men."

5. Till, ringing, singing on its way,
   The world revolved from night to day,
   A voice, a chime, a chant sublime,
   Of peace on earth, good will to men!

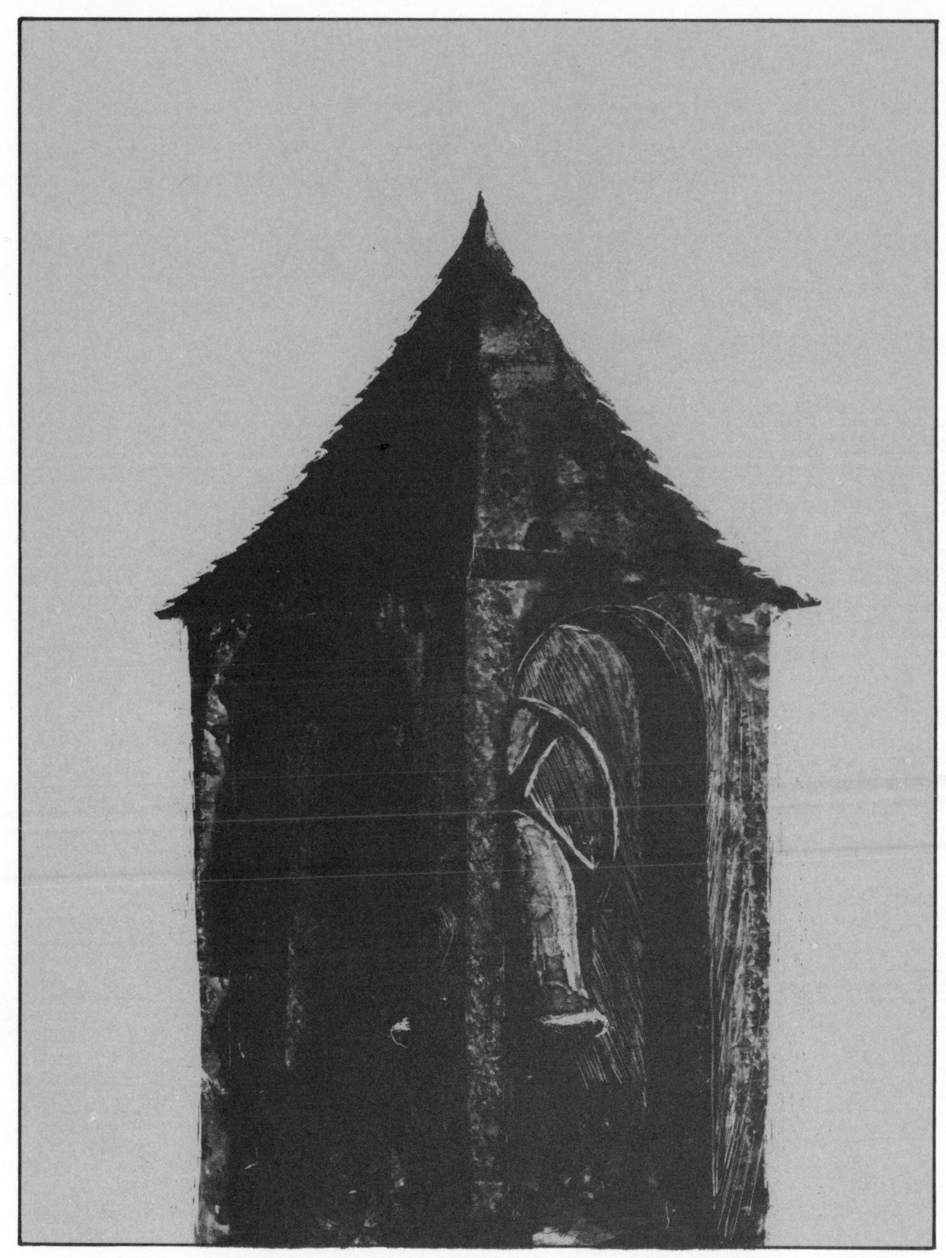

PROGRAM GUIDE: *Traditional American hymn; Christmas*

Henry Wadsworth Longfellow (1807-1882) was the most popular of our nineteenth-century poets. His brother became well known as a hymnwriter. This Christmas poem, with a most unusual and melancholy theme, became one of the few successful hymns by Henry. Longfellow lost his first wife in 1835 and his second wife, in a tragic accident, in 1861. A period of deeper melancholy for the poet followed. These particular lines, according to some sources, were written when Longfellow learned of the serious injury of his son in battle. It was originally set to another, passable tune by Henry Bishop. However, this tune by J. Baptiste Calkin (1829-1905) later became established with the text, and seems to enhance its power. The mood is one of personal sorrow and hope: "God is not dead."

60

I Know Where I'm Going

British Folk Song

Moderately slow with feeling
legato
G6 G D7 D G6 G G G6 G D D7
I know where I'm go-ing, And I know who's go-in' with me;
legato
Coda
G G7 Em7 Em Am D D7 C G
I know who I love, And he knows who I'll mar-ry. John-ny.
Coda

2. I'll give up silk stockings,
   And shoes of bright green leather,
   Combs to buckle my hair,
   And rings for every finger.

3. Feather beds are soft,
   And painted rooms are bonnie;
   But I would trade them all
   For my handsome, winsome Johnny.

4. Some say he's a bad one,
   But I say he is bonnie.
   Fairest of them all
   Is my handsome, winsome Johnny.

Repeat first verse.

PROGRAM GUIDE: *British folk song; romantic*

Why not give the men a rest, and a chance to appreciate the beauty of the ladies' voices? Ask the ladies to sing "I Know Where I'm Goin' " softly, tenderly, and with feeling. They should use a *legato* phrasing as indicated on the vocal score. *Legato* means smooth and connected, without breaks between the successive tones. The proper application of legato phrasing greatly enhances the performance. If everything works out right, that little "Johnny" tag at the end, which resolves the harmony, should bring a few sighs of appreciation from the men. This is a good song to sing after "The Gypsy Rover" (number 47) since the historical relationship of the two songs is obvious and the coupling appropriate. If your singers are not familiar with this arrangement of the song, you should point out that a *coda* is something that happens only at the very end of a song after all else has been sung and done. Otherwise you may pick up a stray "Johnny" at the end of an earlier verse and spoil the effect. If you have sure-pitch harmonizers among the ladies, ask them to sing, at the coda:

John - ny.

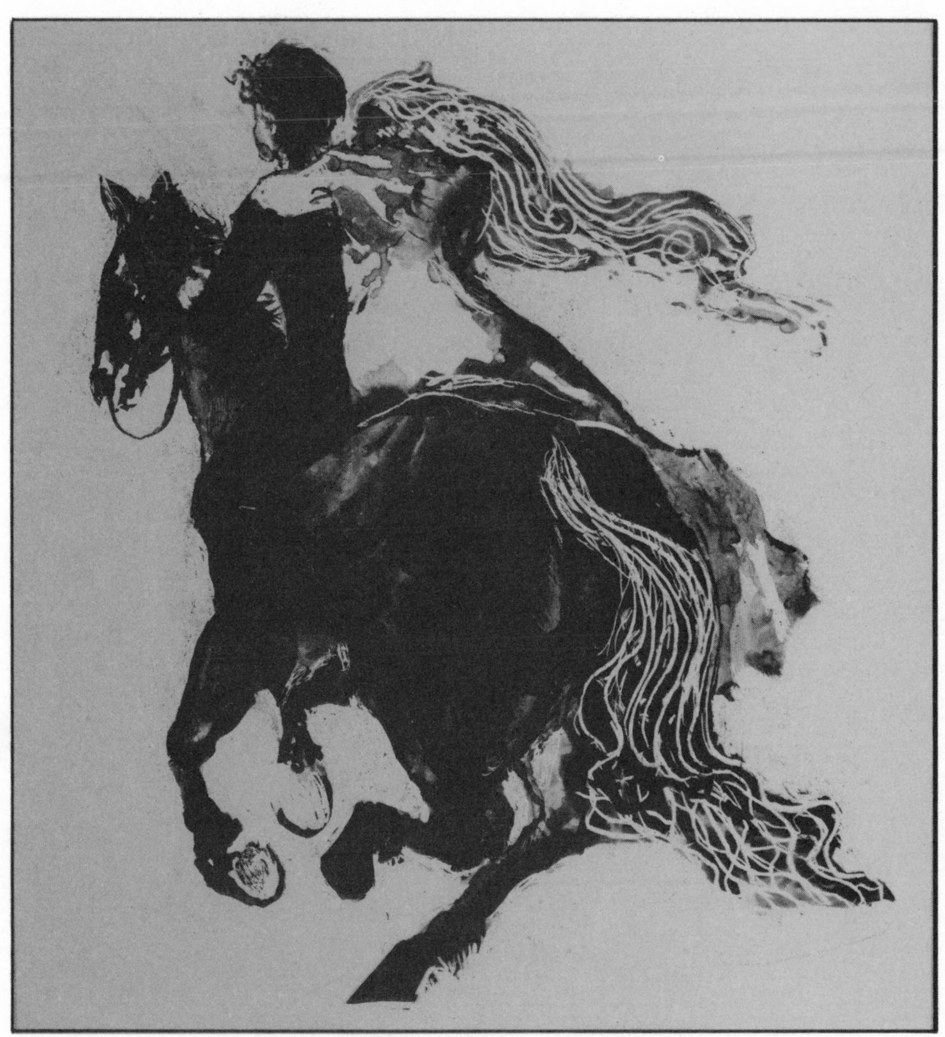

61

I Love the Mountains

American Folk Song

Vamp (Repeat until ready)

Women

F Dm

Men

Boom de ah da, boom de ah da,

Vamp

3

Gm C7 F Dm

I love the moun - tains.

3

boom de ah da, boom de ah da da, Boom de ah da, boom de ah da,

Gm C7 F Dm

I love the roll - ing hills, I love the flow - ers.

3

boom de ah da, boom de ah da da, Boom de ah da, boom de ah da,

Gm
C7
F
Dm
I love the daf - fo-dils. I love the fire side,
boom de ah da, boom de ah da da, Boom de ah da, boom de ah da,
When all the lights are low.
boom de ah da, boom de ah da da, Boom de ah da, boom de ah da,
Boom, Boom!
Boom de ah da, boom de ah da da, Boom, Boom, Boom; Boom, Boom!

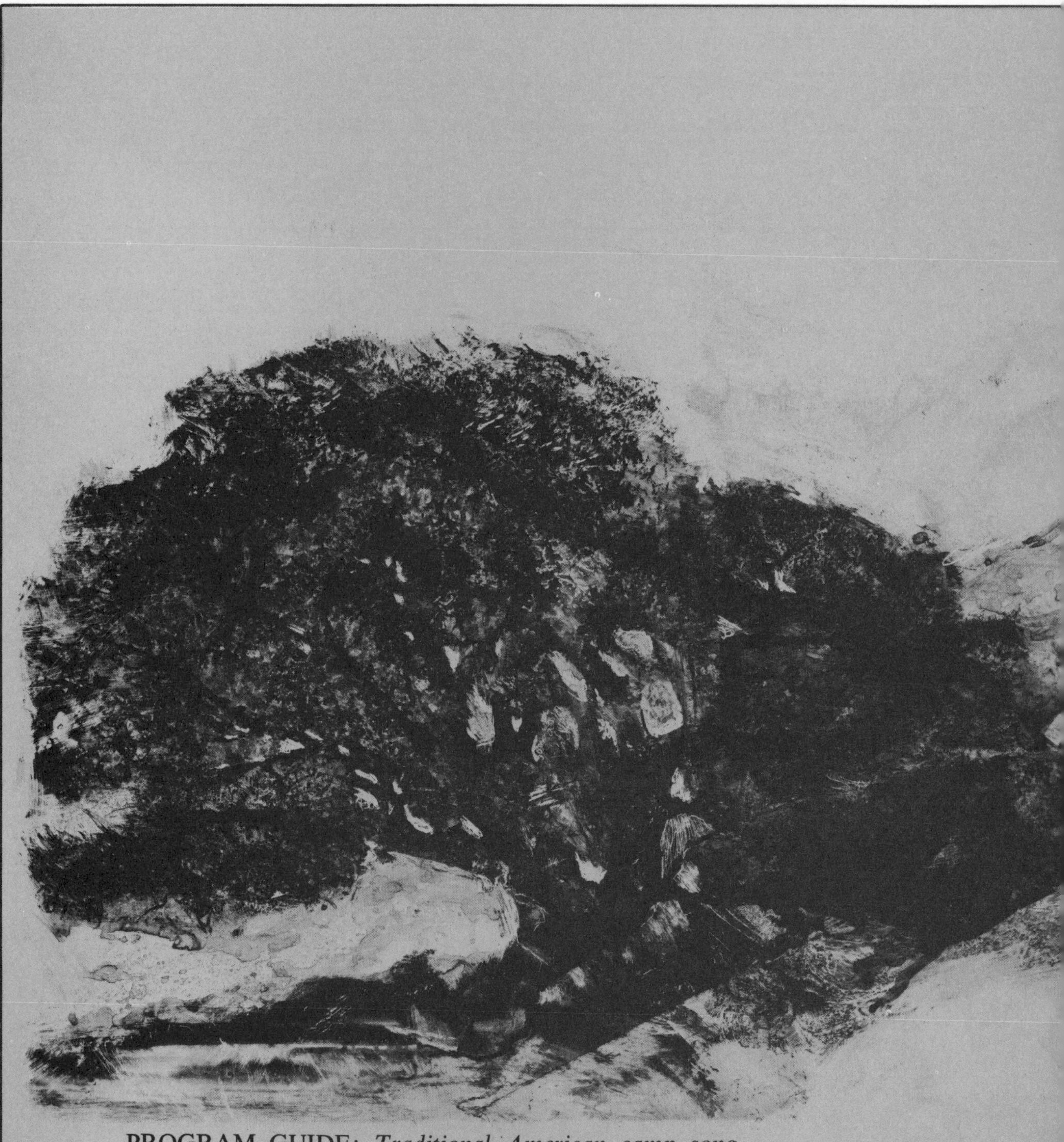

PROGRAM GUIDE: *Traditional American camp song*

A two-measure, popular-music chord progression and jazz accompaniment pattern (known as vamping) was blown up into a popular camp song by some inspired nut. It provides a great vehicle for easy two-part singing. Divide the singers into two groups, vampers and campers. Assign the bass pattern (second line of vocal score) to the vampers and the melody (first line of vocal score) to the campers. Run through the vamp introduction at a medium shuffle-beat tempo until the bass part is solid, then turn the campers loose on the melody. Once may not but probably should be enough! Well, maybe twice—now that we know it.

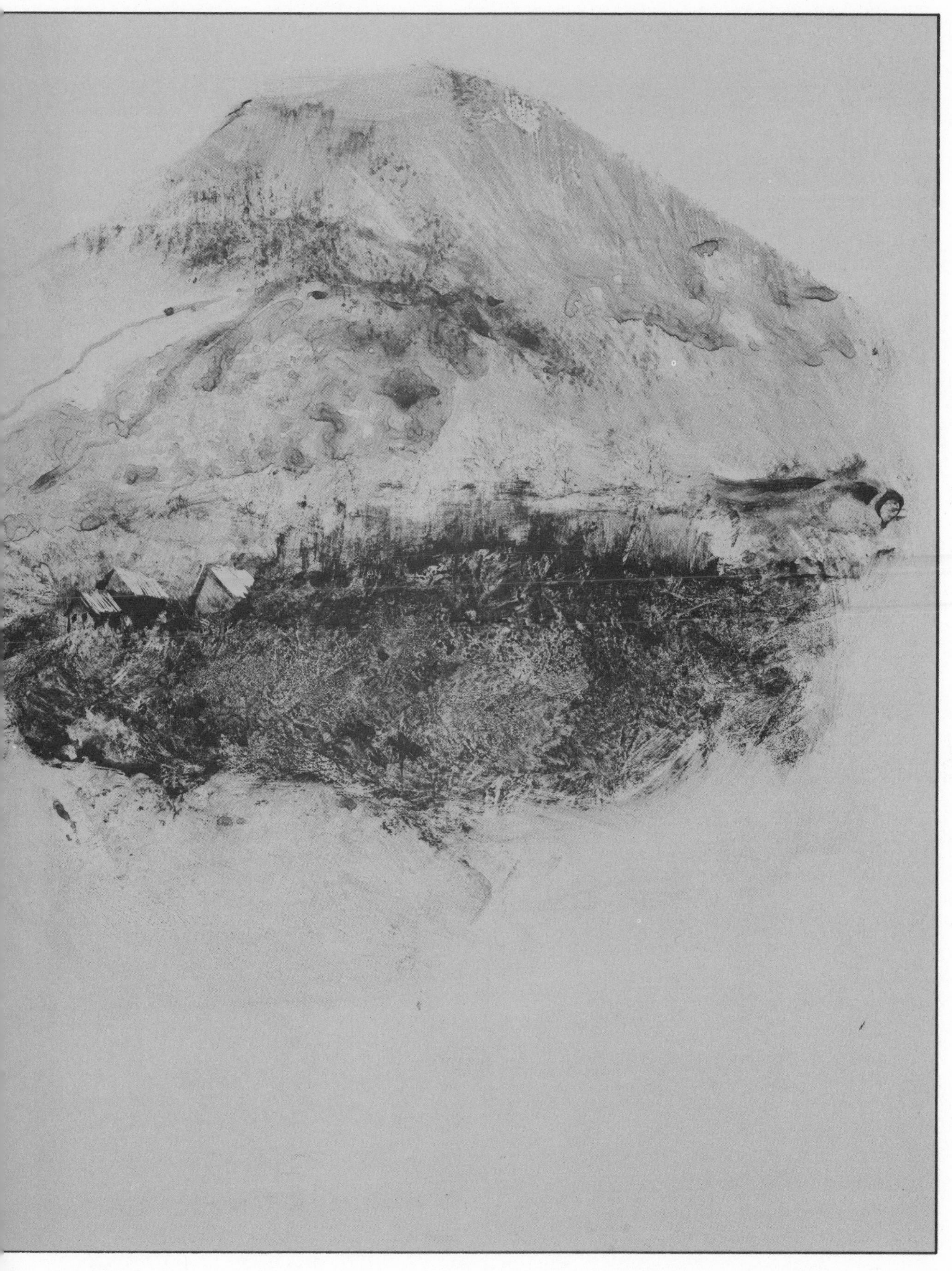

62

I Saw Three Ships

English Folk Song

Brightly

F B♭ F C7 F C7 F

I saw three ships come sail-ing in on Christ-mas Day, on Christ-mas Day, I

F B♭ F B♭ F C7 F

saw three ships come sail - ing in on Christ-mas Day in the morn - ing.

2. And what was in those ships all three,
   On Christmas Day, on Christmas Day?
   And what was in those ships all three,
   On Christmas Day in the morning?

3. The wise man three were in those ships,
   On Christmas Day, on Christmas Day.
   The wise men three were in those ships,
   On Christmas Day in the morning,

Continue, as above:

4. Pray, whither sailed those ships all three?
5. Oh, they sailed in to Bethlehem.
6. And all the angels in heaven shall sing.
7. And all the bells on earth shall ring.
8. And all the souls on earth shall sing.
9. Then let us all rejoice and sing.

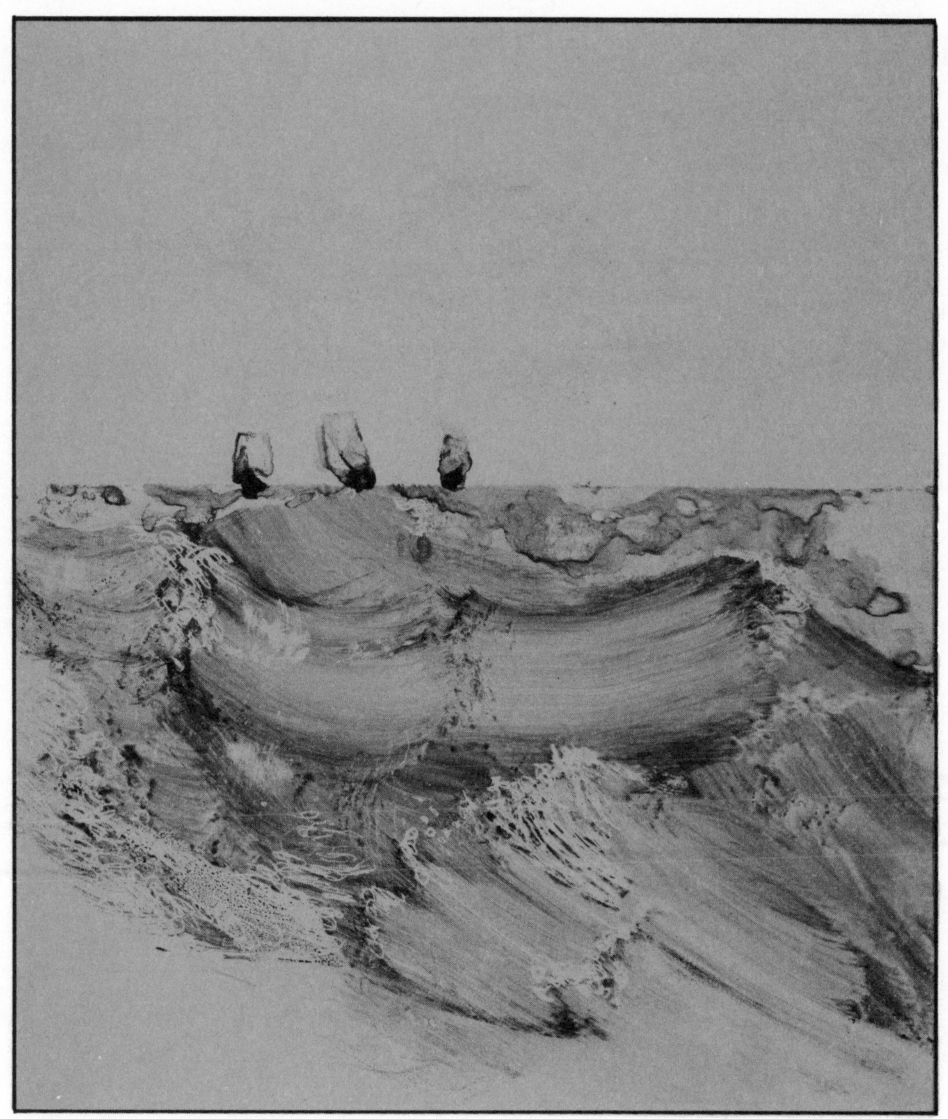

PROGRAM GUIDE: *English folk song; Christmas*

This popular Christmas folk song is based on an old legend: After the three wise men died, Empress Helena moved their bodies to Byzantium, and later to Milan. In 1162, three ships commanded by Frederick Barbarossa carried the skulls of the "wise men" to Cologne. In the song, Cologne becomes Bethelehem and, in some versions, the cargo is changed to:

> The Virgin Mary and Christ were there,
> On Christmas Day, on Christmas Day, etc.

(In still other versions the verse becomes "Three pretty girls were carried there.") It's all very confusing, but that's the way legends and folk songs are. This folk carol is English, but you can hear a little bagpipe drone underlying the melody if you listen closely. The song should be performed at the tempo of a slow walk, two beats to the measure. You might divide the singers into two groups. Have the first group sing verses 1, 3, and 5. Ask the second group to sing verses 2, 4, and 6. Then have both groups sing one or all of the last three verses together.

63

I'm Gonna Sing When the Spirit Says Sing

American Negro Spiritual

Brightly
G
I'm gon-na sing when the spir-it says sing. I'm gon-na
D7
G
sing, when the spir-it says sing. I'm gon-na sing when the spir-it says
(Melody in lower notes)
C
G
D7
G
sing, And o - bey the spir-it of the Lord.

2. I'm gonna shout when the spirit says shout,
I'm gonna shout when the spirit says shout,
I'm gonna shout when the spirit says shout,
And obey the spirit of the Lord.

Additional verses:

Preach.

Pray.

PROGRAM GUIDE: *American Negro spiritual*

This very simple Negro spiritual is often used to open a singing program. It's easy and lively, conducive to natural harmonizing, and the words are easy to remember. Once you learn the basic sentence of the song, all you have to do is zip in a new word with each verse. I've suggested a simple harmony part in the upper notes of the last two measures, for those who need to see it in writing. Set up a rhythm section with four or more handclappers and try this pattern:

Beat	4	1 2 3 4	1 2 3 4
Clappers	♪ ♫	♩ ♫ ♫ ♩	♩ ♫ ♫♫
Singers	I'm gon- na	sing when the spir - it says	sing, I'm gon - na

Beat	1 2 3 4	1 2 3 4	1 2 3 4
Clappers	♩ ♫ ♫ ♩	♩ ♫ ♫♫	♩ ♫ ♫ ♩
Singers	sing when the spir-it says	sing, I'm gon-na	sing when the spir-it says

Beat	1 2 3 4	1 2 3 4	1 2 3
Clappers	♩ ♫ ♫♫	♩ ♩ ♫♫	♩ ♩ ♪
Singers	sing, And o -	bey the spir- it of the	Lord.

64

I'm on My Way

American Gospel Song

Moderately fast
F
C7
I'm on my way and I won't turn back,
R. H.
L.H.
F
I'm on my way and I won't turn back,
F
B♭
I'm on my way and I won't turn back,

F
C7
F
B♭
F
I'm on my way, great God, I'm on my way.

2. I asked my brother to come with me,
   I asked my brother to come with me,
   I asked my brother to come with me,
   I'm on my way, great God, I'm on my way.

   Continue, as above:

3. If he won't come, I'll go alone.
4. I asked my sister to come with me.
5. If she won't come, I'll go alone.
6. I'll ask my boss to let me go.
7. If he says no I'll go anyhow.
8. I'm on my way to freedom land.

   Optional verses:

   I asked the judge to come with me.

   But he was guilty, just like me.

   I asked a rich man to come with me.

   But he was too busy to take the time.

PROGRAM GUIDE: *American gospel song*

Here is another gospel favorite you may keep going as long as you and your singers wish. You just keep tacking on verses about people you want to have go along with you. I've indicated twelve of the more popular verses, and you're welcome to add several hundred of your own. In camp situations, or on a bus trip or hike, you can help pass the time by making up verses. However, in most situations it's better to call a halt before everyone gets worn out and starts singing:

> I asked myself to go along.
> But I'm too tired from singing this song.

Four or five verses ought to be enough to satisfy most. It is customary to repeat the first verse at the end. Use a medium bounce tempo, not too fast.

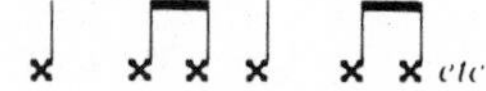
etc.

65
In the Pines

American Folk Song

Moderately slow

Verse

Em Am Em

True love, true love, don't lie to me, Tell me

B7 Em

where did you sleep last night? ——— I slept in the

Am Em B7
pines, where the sun nev-er shines And I shiv-ered when the cold wind

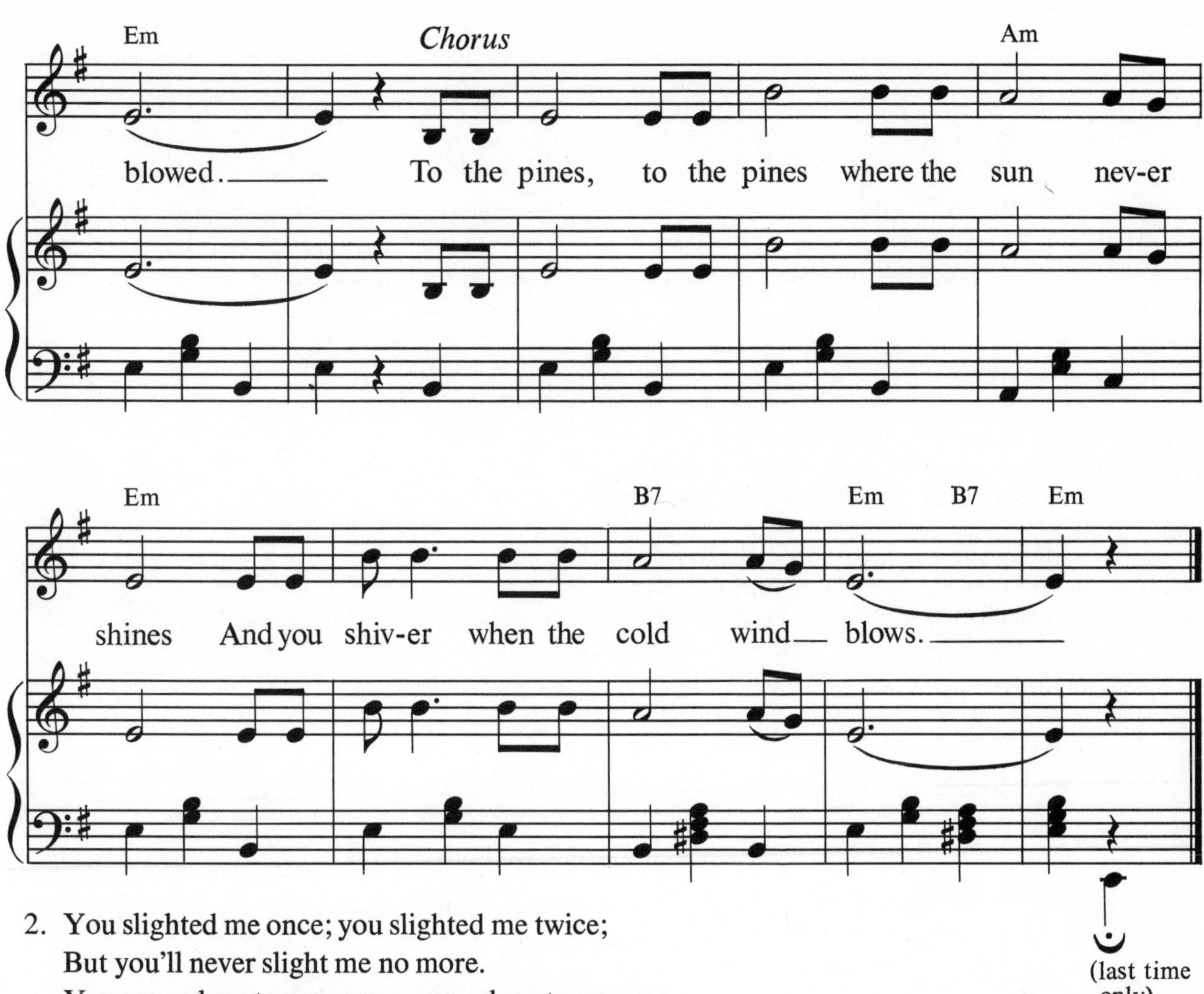
Em
Chorus
Am
blowed. To the pines, to the pines where the sun nev-er
Em
B7
Em B7 Em
shines And you shiv-er when the cold wind blows.
(last time only)

2. You slighted me once; you slighted me twice;
But you'll never slight me no more.
You caused me to weep; you caused me to mourn;
You caused me to leave my home. (*Chorus*)

3. Them long steel rails with short crossties
Gonna carry me away from home.
That lonesome track gonna take me back
Where a man can call his soul his own. (*Chorus*)

4. The longest train I ever saw
Was on the Georgia line.
The engine passed at five o'clock;
The caboose done passed at nine. (*Chorus*)

5. The longest day I every saw,
Ever since I started to roam,
Was the day I left my own true love,
The day I left my home. (*Chorus*)

6. Now, don't you hear those mournin' doves
Flyin' from pine to pine,
Mournin' for their own true love
Just like I mourn for mine. (*Chorus*)

PROGRAM GUIDE: *American folk song; blues-style lament*

This unique, moody, blues-style song from the southern mountain country may have been created originally out of a fragment from another song. Songs are sometimes born this way. A fragmentary lyrical phrase catches and holds the conscious or unconscious attention of an inventive singer. It works its way around in his mind and one day emerges with a melodic strain to accompany it. The melody may have evolved from the original song or from some other song or may simply be a freewheeling tune lying dormant in the mind of the composer until its creation. The important thing is that the emerging tune and lyric fit well, are appealing, and are worthy of repetition. That's certainly true of "In the Pines"; it's well worth repeating. Whether or not it started out as a fragment, it has grown by picking up floating verses, phrases, and ideas from other songs through the creative, loving attention of many an unknown folk lyricist. The relatives of "In the Pines" include "On Top of Old Smoky" (number 105), "Lonesome Road" (number 81), "Nine Hundred Miles" (number 89), and "The Wagoner's Lad."

Use a slow tempo and ask your singers to sing softly to enhance the mood. You may vary the voices used between the men and women, if you wish, following the natural assignments based on the lyrics. If you have three good harmonizers, ask them to sing this background:

Loo

66

It Came upon the Midnight Clear

Edmund H. Sears *Richard Storrs Willis*

B♭ D7 E♭ B♭ E♭ B♭ E♭ C7 F7
p
It came up-on the mid-night clear, That glo - rious song of old, From
p
B♭ D7 E♭ B♭ E♭ B♭ E♭ F7 B♭
mf
an - gels bend - ing near the earth, To touch their harps of gold: "Peace
mf
D D7 Gm D Gm F C7 F F7
pp
on the earth, good will to men, From heaven's all gra - cious King." The
pp

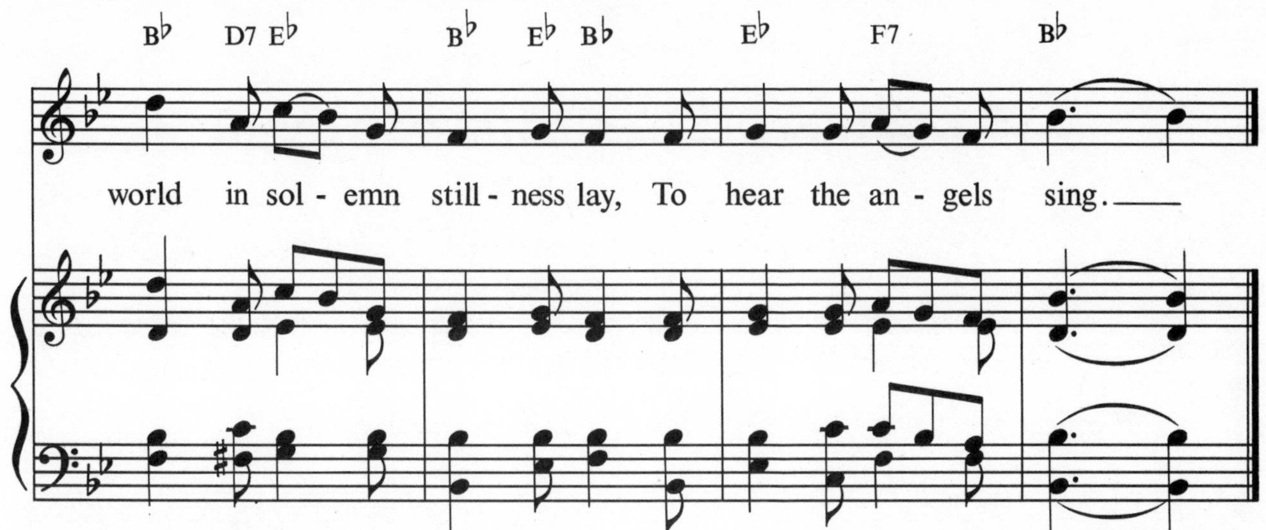
B♭ D7 E♭ B♭ E♭ B♭ E♭ F7 B♭
world in sol - emn still - ness lay, To hear the an - gels sing.

2. Still through the cloven skies they come
With peaceful wings unfurled,
And still their heavenly music floats
O'er all the weary world:
Above its sad and lowly plains
They bend on hovering wing,
And ever o'er its Babel sounds
The blessed angels sing.

3. O ye, beneath life's crushing load,
Whose forms are bending low,
Who toil along the climbing way
With painful steps and slow,
Look now! for glad and golden hours
Come swiftly on the wing:
O rest beside the weary road,
And hear the angels sing.

4. For lo! the days are hastening on,
By prophets seen of old,
When with the evercircling years,
Shall come the time foretold,
When peace shall over all the earth
Its ancient splendors fling,
And the whole world send back the song
Which now the angels sing.

PROGRAM GUIDE: *Traditional American hymn; Christmas*

The words and music to this popular Christmas hymn came from two different schools, in more ways than one. They got together a little over a century ago, despite the fact that the author and composer did not have each other in mind when the separate parts were conceived. (This is not uncommon, however, in hymnmaking, or hymn-remaking, as it were.) The words were written as a poem by Edmund H. Sears (1810-1876), a Unitarian clergyman trained at Harvard. The poem was published in the *Christian Register* in 1849. The third stanza reflects the impact of the industrial revolution on New England. The music was written to accompany another hymn text ("See Israel's Gentle Shepherd Stand") by Richard S. Willis (1819-1900), a Yale man who was also a student of Felix Mendelssohn. The theme is typical of many religious songs of the 1800s, with its promise of salvation for a troubled world. Sears interpreted Unitarian creed in his own fashion without getting into trouble with his parishioners: "I believe and preach the divinity of Christ."

You can add to the effectiveness of the performance by observing the dynamics indicated on the score.

67

I've Been Workin' on the Railroad

American Folk Song
Adapted by J.F.L.

Moderately fast
F
B♭
F
I've been work-in' on the rail - road, All the live-long day;
F
G7
C7
I've been work-in' on the rail - road, Just to pass the time a - way.

C7 F B♭ A7
Don't you hear the whis-tle blow - in'? Rise up so ear-ly in the morn.
B♭ F G7 F C7 F
Don't you hear the cap-tain shout - in', "Din - ah, blow your horn."
F B♭ G7 C7
Di-nah, won't you blow, Di-nah, won't you blow, Di-nah, won't you blow your

F C7 F
B♭ G7
horn?
Di-nah, won't you blow,
Di-nah, won't you blow,
C7
F
Di-nah, won't you blow your horn?
Some-one's in the kitch-en with
F
C7
Di - nah,
Some-one's in the kitch-en, I know.

F
B♭
F
C7
Some-one's in the kitch-en with Di - nah,
Strum-min' on the old ban -
F
jo.
Fee fi fid-dle-ee - i - o,
Fee fi
C7
F
B♭
F
C
fid-dle-ee-i - o,
Fee fi fid-dle-ee-i - o,
Strum-min' on the old ban-

F C7 F
jo. Now you may think that there ain't no more.
C7 F
Oh, you may think that there ain't no more.
B♭ F
Now you may think that there ain't no more, well, there ain't!

PROGRAM GUIDE: *American folk song; camp song*

The best-known of all the camp songs continues to grow longer over the years as campers keep thinking of new tags to add on at the end. That's why this more-or-less complete, as of the moment, arrangement stretches out over so much space. Even so, I've left out at least two of the tags:

No one's in the kitchen with Dinah,
No one's in the kitchen I know.
No one's in the kitchen with Dinah,
'Cause Dinah's got B. O.

Someone's in the kitchen with Dinah,
Someone's in the kitchen I know.
Someone's in the kitchen with Dinah,
'Cause I can't hear the old banjo.

Lifebuoy soap advertising coined the B. O. identification for body odor. You may put these verses back in if you wish, adding them just before the last tag. The song seems to have started out as a minstrel song, but the origin is now rather obscure. The tempo is lively, of course.

68
Jacob's Loader

American White Spiritual
Adapted by J.F.L.

Slowly
C
G7
We are climb-ing Ja-cob's lad-der, We are
F
C
C7
climb-ing Ja-cob's lad-der, We are climb-ing
F
C
G7
C
Ja-cob's lad-der, Sol-diers of the cross.

2. Each rung takes us higher, higher,
   Each rung takes us higher, higher,
   Each rung takes us higher, higher,
   Soldiers of the cross.

   Continue, as above

3. Sinner, do you love my Jesus?

4. If you love him, why not serve him?

5. We are climbing higher, higher.

PROGRAM GUIDE: *American white spiritual*

Spirituals were created and sung by both Negroes and whites in the nineteenth century. Since many of the same spirituals were sung by both, it has been difficult to decide how some of them originated. "Jacob's Ladder" is one that is difficult to pin down, although it probably started out as a white Sunday school song. Some singers prefer the ecumenical line "Brothers in our land" to "Soldiers of the Cross." If you take this approach, you may wish to use the following verses and others of your own invention:

Every new man makes us stronger.
We have worked in dark and danger.

Also, some singers know the second line as:

Every round goes higher, higher.

"Jacob's Ladder" has long been a favorite at church and camp meetings. It has also been adapted for union ("We are Building a Strong Union") and political ("We Are Building a People's Party") singing. It's a great number to end a session around a campfire in the evening or at a sunrise breakfast. Sing it softly, with a slight crescendo as the melody rises, diminuendo as it falls. Natural harmony should be encouraged.

69

Jingle Bells

James S. Pierpont

Brightly
Chorus
(Melody in upper notes)
G
Jin-gle bells, jin-gle bells, jin-gle all the way!
C G A7 D7 G
Oh, what fun it is to ride in a one-horse o-pen sleigh! Jin-gle bells, jin-gle bells,
C G D7 G
jin-gle all the way! Oh, what fun it is to ride in a one-horse o-pen sleigh!
Fine

G
C
Dash-ing through the snow In a one-horse o - pen sleigh,
Am
D7
G
G
O'er the fields we go, Laugh-ing all the way. Bells on bob-tail ring,
C
Am
D7
G
D7
D.C.
Mak-ing spir-its bright. Oh, what fun it is to sing A sleigh-ing song to-night. Oh,
D.C.

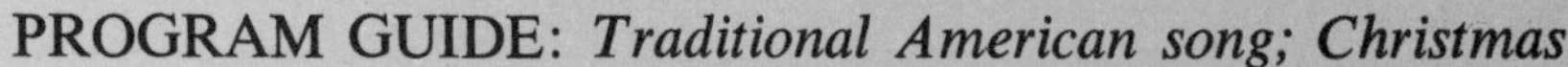

PROGRAM GUIDE: *Traditional American song; Christmas*

In the year 1857 Mardi Gras was first observed in New Orleans, the Atlantic Monthly was founded in Boston, and baseball became a national sport. Two of the big songs from that year were musical settings of poems: Alfred Lord Tennyson's "Come Into the Garden, Maud" and Henry Wadsworth Longfellow's "The Village Blacksmith." But the most durable song to come from the year was the perennial Christmas favorite "Jingle Bells," by James S. Pierpont. Although one-horse open sleighs are long out of fashion, the song remains a fresh and universally appealing expression of joy and cameraderie on a festive occasion. Sing it with a lively, moderately fast tempo, and bring along some bells to jingle if you can. I've indicated a harmony part for the choruses (see the lower notes of the vocal score). Pierpont's second verse no longer adds much to the song and, for that reason, I have omitted it from the singer's edition. Here is how it goes, in the event you need it:

A day or two ago
I thought I'd take a ride,
And soon Miss Fannie Bright
Was seated by my side.
The horse was lean and lank.
Misfortune seemed his lot.
He got into a drifted bank,
And then we got upsot!

The routine is chorus, verse, chorus.

70
Johnny, I Hardly Knew You

Irish Folk Song

Slowly

Gm Cm C Cm Gm Cm7

With your guns and drums and

C7 Cm7 Dm Gm Cm7

drums and guns, hoo - roo, hoo - roo, With your guns and drums and

C7 Cm7 B♭ D7 Gm

drums and guns, hoo - roo, hoo - roo, With your guns and drums and

Cm
Gm
D7
drums and guns, The en - e - my near - ly slew you, Oh, my
Gm
Cm
Gm
D7
ten.
Gm
Cm7
Gm
dar - ling dear, you look so queer, Oh John-ny, I hard - ly knew you.
ten.

2. Where are your eyes that were so mild, hooroo, hooroo,
Where are your eyes that were so mild, hooroo, hooroo,
Where are your eyes that were so mild
When my heart you first beguiled;
Oh, why did you run from me and the child?
Johnny, I hardly knew you.

Continue, as above:

3. Where are your legs that used to run, *etc.*
When first you went to carry a gun?
Indeed your dancing days are done.
Oh, Johnny, I hardly knew you.

4. You haven't an arm you haven't a leg, *etc.*
You're a hopeless shell of a man with a peg.
And you'll have to be put with a bowl to beg.
Oh, Johnny, I hardly knew you.

5. It's glad I am to see you home, *etc.*
My darlin', you're so pale and wan.
So low in flesh, so high in bone . . .
Oh, Johnny, I hardly knew you.

6. They're rollin' out the drums again, *etc.*
But they'll never take my sons again,
No, they'll never take my sons again,
Johnny, I'm swearin' to you.

PROGRAM GUIDE: *Irish folk song; peace*

There are two antithetical songs for greeting Johnny when he returns from war. They share the same tune, but the moods and themes are in direct contrast to each other. The contrast is summed up in the slight turn of a word from *hurrah* to *hooroo.* Although "When Johnny Comes Marching Home" is the better-known version in America, the Irish anti-war version may have come first and served as the pattern for Patrick Gilmore's version from the Civil War (written under the pseudonym Louis Lambert and published in 1863). The tune dates back to very old versions of the "The Three Ravens" (also known as "Billie Magee Magaw").

I've used a dirgelike setting to emphasize the morose quality of the Irish version. You can add variety in performance by assigning this voice pattern throughout:

Women: With your guns and drums and drums and guns,

Men: Hooroo, hooroo.

Women: With your guns and drums and drums and guns,

Men (or all): Hooroo, hooroo.

All: With your guns and drums and drums and guns
The enemy nearly slew you.

Women: Oh, my darling dear, you look so queer,
Oh, Johnny, I hardly knew you.

The tempo should be moderately slow, as in a funeral march, but it can be varied at your direction for emotional effect if you have an attentive and cooperative group. Notice the *fermata* (hold) on the word *you* in the 12th measure (counting after the two-measure introduction) and the *tenuto* on *queer* in the 14th measure. The *tenuto* should be held slightly longer than its normal duration, but not as long as the *fermata.* If you are using instrumental accompaniment, the two-measure introduction can be effectively repeated before each verse. In addition to varying the tempo *ad lib* (at liberty, with irregular rhythm), you may wish to vary the dynamics also, following the mood of the words.

If you want to try making a big production number out of *Johnny,* have the men sing, "When Johnny Comes Marching Home" (number 155) and the women sing, "Johnny, I hardly knew You," alternating verses, as follows:

1. Men sing verse 1 of "When Johnny . . ."
2. Women sing verse 1 of "Johnny, I . . ."
3. Men sing verse 2 of "When Johnny . . ."
4. Women sing verse 2 of "Johnny, I . . ."

The singing may continue in this alternating fashion through the fourth verses of the two songs, ending with the ladies singing either or both of the fifth and sixth verses of "Johnny, I. . . ."

Or this short version may be used:

1. Men—1
2. Women—2
3. Men—2
4. Women—4

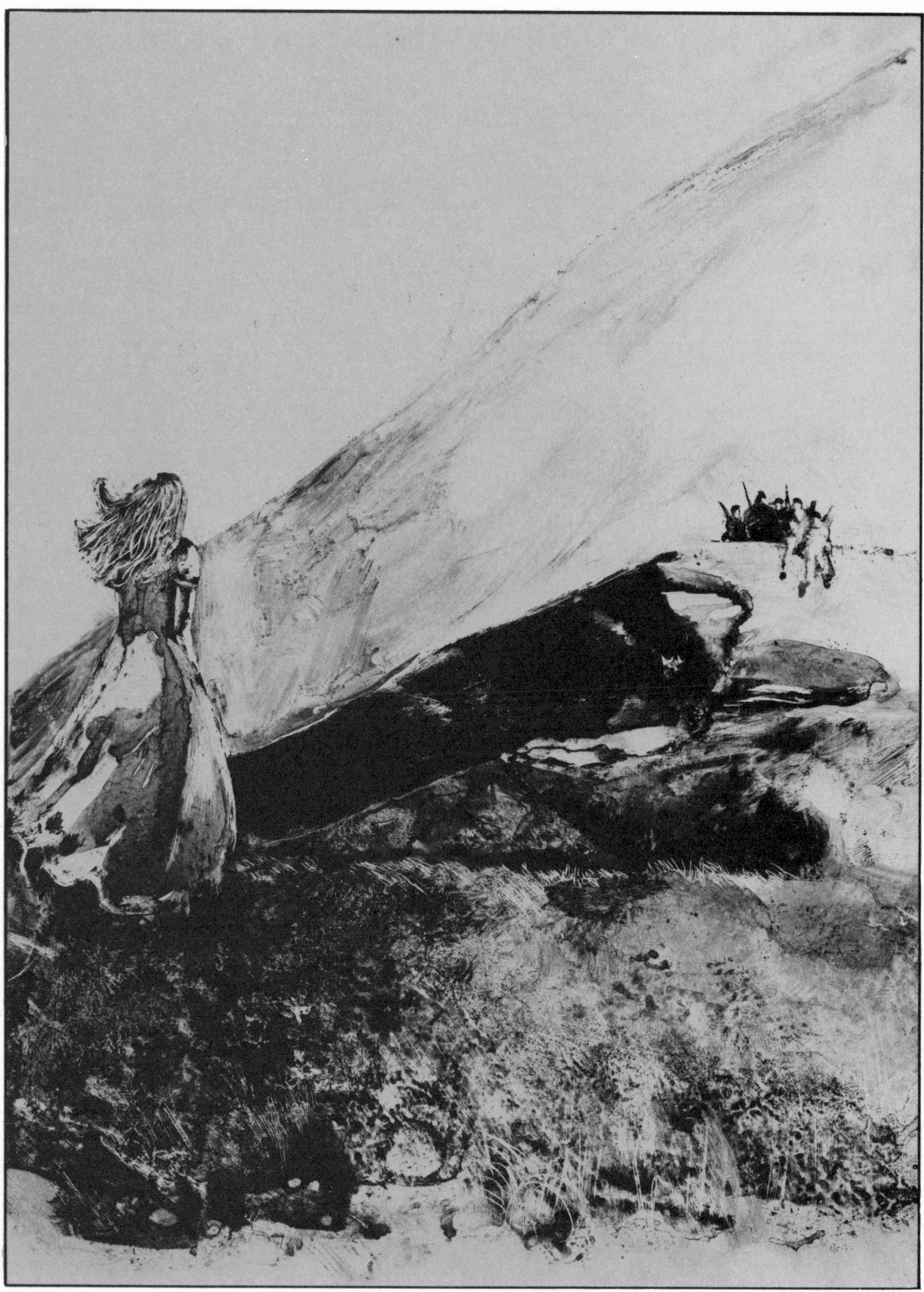

71

Joshua Fought the Battle of Jericho

American Negro Spiritual

Moderately fast and rhythmic
Chorus
Dm
A7
Josh-ua fought the bat-tle of___ Jer-i - cho,_ Jer-i - cho,_
Dm
Jer-i - cho._ Josh-ua fought the bat-tle of___ Jer-i - cho,_ And the
A
Dm
Fine
Verse
Dm
walls came tum-b'lin' down. You may talk a-bout your kings of
(Solo cues)
Fine

Dm
Gid-e-on, You may talk a-bout your men of Saul, But there's
A7
Dm
D.C. al Fine
none like good old Josh-ua, At the bat-tle of Jer-i-cho.
D.C. al Fine

2. Well, the Lord done told old Joshua:
"You must do just what I say,
March 'round that city seven times
And the walls will tumble away."

3. So up to the walls of Jericho,
He marched with spear in hand,
"Go blow them ram horns," Joshua cried,
'Cause the battle is in my hand."

4. Then the lamb, ram, sheep horns began to blow,
And the trumpet began to sound,
Joshua told the children to shout, that mornin'
And the walls came tumblin' down.

PROGRAM GUIDE: *American Negro spiritual*

The cross section of Negro religious music in this book demonstrates the versatility and rich variety of styles employed by Negro composers. "Joshua" is a classic example, with a dramatic story told in the musical setting of a spirited march. It is a perfect marriage of words, music, and mood, and should be performed with this in mind. If you have a strong bass soloist in the group ask him to sing the verses. If you have two bass soloists, you may wish to make more of a production out of the number by adding these two verses (not shown in singer's edition) at the beginning to enhance the performance:

Good morning, brother pilgrim,
Pray tell me where you're bound?
Oh, tell me where you been traveling to
On this enchanted ground.

My name it is Poor Pilgrim,
To Canaan I am bound,
Traveling through this wilderness
On this enchanted ground.

The routine is chorus, verse, chorus, verse, chorus, ending on a chorus. But if you add the soloists as suggested above, you may want to start with the two special verses together, either before or after an initial chorus.

72

Joy to the World

Isaac Watts

Arr. from George F. Handel
by Lowell Mason

Majestically
C Dm C G7 C F
Joy to the world! the Lord is come; Let earth re-
G7 C
ceive her King; Let ev-ery heart prepare him
room, And heaven and na-ture sing,
G
And heaven and na-ture

G7
C
F
C
Dm
C
G7
C
sing, And_ heaven, and heaven_ and na - ture sing.

2. Joy to the world! the Savior reigns.
Let men their songs employ;
While fields and floods, rocks, hills, and plains
Repeat the sounding joy,
Repeat the sounding joy,
Repeat, repeat the sounding joy.

3. He rules the world with truth and grace,
And makes the nations prove
The glories of his righteousness,
And wonders of his love,
And wonders of his love,
And wonders, wonders of his love.

PROGRAM GUIDE: *Traditional American hymn; Christmas*

The text is a paraphrase of the ninety-eighth psalm, written by Isaac Watts (1674-1748), a religious poet theologian generally accepted as the "father of English hymnody." Watts was a pioneer in writing hymn texts based on the psalms. The tune evidently was developed (adapted and arranged) from various parts of Handel's *Messiah* by Lowell Mason (1792-1872). Mason was fond of using the descending major scale and employed it in another of his hymns, "My Faith Looks Up to Thee" (see number 85). A majestic tempo that is not too slow is appropriate.

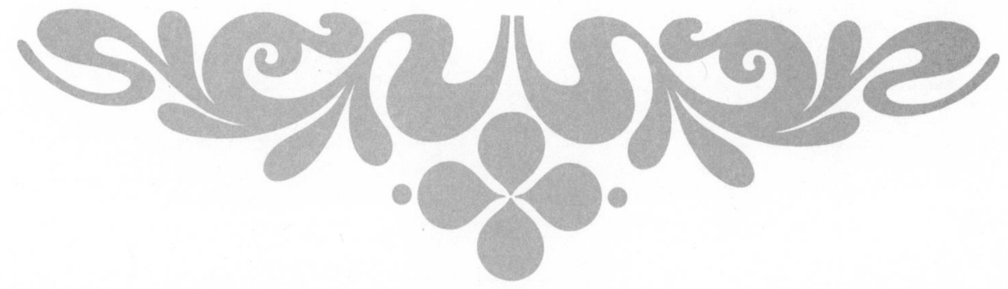

73

Just a Closer Walk with Thee

American Gospel Song

Moderately
B♭
C7
F7
Just a clos - er walk with thee,
Walking bass - legato
F7
B♭
Grant it, Je - sus, is my plea.
B♭7
E♭
Dai - ly walk - ing close with thee;
Let it

B♭
F7
B♭
be, dear Lord, let it be.
(Omit Last Time)

2. I am weak but thou art strong;
Jesus, keep me from all wrong;
I'll be satisfied as long,
As I walk, dear Lord, close to thee.

3. Through this world of toil and snares,
If I falter, Lord, who cares?
Who with me my burden shares?
None but thee, dear Lord, none but thee.

4. When my feeble life is o'er,
Time for me will be no more;
Guide me gently, safely on,
To thy shore, dear Lord, to thy shore.

PROGRAM GUIDE: *Traditional American gospel song*

A forthright message to a highly personal God, and a moody, bluesy tune have made this popular gospel song a longtime favorite of singers and jazz musicians. I've provided a walking bass in the accompaniment to help establish the right feel and sound for "Closer Walk." An easy, relaxed walking tempo is called for, along with more subdued dynamics. If you have three good harmonizers in the group you might have them echo the lyrics of the rest of the singers, using this rhythmic chant:

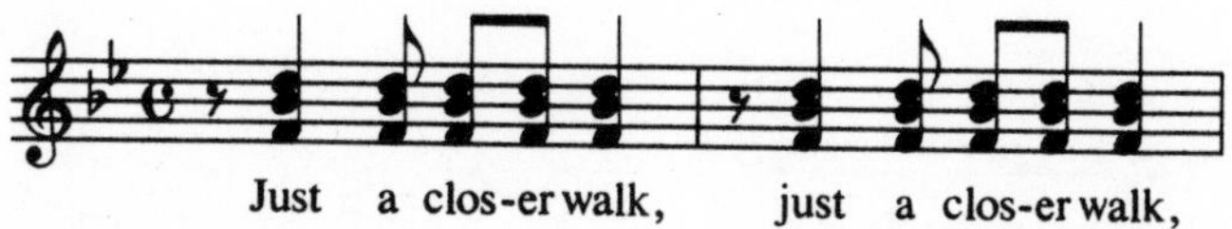
Just a clos-er walk, just a clos-er walk,

and so on, changing the harmony notes to follow the progression of the chords, and the chanted words to follow the lyrics. Some singers like to repeat the first verse as a chorus after the second, third, and fourth verses.

74

The Keeper Would A-Hunting Go

English Folk Song

Briskly
C G7 C F C G7 C F C
The keep-er would a - hunt-ing go, And un-der his coat he car-ried a bow,
C G7 C
All for to shoot at a mer-ry lit-tle doe, A - mong the leaves so__ green, O
C G7
Group One Two One Two All
Jack-ie boy! Mas-ter! Sing ye well? Ver-y well! Hey down! Ho down! Der-ry, der-ry down, A-

C G7 C G7 C G7 C
mong the leaves so__ green, O To me hey down, down, To me ho down, down.
C G7 C G7 C
Hey down, ho down, der-ry der-ry down A - mong the leaves so__ green O.

2. The first doe he shot at he missed;
The second doe he trimmed he kissed;
The third doe went where nobody wist
Among the leaves so green, O.

3. The fourth doe she did cross the plain;
The keeper fetched her back again;
Where she is now she may remain
Among the leaves so green, O.

4. The fifth doe she did cross the brook;
The keeper fetched her back with his crook;
Where she is now you must go and look
Among the leaves so green, O.

5. The sixth doe she ran over the plain;
But he with his hounds did turn her again,
And it's there he did hunt in a merry, merry vein
Among the leaves so green, O.

PROGRAM GUIDE: *English folk song*

What the keeper hunts in the version we sing today and what he hunted in ye olde English version are two different things (for the other version see my book *The Folk Song Abecedary*). But regardless of the quarry this is a fine singers' song. To make the most of it you should divide the singers into two groups and assign the parts, as indicated, on the vocal score. You may also use soloists, if you prefer, for those brief calls and responses. Go a-hunting at a lively, brisk tempo.

75
Kookaburra

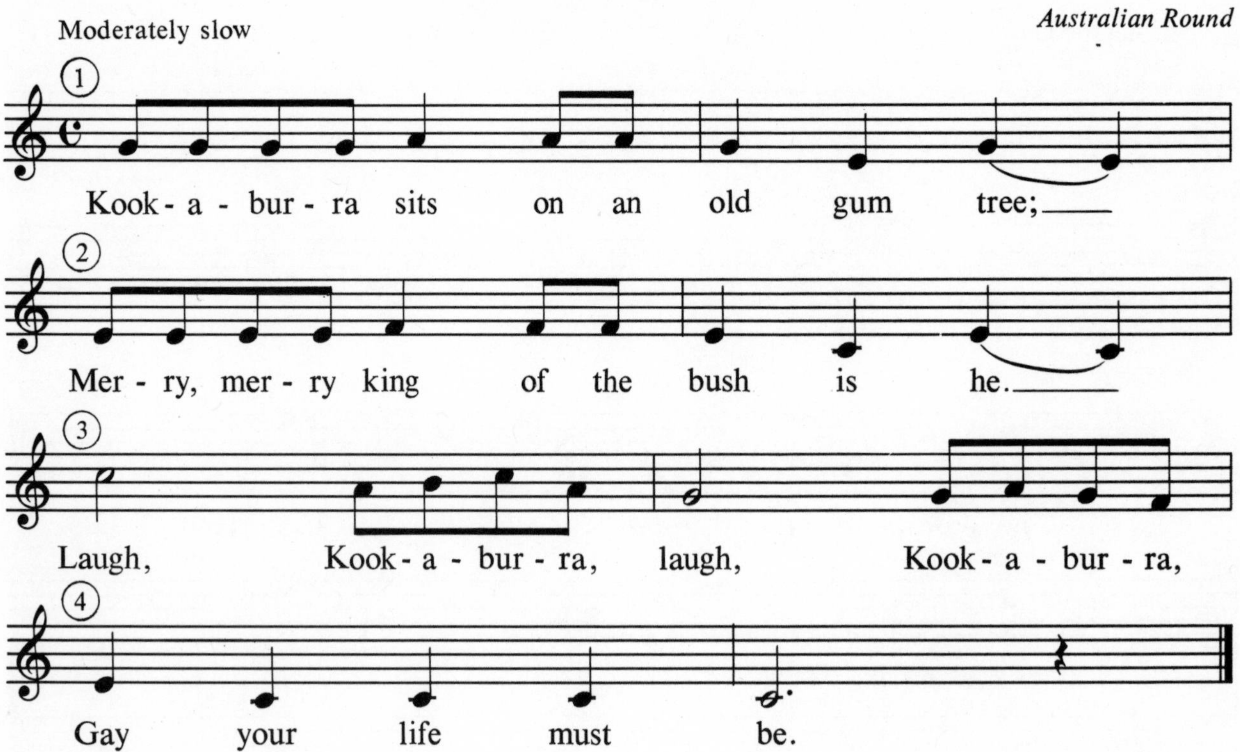
Moderately slow
Australian Round
1
Kook - a - bur - ra sits on an old gum tree;
2
Mer - ry, mer - ry king of the bush is he.
3
Laugh, Kook - a - bur - ra, laugh, Kook - a - bur - ra,
4
Gay your life must be.

Divide the group into four sections. Each section sings the entire round the agreed-upon number of times, beginning at point 1 when the preceding section reaches point 2. Thus the round begins and ends with one section singing alone: section 1 at the beginning and Section 4 at the end.

PROGRAM GUIDE: *Traditional Australian round*

The Kookaburra (*Dacelo gigas*) is the Australian kingfisher, or laughing jackass, which is known for its loud, harsh cry that resembles laughter. This laughable, four-part round, as you might expect, also comes from Australia. The tempo is moderately slow with two beats to the measure. It's a fine round for outdoor settings.

76

Kum Ba Ya

African Folk Song
Adapted by J.F.L.

Slowly
D G D
Kum ba ya, my Lord, Kum ba ya. Kum ba
D G A7 D G
ya, my Lord, Kum ba ya. Kum ba ya, my Lord, Kum ba
D G D A7 D
ya. Oh, Lord, Kum ba ya.

Verses (same tune as chorus):

1. Someone's crying, Lord, kum ba ya,
   Someone's crying, Lord, kum ba ya,
   Someone's crying, Lord, kum ba ya,
   Oh, Lord, kum ba ya.

Chorus

Continue, as above:

2. Someone's singing, Lord, etc.
3. Someone's praying.
4. Someone's hoping.

PROGRAM GUIDE: *African folk song; brotherhood*

There is a widely circulated theory that this African song is a transmogrified version of an American Negro spiritual, "Come By Here, Lord." That is, so the story goes, the spiritual was taken from the United States by missionaries to Africa, learned and changed by the Africans, and then eventually brought back here in its new version. Since returning to the United States, "Kum Ba Ya" has been picking up new verses by the dozen as it has circulated widely among enthusiastic singers. As the world gets smaller and cultures mix, this unique kind of tradition swapping is bound to take place, as it has in the past, except that more cultures are likely to be involved in the swapping. The words are pronounced *koom bah yah* and the song is sung very slowly, *six* even beats to the measure, with dignity. I've listed four popular verses (sung to the same tune as the chorus) in the singer's edition. Here are some more:

The world's in danger, Lord, kum ba ya, etc.

Tell the leaders, etc.

We must act now, etc.

Sing out loud and clear, etc.

77

Let Me Fly

American Negro Gospel Song

Verse
G C G C G C G C G C G C
Way down yon-der in the mid-dle of the field, An - gel work-in' on the
G C G C G C G C G C G C
char - iot wheel. Not so par - ti - cu - lar 'bout work-in' at the wheel, But I
Chorus
G C G C G C G C G
just want - a see how the char - iot feels. Now let me fly,

G Bm

Now, let me fly.________ Now

C D7 Em G C D7 G C G C G (C)

let me fly_ in - to Mount Zi - on, Lord, Lord.______

(Omit last time)

2. I got a mother in the promised land,
Ain't gonna stop till I shake her hand.
Not so particular 'bout shakin' her hand,
But I just wanta go up in the promised land.

3. Meet that hypocrite on the street,
First thing he'll do is show his teeth.
Next thing he'll do is to tell a lie,
And the best thing to do is to pass him by.

PROGRAM GUIDE: *American Negro gospel song*

If you are not familiar with this rousing, humorous gospel song, the joy of singing it will more than repay the effort of learning it. Set a bright tempo and give it a chance. It's a shouter, and the men should come through strong for you, even on the high notes in the chorus (the basses will want to drop an octave on "let me fly" the second and third time, so you might as well warn them in advance). The tenors and the ladies should have no problems with the range.

78
Let My Little Light Shine

Moderately fast

American Negro Gospel Song

Chorus
G
This lit-tle light of mine,
I'm gon-na let it shine;
G7
C
This lit-tle light of mine,
I'm gon-na let it shine;
G
This lit-tle light of mine,

G
B7
Em
I'm gon-na let it shine; Ev - 'ry -
G
E♭7
G
day, ev - ery - day, ev - ery - day, ev - ery -
A7
G
D7
Divide
G
D7
Fine
Verse
D7
day, Gon-na let my lit-tle light shine. On
Fine
(Omit Last Time)
G
G7
C
Mon-day he gave me the gift of love. On Tues-day peace came
R.H.
L.H.

C7
G
G7
from a-bove. On Wednes-day told me to have more faith. On
A7
D7
G
Thurs-day gave me a lit-tle more grace. On Fri-day told me to
G7
C
C7
watch and pray. On Sat-ur-day told me just what to say. On
G
Em
A7
D7
G
D.C.
Sun-day gave me pow-er di-vine just to let my lit-tle light shine.
D.C.

PROGRAM GUIDE: *American Negro gospel song*

Here is another popular gospel song that will really swing if you let it. Use a moderately fast, relaxed beat. Don't hesitate to turn the verse over to an able soloist. But be careful, this song is tricky and unless your singers are familiar with it, the syncopation, phrasing, and blues notes can give them a difficult time. If you have four sure-fire harmonizers, encourage them to answer (echo) the "everydays," using the notes assigned to that responsibility in the piano score (see measures 12, 13, and 14). At the divide (where voices are assigned different pitches) in the last two measures of the chorus, follow your own judgment on what the singers should do. With no divide the melody is:

shine.

Also, why not set up a rhythm section for the clappers. Try this pattern, or one of your own choosing.

But it's best if your clappers improvise.

79

Little Black Train Is A-comin'

American Negro Spiritual

Moderately fast
Introd.
R.H.
L.H.
Verse
Dm A7 Dm A7 Dm
God told Hez-e - ki-ah, In a mes-sage from on high: "Go
Dm A7 Dm A7 Dm
set your house in or-der For you will sure-ly die." He

Dm A7 Dm A7 Dm
turned to the wall a - weep-ing, oh, see the king in tears. He
Dm A7 Dm A7 Dm
got his bus-i-ness fixed all right, God spared him fif-teen years.
Chorus
Dm A7
Lit-tle black train is a - com-ing. Get all your bus-'ness right. Go
Dm Dm A7 Dm A7 Dm
set your house in or-der, For the train may come to - night.
(Omit last time)

2. Go tell that ballroom lady,
All filled with worldly pride,
That a little black train is coming,
Get prepared to take a ride.
For the little black train and engine,
Caboose and baggage car,
And all the folks a-riding
Got to stop at the judgment bar.

Chorus

3. Did you see that man in darkness?
Hid from the gospel light?
Did you hear him scream for mercy
When the train came moving in sight?
The devil had him in shackles,
Wrapped around his soul so tight,
No time to fix his business
When the train rolled in that night.

Chorus

PROGRAM GUIDE: *American Negro spiritual*

Here is another Sunday school Bible lesson told in a musical form reminiscent of "Joshua Fought the Battle of Jericho," but well able to stand on its own merit. A moderately fast tempo is appropriate, but not so fast that you lose the rhythmic effect. You may wish to pass the verses around among soloists, or divide them between the ladies and the men. Here's a two-measure rhythmic pattern for your clappers;

etc.

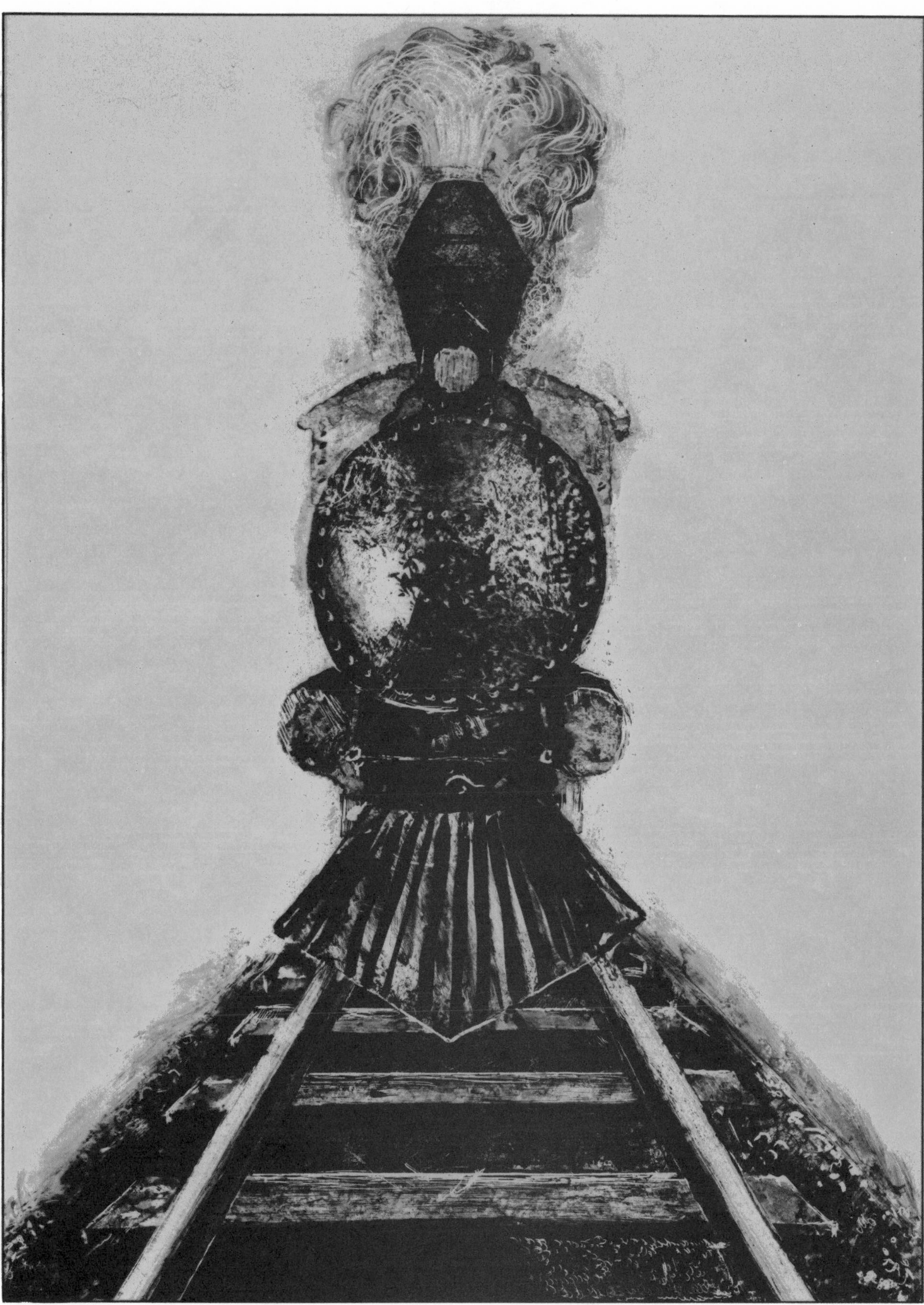

80
Lolly Too Dum

American Folk Song

Moderately fast
B♭
As I went out one morn-ing to take the morn-ing air, Lol-ly
F7
B♭
too dum, too dum, Lol - ly too dum day. As
B♭
E♭
I went out one morn-ing to take the morn-ing air, I

B♭
o - ver - heard a moth - er A - scold - ing her daugh - ter fair, Lol - ly
B♭
F7
B♭
too dum, too dum, Lol - ly too dum day.

2. "You better go wash them dishes,
And hush that clattering tongue,
Lolly too dum, too dum, lolly too dum day.
I know you want to get married
And that you are too young."
Lolly too dum, too dum, lolly too dum day.

Continue, as above:

3. "Oh, pity my condition
As you would your own,
For seventeen long years
I've been sleeping all alone."

4. "Yes, I'm seventeen and over,
And that you will allow—
I must and I will get married
For I'm in the notion now."

5. "Supposin' I was willin'.
Where would you get your man?"
"Why, Lordy mercy, Mammy,
I'd marry handsome Sam."

6. "Supposin' he should slight you
Like you done him before?"
"Why, Lordy mercy, Mammy,
I could marry forty more."

7. "There's peddlers and there's tinkers
And boys from the plow,
Oh Lordy mercy, Mammy,
I'm gettin' that feeling now!"

8. "Now my daughter's married
And well fer to do,
Gather 'round young fellers,
I'm on the market too."

9. "Lordy mercy, Mammy,
And who would marry you?
Ain't no man alive wants
A wife as old as you."

10. "There's doctors and there's lawyers
And men of high degree,
And some of them will marry
And one will marry me."

11. "Now we both are married
And well fer to be.
Ha ha ha, you pretty young girls,
That feeling's off of me."

PROGRAM GUIDE: *American folk song; humorous; dialogue*

Folk music abounds with variations on this familiar theme. First, mother has problems with her daughter who is overly eager to get married. But once the daughter leaves the nest mother gets ideas of her own, and it's daughter's turn to worry. Dialogue songs are meant to be sung as dialogue. Find an expeditious way, like pointing, to divide your group into mothers and daughters (men make good daughters, but any arrangement will do if your singers are crazy enough).

All: Verse 1.
Mothers: Verse 2, first part of verses 5, 6, 7, and all of verses 8, 10, and 11.
Daughters: verses 3 and 4, last part of verses 5, 6, 7, and all of 9.

You may want to mark these parts in your book for easy reference and for reminder cues as needed. If you have a couple of actors in your group who are always good for a laugh, you might let them sing the roles as solos, with everybody else chiming in on the *lolly-too-dums* (which everyone should do, in any event). This song seems to work best with very young or mature groups with an easy sense of humor. You may have a little difficulty with in-between-agers. In other words, it should be programmed selectively.

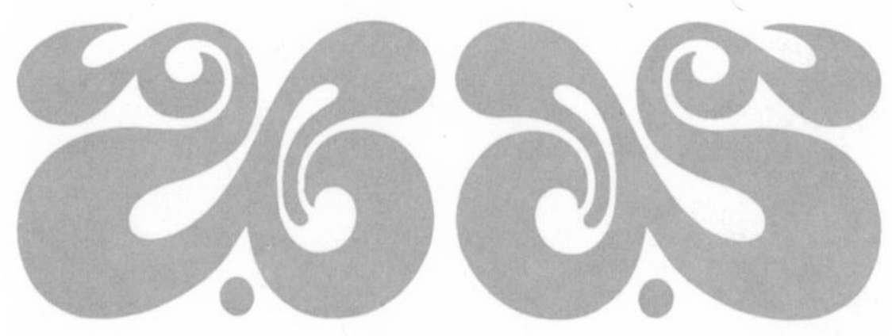

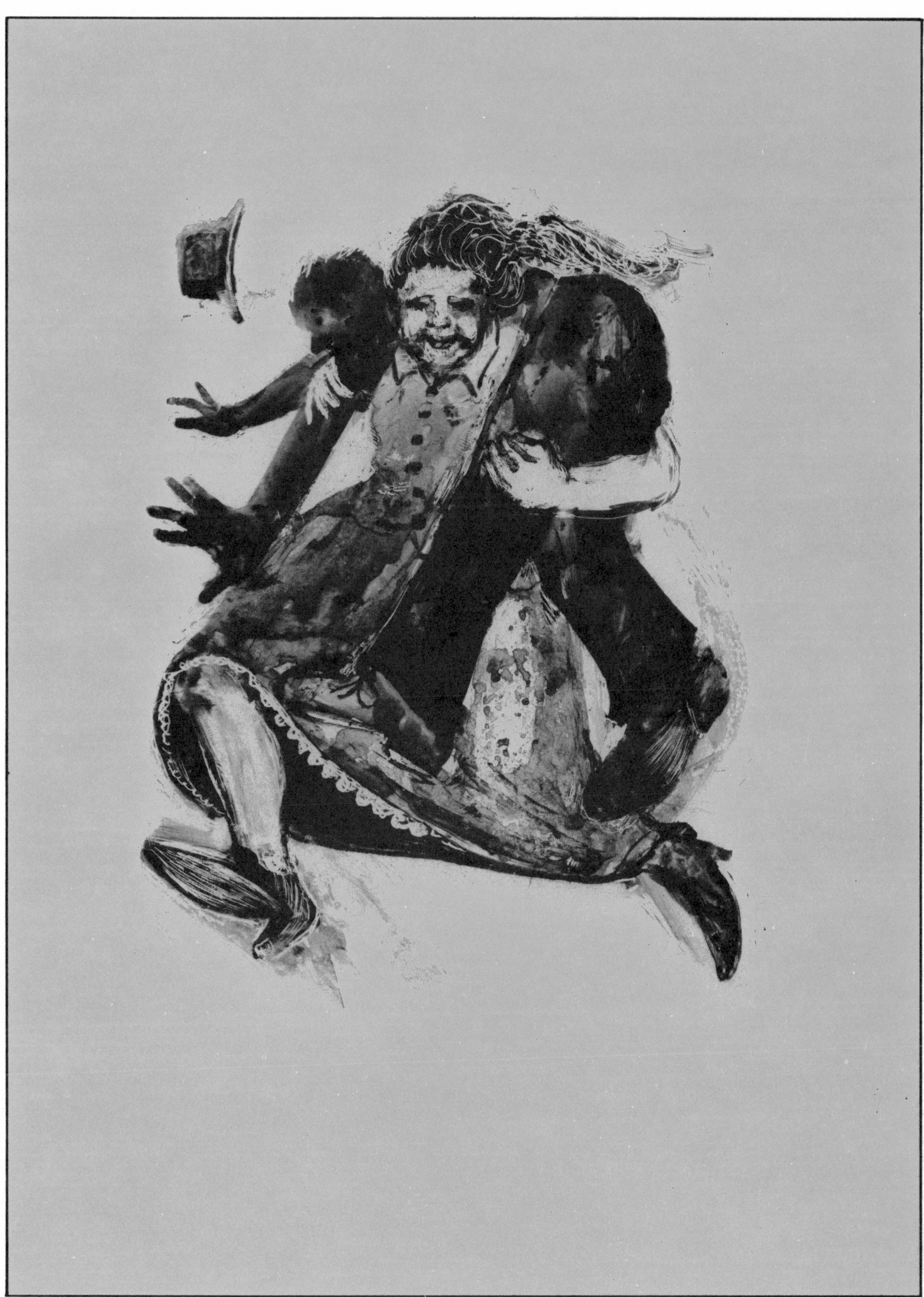

81
Lonesome Road

American Negro Folk Song

Moderately slow

F F7 B♭ B♭m

Look down, look down that lone - some road, Hang

legato, walking bass

F C7 F

down your head and cry.____ The

F F7 B♭ B♭m

best of friends must part some - time, Then

F
C7
F
why not you and I?
(Omit last time)

2. Look down, look down that lonesome road,
Before you travel on;
Look up, look up and greet your Maker,
'Fore Gabriel blows his horn.

3. Look down, look down, it's weary walkin',
Trudgin' down that lonesome road.
Look up, look up and greet your Maker,
'Fore Gabriel blows his horn.

Repeat first verse.

PROGRAM GUIDE: *American Negro folk song; blues style*

"Lonesome Road" has been a favorite of singers, concert performers, and jazz musicians. It's not real blues, but it has a blues feeling and sound to it, so take it slow and easy and let it wail. If you can't hear the walking bass in the piano, you may be wailing too loud.

82
Lonesome Valley

American Folk Hymn

Slowly
Dm
B♭
1. Je - sus walked this lone-some val - ley, He had to
F
C
F7
3
walk it by him - self, Oh, no-bod-y else could walk it
B♭
C
B♭
F
for him. He had to walk it by him - self.

2. You must go and stand your trial,
You have to stand it by yourself.
Oh, nobody else can stand it for you,
You have to stand it by yourself.

3. We must walk this lonesome valley,
We have to walk it by ourselves.
Oh, nobody else can walk it for us,
We have to walk it by ourselves.

PROGRAM GUIDE: *American folk hymn; white spiritual*

"Lonesome Valley" is a modal white spiritual. It should be performed at a relatively slow tempo with this arrangement. However, guitar accompaniment can add a nice rhythmic thrust with a strum based on doubled time values. Sing it softly and let those modal chord changes be heard. If you want a fourth stanza, repeat the first verse at the end.

83

Mary and Martha

American Negro Spiritual

Moderately fast
Verse
F
C7
F
Mar-y and Mar-tha jus' gone 'long, Mar-y and Mar-tha jus' gone 'long,
F
(Melody in lower notes)
C7
C7
Mar-y and Mar-tha jus' gone long To ring them charm-ing bells. Cry-in',
Chorus
F
C7
F
"Free grace, un-a-dy-in' love, Free grace, un-a-dy-in' love,

(Melody in lower notes)
F
C7
F
C7
F
Free grace, un-a - dy - in' love", To ring them charm - ing bells.

2. Father and mother jus' gone 'long,
   Father and mother jus' gone 'long,
   Father and mother jus' gone 'long,
   To ring them charming bells.

Continue, as above:

3. Preacher and the elder jus' gone 'long.
4. Everybody jus' gone 'long.

PROGRAM GUIDE: *American Negro spiritual*

When you're in the mood for a very simple, unadorned, but thoroughly pleasant spiritual, this Negro Sunday school song could be the one. All it requires is a quiet, joyful, natural, relaxed performance. I've added a light, two-part finish that is easy to teach, and can be picked up quickly and easily by your ladies (see last two measures of verse and chorus). Here's a simple clapping pattern for your rhythm section:

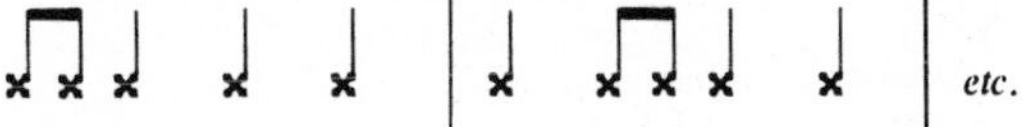
etc.

84

Michael, Row the Boat Ashore

American-West Indian Folk Song

Moderately slow calypso
D
G
Mi-chael, row the boat a - shore, Al - le - lu -
D
F♯m
G
A7
D
ia. Mi-chael, row the boat a - shore, Al - le - lu - ia.

2. Michael's boat's a music boat, Alleluia,
   Michael's boat's a music boat, Alleluia.

3. Sister, help to trim the sail, Alleluia,
   Sister, help to trim the sail, Alleluia.

4. Jordan's River is chilly and cold, Alleluia,
   Kills the body but not the soul, Alleluia.

5. Jordan's River is deep and wide, Alleluia,
   Meet my mother on the other side, Alleluia.

6. Gabriel, blow the trumpet horn, Alleluia,
   Blow the trumpet loud and long, Alleluia.

7. Brother, lend a helping hand, Alleluia,
   Brother, lend a helping hand, Alleluia.

8. Michael's boat's a gospel boat, Alleluia,
   Michael's boat's a gospel boat, Alleluia.

PROGRAM GUIDE: *American/West Indian folk song*

U.S. folk song revivalists found *Michael* in the Georgia Sea Islands and circulated the song widely and fervently in the 1960s. As it is usually performed today, the song is a melding of spiritual, calypso, and sea-song styles. It seems to have originated in the United States as a spiritual sung by the slave crews on plantation riverboats. You can find it in the earliest-known source of the folk songs created by American Negroes, *Slave Songs of the United States,* by William Francis Allen, Charles Pickard Ware, and Lucy McKim Garrison, published in 1867. Charles Ware notes that "Michael" was one of the rowing songs used when the load was heavy or the boat was going against the tide. The name Michael refers to the archangel Michael. Take it moderately slow and easy, letting the calypso beat take care of the rhythmic thrust. Select the number of verses you want to sing, and finish with a repetition of the first verse. If you want to psych your singers into a pretty two-part performance, divide them into groups. Then teach each group a "new melody" for the song as shown below, using the upper notes for one group and the lower notes for the other. When you put the two together, after a brief rehearsal, they will love you.

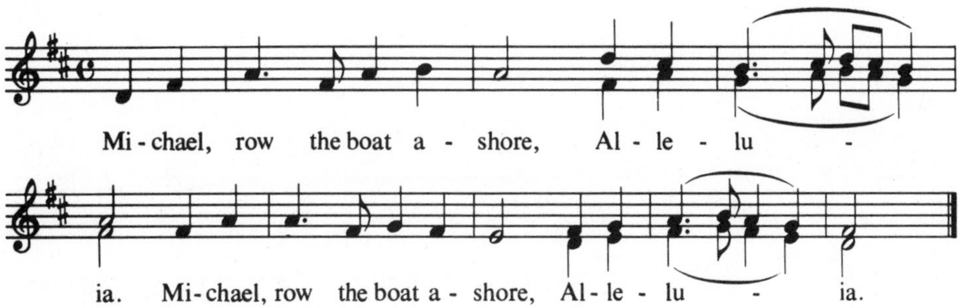
Mi - chael, row the boat a - shore, Al - le - lu - ia.
Mi-chael, row the boat a - shore, Al - le - lu - ia.

85
My Faith Looks up to Thee

Ray Palmer *Lowell Mason*

Moderately
E♭
B♭7
My faith looks up to thee, Thou Lamb of Cal - va - ry,
E♭ F7 B♭ E♭ Fm7 E♭ A♭ E♭ Fm7
Sav - ior di - vine! Now hear me while I pray, Take all my
E♭ A♭ E♭ E♭maj7 A♭ E♭ A♭ E♭ Fm7 B♭ E♭
guilt a - way, O let me from this day Be whol - ly thine.

2. May thy rich grace impart
Strength to my fainting heart,
My zeal inspire;
As thou hast died for me,
O may my love to thee
Pure, warm, and changeless be,
A living fire!

3. While life's dark maze I tread,
And griefs around me spread,
Be thou my guide;
Bid darkness turn to day,
Wipe sorrow's tears away,
Nor let me ever stray
From thee aside.

4. When ends life's transient dream,
When death's cold, sullen stream
Shall o'er me roll;
Blest Savior, then, in love,
Fear and distrust remove;
O bear me safe above,
A ransomed soul!

PROGRAM GUIDE: *Traditional American hymn*

Lowell Mason (1792-1892) gave up a banking career at the age of thirty-seven to become one of America's most influential music educators. He pioneered the teaching of music in public schools and the holding of music teachers' conventions. He also compiled and edited many widely used hymnals. He is best known today for several popular hymn tunes that are still going strong. These include the tunes associated with "Nearer My God to Thee" and "My Faith Looks Up to Thee." He also had a hand in fashioning the tune to which we sing "Joy to the World" (number 72). Mason wrote the hymn tune *Olivet* for "My Faith Looks Up to Thee" in 1824. The text was written by Ray Palmer (1808-1887) when he was only twenty-one. Palmer, who was very devout, stated that he "ended the last line with tears." A moderate tempo is appropriate.

86
My Gal Sal

Paul Dresser

Moderately
F
B♭
F
They called her friv-o - lous Sal, A pe - cu - liar
B♭
F
A7
sort of a gal, With a heart that was mel-low, An
Dm
G7
C7
all-round good fel - low Was my old pal.

F
B♭
F
Your trou-bles, sor-rows, and care She was
A7
Dm
F7
B♭
F
A7
al - ways will-ing to share; A wild sort of dev- il, But
D7
Gm
G7
C7
F
dead on the lev-el, Was my gal Sal.

PROGRAM GUIDE: *Traditional American popular song*

Tune up your player piano, dust off the piano roll, and listen to a song about a hard-boiled girl with a heart of gold. Paul Dresser's hit song was published in 1905, the same year that Orville Wright made the first officially recorded airplane flight, Ty Cobb joined the Detroit Tigers, and the Staten Island ferry made its first run. Theodore Roosevelt was President, and tough guys—including Sal—were in vogue. Turn the piano switch to moderato and sit back and let it happen to you.

87

My Home's Across the Smoky Mountain

American Folk Song

F
My home's a - cross the Smok-y Moun - tains, My
R. H.
L. H.
C7
F
home's a - cross the Smok-y Moun - tains, My
F
home's a - cross the Smok-y Moun - tains, And I'll

C7
F
nev - er get to see you an - y - more, more, more, And I'll
C7
F
nev - er get to see you an - y - more.
(Omit Last Time)

2. Goodbye, my honey, sugar darlin',
Goodbye, my honey, sugar darlin',
Goodbye, my honey, sugar darlin',
And I'll never get to see you anymore, more, more,
And I'll never get to see you anymore.

3. I love my honey, feed her candy,
I love my honey, feed her candy,
I love my honey, feed her candy,
And I'll never get to see her anymore, more, more,
Oh, I'll never get to see her anymore.
Repeat first verse.

PROGRAM GUIDE: *American folk song*

This backwoods country song grew up about two haircuts away from town. But you sure can raise cane with it when you go into town on Saturday night to watch the new traffic light change. It's green, yellow, RED, and I'll never get to see her anymore, more, more. Let's hit it at an up-tempo and let the devil take the hindmost. One, two, what're we gonna' do: My home's across the Smoky Mountains, etc.

88

New River Train

New lyrics by J.F.L.

American Folk Song

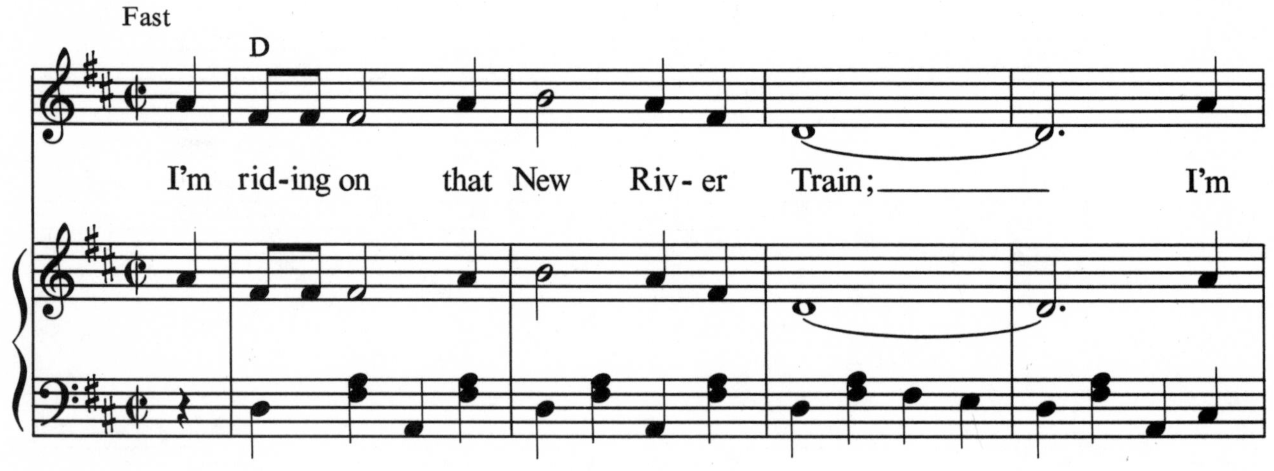
Fast
D
I'm rid-ing on that New Riv-er Train; I'm

D
A7
rid-ing on that New Riv-er Train;

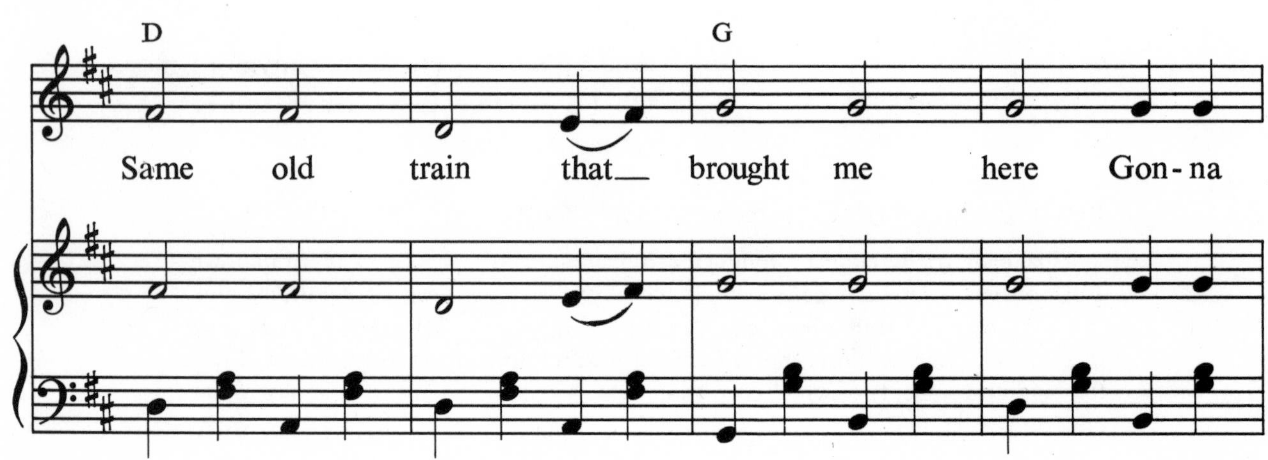
D
G
Same old train that brought me here Gon-na

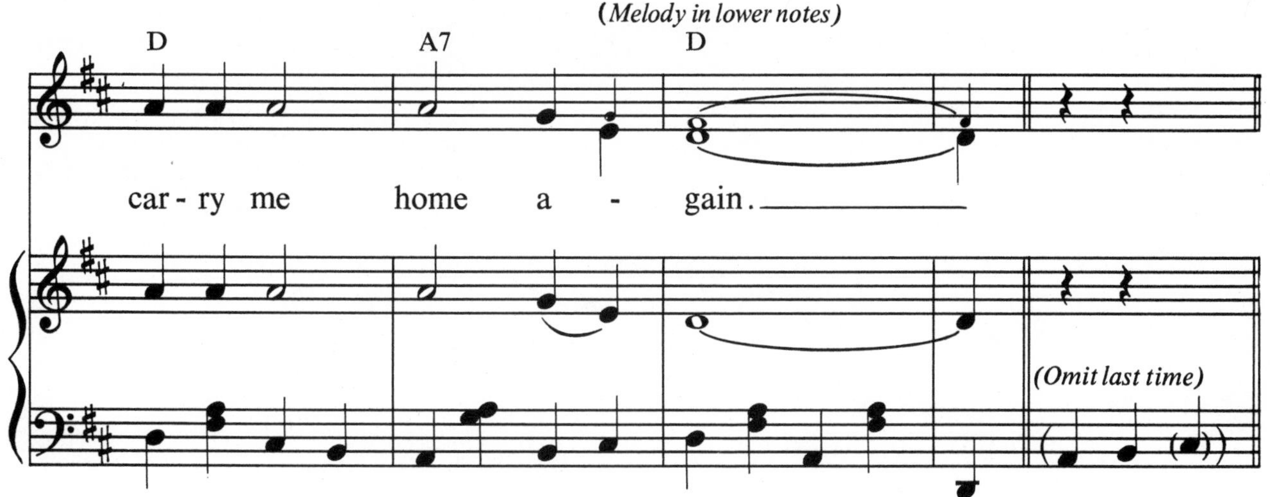
(Melody in lower notes)
D
A7
D
car - ry me home a - gain.
(Omit last time)

2. Oh, baby, remember what you said;
   Oh, baby, remember what you said;
   Remember what you said: You would
   rather see me dead
   Than ridin' on that New River Train.

3. Oh, darlin', you can't love one,
   Oh, darlin', you can't love one;
   You can't love one and have any fun,
   Oh, darlin', you can't love one.

Continue, as above:

4. You can't love two and your little heart be true.
5. You can't love three and still love me.
6. You can't love four and love me anymore.
7. You can't love five and still stay alive.
8. You can't love six and not get in a fix.
9. You can't love seven if you want to go to heaven.
10. You can't love eight 'cause you'll make somebody wait.
11. You can't love nine and keep 'em all in line.
12. You can't love ten and stay out of the county pen.
13. You can't love eleven—you should've stopped at seven.

PROGRAM GUIDE: *American folk song; humorous, counting song*

Counting songs started out as aids to slow learners. But most slow learners changed the "official" versions to something less respectable when they graduated. "New River Train," with a country music motif, is one of the nicer types among the postgraduates. Use a bright tempo and feel free to make up your own verses, instead of using mine. You can pass the singing and the line-inventing chores around if you want to. Let your harmonizers pick up the easy harmony notes at the finish, if you wish.

89
Nine Hundred Miles

American Folk Song

Moderately slow
Cm
Fm
Cm
Well, I'm walk-ing down this track, I've got tears in my eyes,
legato
A♭
E♭
Cm
Chorus
Tryin' to read a let-ter from my home, And if this
Cm
Fm
Cm
train runs me right, I'll be home to-mor-row night, 'Cause I'm

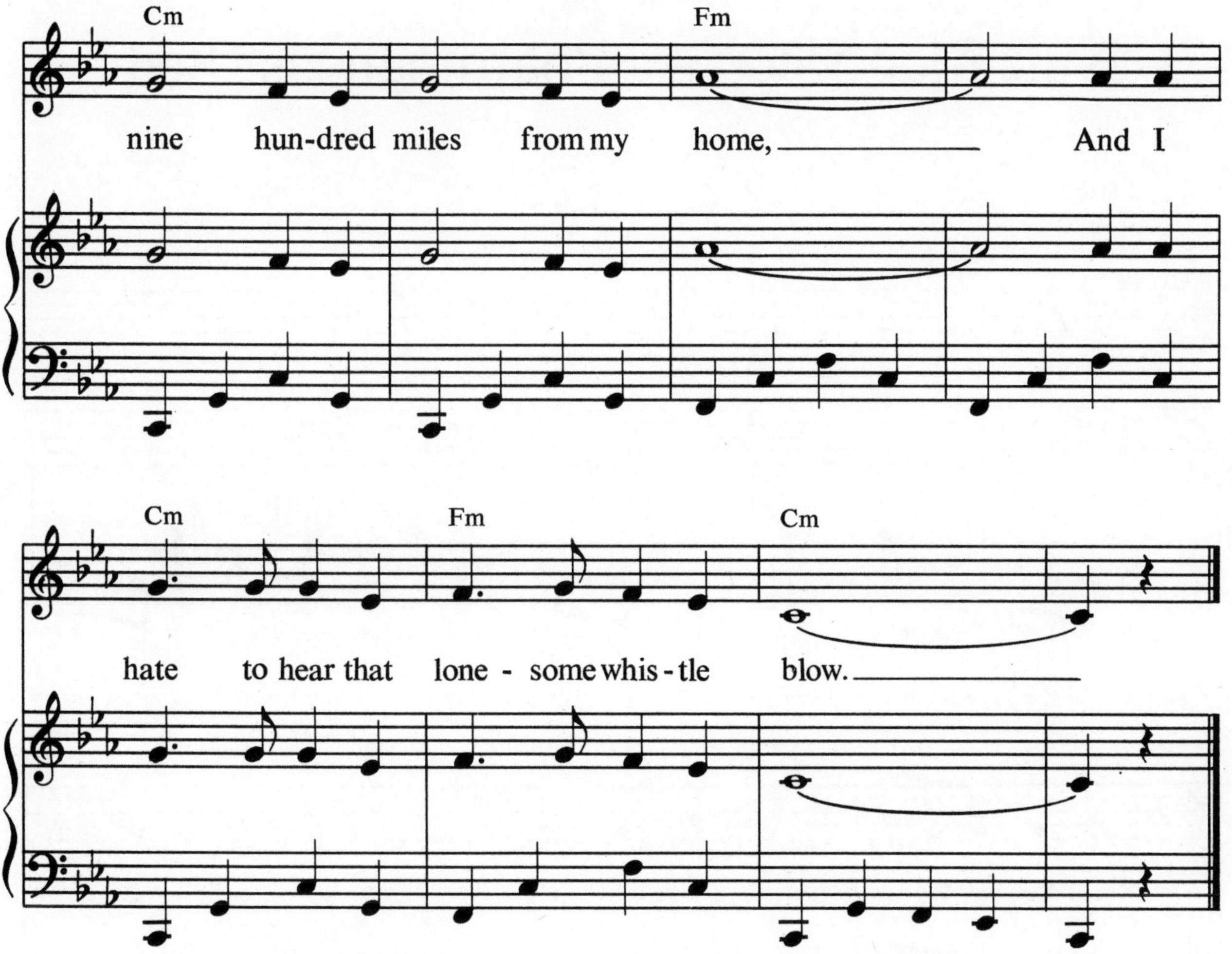
Cm
Fm
nine hun-dred miles from my home, And I
Cm
Fm
Cm
hate to hear that lone - some whis - tle blow.

2. I will pawn you my watch;
   I will pawn you my chain;
   Pawn you my gold diamond ring.

   Chorus

3. If my woman tells me so,
   I will railroad no more;
   I'll hang around her shanty all the time.

   Chorus

4. Now this train I ride on
   Is a hundred coaches long;
   Travels back a hundred miles or more;

   Chorus

PROGRAM GUIDE: *American folk song*

"Nine Hundred Miles" is a relative, as folk song relationships go, of "In the Pines" (number 65) and "Lonesome Road" (number 81). One of the characteristics of a folk song is that the folk song writers never seem to tire of remaking them to suit different ideas and tastes. When fine rewrites like this come along we are thankful. Use a moderately slow tempo, let the arpeggios in the accompaniment (piano or guitar) carry the momentum, and keep the voices subdued.

90

Nine Men Slept in a Boardinghouse Bed

American Folk Song

Briskly
Introd.
F
C7
F
C7
Humorously
F
C7
F
Nine men slept in a board-ing house bed, Roll o - ver, roll o - ver, They
F
C7
F
all rolled o-ver when an-y-one said, "Roll o - ver, roll o - ver."

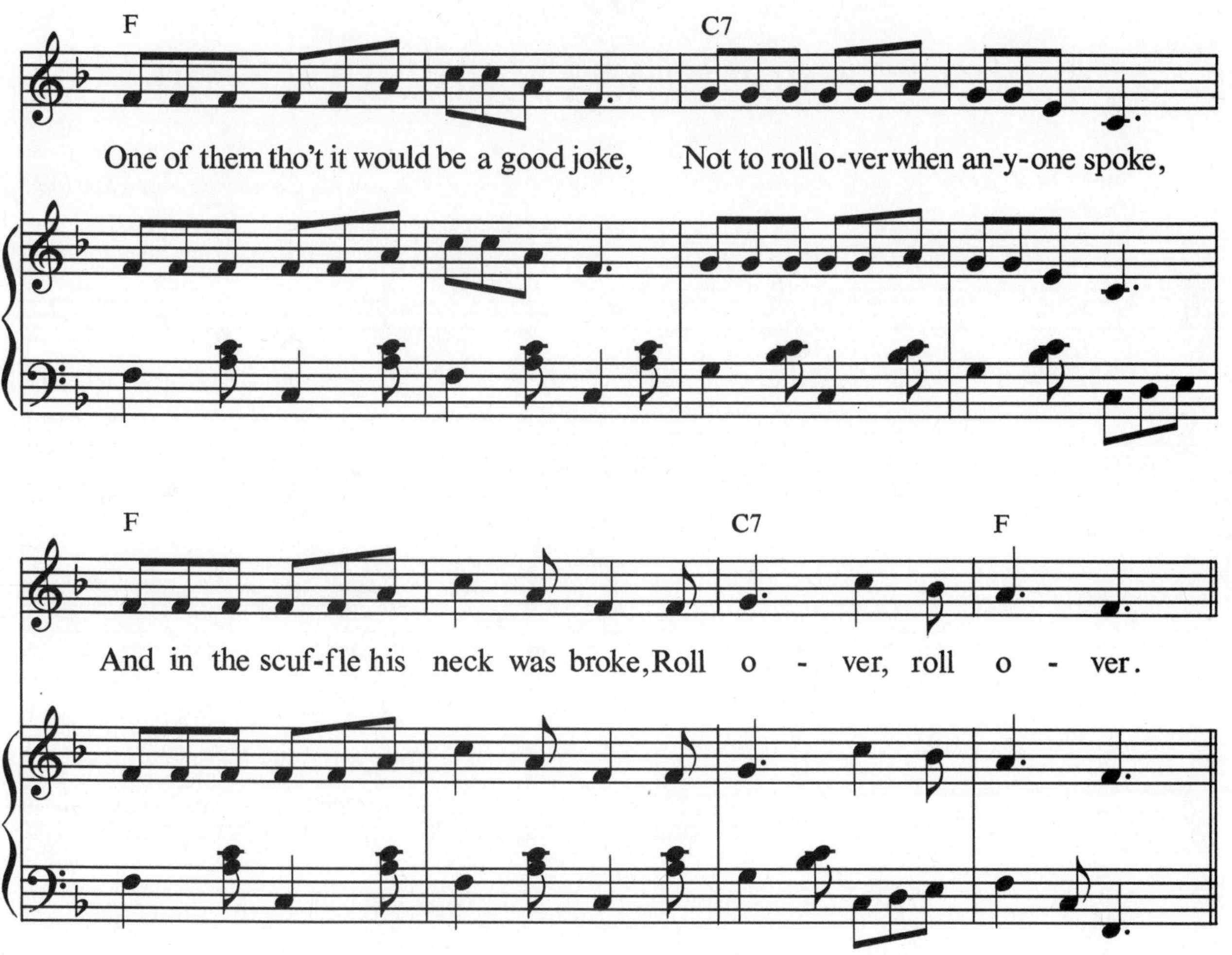
F
C7
One of them tho't it would be a good joke, Not to roll o-ver when an-y-one spoke,
F
C7
F
And in the scuf-fle his neck was broke, Roll o - ver, roll o - ver.

2. Eight men slept in a boardinghouse bed,
   Roll over, roll over.
   They all rolled over when anyone said,
   "Roll over, roll over."
   One of them thought it would be a good joke,
   Not to roll over when anyone spoke,
   And in the scuffle his neck was broke,
   Roll over, roll over.

Continue, as above, until the bed is empty:

3. Seven men slept. . . .

PROGRAM GUIDE: *Traditional American camp song; humorous, counting song*

It's easy to see why this is a popular camp song—mayhem! First you put nine men in a bed, pile on, and then you roll them out one verse and one man at a time. Use a lively march tempo.

91

Nobody Knows the Trouble I've Seen

Moderately slow
Chorus
American Negro Spiritual
F
B♭
F
B♭
No-bod - y knows the trou-ble I've seen, No-bod - y knows but
legato
F
B♭
F
Je - sus. No-bod - y knows the trou-ble I've seen,
F
C7
F
Fine
Leader
F
Glo - ry hal - le - lu - jah! Some - times I'm up, some -
Fine

(Melody in lower notes)
Response
C7
Leader
times I'm down, Oh, yes, Lord; Some -

Response
(Melody in lower notes)
F
C7
F
D.C.
times I'm al - most to the ground, Oh, yes, Lord!
D.C.

2. Now you may think that I don't know,
   Oh, yes, Lord,
   But I've had my troubles here below,
   Oh, yes, Lord!

   Chorus

Continue, as above:

3. One day when I was walkin' along,
   The sky opened up and love came down.

4. What makes old Satan hate me so?
   He had me once and had to let me go.

5. I never shall forget that day,
   When Jesus washed my sins away.

PROGRAM GUIDE: *American Negro spiritual*

Use a moderately slow pace for this powerful Negro spiritual. I've suggested harmony notes for the responses in the verse, but if your group is loaded with talent, encourage the harmonizers to enrich the chord (either by ear or by borrowing tones from the piano score). You may assign the calls in the verse to one or two male or female soloists. Otherwise, divide the calls between the ladies and the men.

92

Now the Day Is Over

Sabine Baring-Gould *Joseph Barnby*

Slowly

B♭ F F7 B♭ Gm D7 Gm

Now the day is o - ver, Night is draw - ing nigh,

C9 Am C F F7 B♭ B♭m C°7(♭5) F7 Cm(+F) F7 B♭

Shad - ows of the eve - ning Steal a - cross the sky.

2. Through the hours of darkness,
May thine angels spread
Their white wings above me,
Watching 'round my bed.

PROGRAM GUIDE: *Traditional English hymn*

The words were written by Sabine Baring-Gould (1834-1924) as an evening hymn for children. The music, composed by Sir Joseph Barnby (1838-1896), is a masterpiece of beauty and economy. It probably has the smallest range of any successful tune in history, no more than three steps of the scale (one of them only a halfstep) and five different tones are employed. The secret of its beauty lies in the movement of the supporting tones, and not in the melodic line itself, though the melody itself is strong. I've included only two verses in the singer's edition, because the other verses are often disappointing to contemporary singers. You may want to repeat the first verse at the end if you sing it as shown. Here are the verses that were omitted:

Jesus, give the weary
Calm and sweet repose;
With thy tenderest blessing,
May our eyelids close.

Grant to little children
Visions bright of thee;
Guard the sailors tossing
On the deep blue sea.

Comfort every sufferer
Watching late in pain;
Those who plan some evil,
From their sin restrain.

(*Note: last verse in singer's edition appears here in the original version.*)

When the morning wakens,
Then may I arise
Pure and fresh and sinless
In thy holy eyes.

This beautiful hymn is particularly appropriate when a prayer or a benediction is called for in an evening or sunset program. It has long been a favorite of campers and campfire singers. It should be sung softly and slowly. If anyone knows or wants to learn those moving harmony parts, give them some encouragement (see piano score for the harmony parts).

93

Now We'll Make the Rafters Ring

Words altered by J.F.L.

Traditional English Round

Majestically

1
2
Now we'll make the raf - ters ring,
3
4
while these songs we all shall sing.

Divide the group into four sections. Each section sings the entire round the agreed-upon number of times, beginning at point 1 when the preceding section reaches point 2. Thus the round begins and ends with one section singing alone: Section 1 at the beginning and Section 4 at the end.

PROGRAM GUIDE: *Traditional English round*

I altered the words of this four-part round slightly to make it useful for those who wish to use the round as a part of a standard program format. Once the round is learned it may be used, from time to time or consistently, to open the singing portion of any program series. If you prefer the original, ask your singers to mark their books accordingly:

Now we'll make the rafters ring,
While we all this round will sing.

Sing it broadly at a very slow, majestic tempo.

94

O Christmas Tree

German Folk Song

Briskly
F C7 F Gm D7 Gm C7 F
O Christ-mas tree, O Christ-mas tree, With faith-ful leaves un - chang-ing. O
F C7 F Gm D7 Gm C7 F
Christ-mas tree, O Christ-mas tree, With faith-ful leaves un - chang-ing. Not
F B♭ C7 F
on-ly green in sum-mer's heat, But al-so win - ter's snow and sleet; O

F
C7
D7
Gm D7 Gm C7
F
Christ-mas tree, O Christ-mas tree, with faith-ful leaves un - chang-ing.

2. O Christmas tree, O Christmas tree,
Of all the trees most lovely; (*Repeat*)
Each year you bring to me delight
Gleaming in the Christmas night.
O Christmas tree, O Christmas tree,
Of all the trees most lovely.

3. O Christmas tree, O Christmas tree,
Your leaves will teach me also (*Repeat*)
That hope and love and faithfulness
Are precious things I can possess.
O Christmas tree, O Christmas tree,
Your leaves will teach me also.

Optional verse:

O Christmas tree, O Christmas tree,
How lovely are your branches. (*Repeat*)
In summer sun or winter snow
A coat of green you always show.
O Christmas tree, O Christmas tree.
How lovely are your branches.

PROGRAM GUIDE: *Traditional German folk song; Christmas*

Our traditional salute to the Christmas tree is adapted from a German folk song, "O Tannenbaum," which was published in Berlin in 1820. The tune has been traced to a 1799 publication and could be as old as the twelfth century. The optional verse shown in the singer's edition is included simply because I prefer it to the more traditional, literal translation shown in the first verse. You may substitute it for the for the first verse if you agree, add it on as a last verse if you prefer, or ignore it entirely. Sing this stouthearted carol briskly, in the German fashion.

Here are the German words:

O Tannenbaum, O Tannenbaum,
Wie treu sind deine Blätter! (*Repeat*)
Du grünst nicht nur zur Sommerszeit,
Nein, auch in Winter, wenn es schneit.
O Tannenbaum, O Tannenbaum,
Wie treu sind deine Blätter!

O Tannenbaum, O Tannenbaum,
Du kannst mir sehr gefallen! (*Repeat*)
Wie oft hat nicht zur Weihnachtszeit
Ein Baum von dir mich hoch erfreut!
O Tannenbaum, O Tannenbaum,
Du Kannst mir sehr gefallen!

O Tannenbaum, O Tannenbaum,
Dein Kleid will mich was lehren! (*Repeat*)
Die Hoffnung und Beständigkeit
Gibt Trost und Kraft zu jeder Zeit.
O Tannenbaum, O Tannenbaum,
Dein Kleid will mich was lehren!

95

O Come, All Ye Faithful

John Francis Wade (?)
Trans. and alt. by Frederick Oakeley

John Francis Wade

Moderately slow
G D G D G C G D Em
O come, all ye faith - ful, joy-ful and tri - um - phant, O
Em D A D G D A7 D
come ye, O come ye to Beth - le - hem;
Refrain
G Am G Am D7 G D G Em Am D Guitar tacet -
Come and be - hold him, born the King of an - gels; O

G D G D7 G D G

come, let us a - dore him, O come, let us a - dore him, O

D7 G D A7 D G C G D7 G

come, let us a - dore him, Christ the Lord.

2. Sing, choirs of angels, sing in exultation,
O Sing, all ye citizens of heaven above!
Glory to God, all glory in the highest;

Refrain

3. Yea, Lord, we greet thee, born this holy morning,
Jesus, to thee be all glory giv'n!
Word of the Father, now in flesh appearing;

Refrain

PROGRAM GUIDE: *Traditional Latin-English hymn*

The text and music of "Adeste Fideles" were transcribed, or possibly composed, by John Francis Wade (1711-1786), an English political refugee who was a teacher and copyist at the Roman Catholic Center in Douay, France. The Reverend Frederick Oakeley, Rector of All Saints' Anglican Church in London, translated the text into English in 1841, about a hundred years after it was discovered or composed (the discovery is much more probable) by Wade. Oakeley's translation was subsequently modified slightly to arrive at the version we sing today. A moderately slow and even tempo is suggested.

The Latin words are:

1. Adeste fideles, laeti triumphantes,
   Venite, venite in Bethlehem!
   Natum videte Regem angelorum:

   Refrain:

   Venite adoremus, venite adoremus,
   Venite adoremus Dominum.

2. Cantet nunc Io! chorus angelorum;
   Cantet nunc aula caelestium:
   Gloria, gloria, in excelsis Deo:

   Refrain.

3. Ergo qui natus die hodierna,
   Jesu, tibi sit gloria!
   Patris aeterni Verbum caro factum:

   Refrain.

The tune is a "fuguing tune," a style that was common in England in the eighteenth century, the soprano being imitated and answered by the tenor in the refrain.

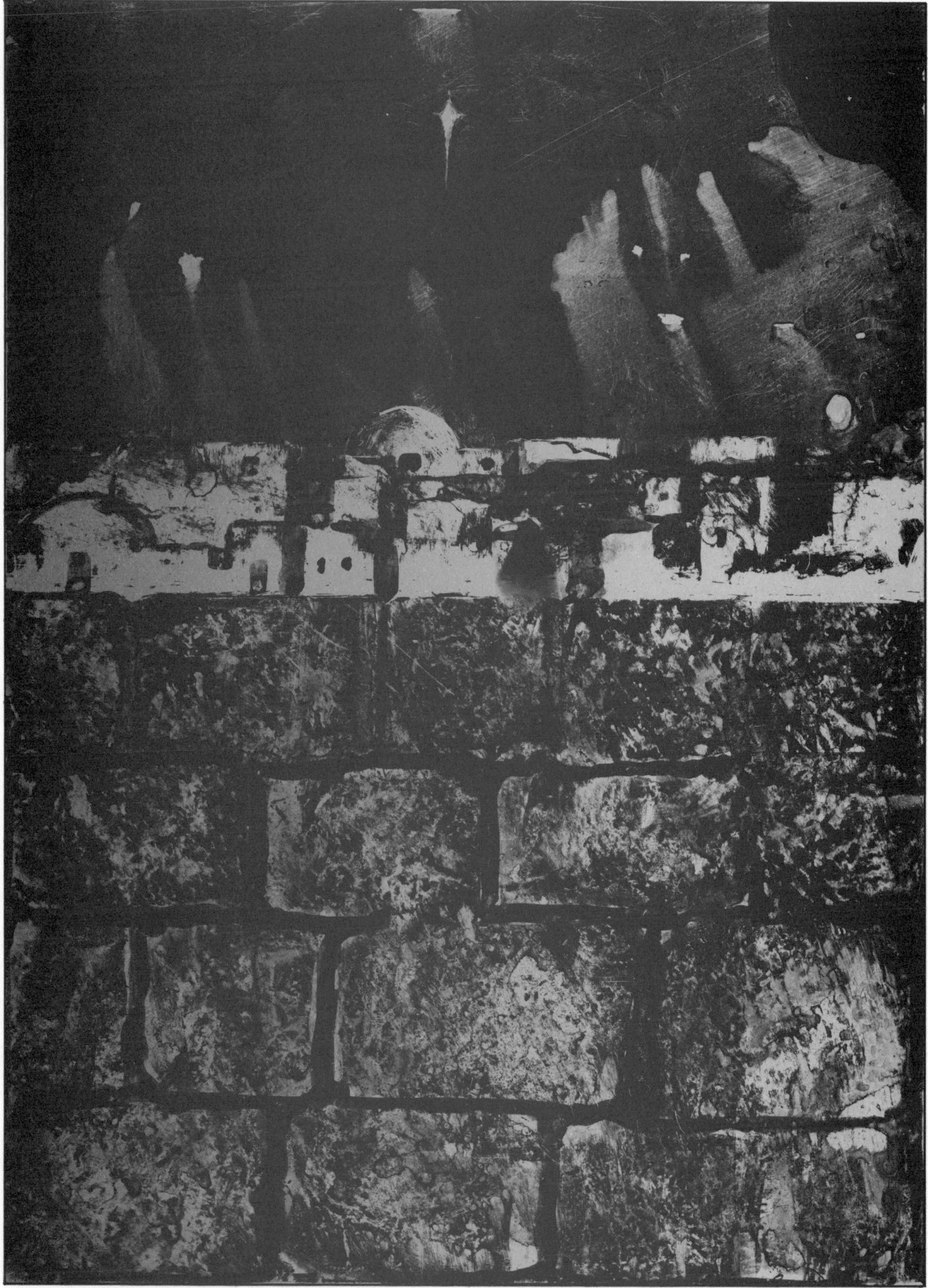

96

O Little Town of Bethlehem

Phillips Brooks
Lewis H. Redner
Moderately
F F°7 F C°7 Gm F Am C7 F
O lit - tle town of Beth - le - hem, How still we see thee lie! A -
F F7 D D7 E♭maj7 Gm F C7 F
bove thy deep and dream - less sleep The si - lent stars go by: Yet
F G°7 G♯°7 A Dm Gm A F
in thy dark streets shin - eth The ev - er - last - ing light; The

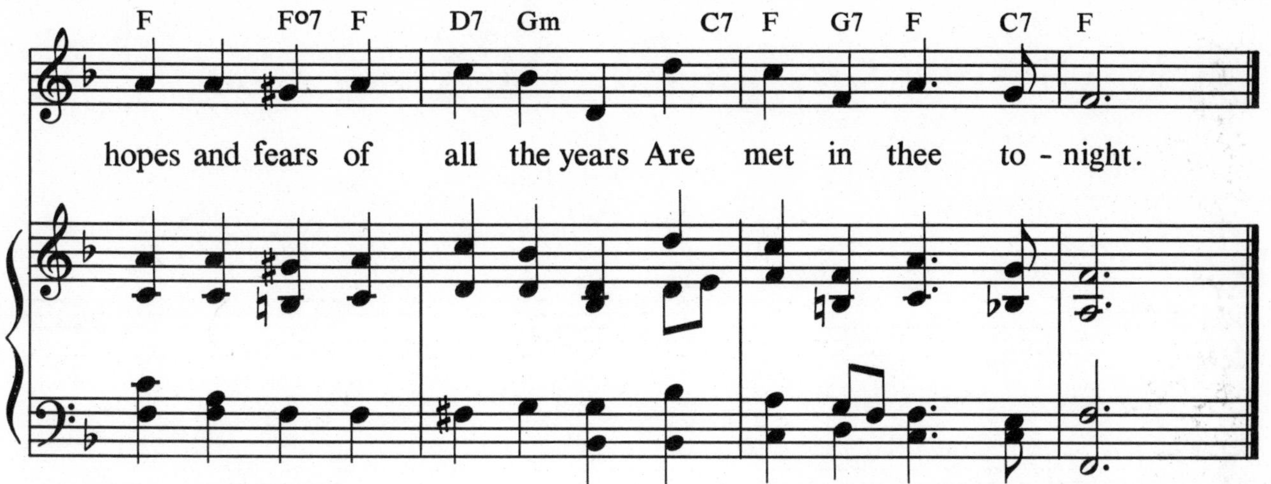
F
F°7
F
D7
Gm
C7
F
G7
F
C7
F
hopes and fears of all the years Are met in thee to - night.

2. For Christ is born of Mary,
And gathered all above,
While mortals sleep, the angels keep
Their watch of wondering love.
O morning stars, together
Proclaim the holy birth,
And praises sing to God the King,
And peace to men on earth!

3. How silently how silently
The wondrous gift is given!
So God imparts to human hearts
The blessings of his heaven.
No ear may hear his coming,
But in this world of sin,
Where meek souls will receive him, still
The dear Christ enters in.

4. O holy Child of Bethlehem!
Descend to us, we pray;
Cast out our sin, and enter in,
Be born in us today.
We hear the Christmas angels
The great glad tidings tell;
O come to us, abide with us,
Our Lord Emmanuel!

PROGRAM GUIDE: *Traditional American hymn; Christmas*

Phillips Brooks (1835-1893), a famous American Episcopal minister, wrote the text of "O Little Town of Bethlehem" in 1868, when he was rector of Philadelphia's Holy Trinity Church. Wanting to write a Christmas carol for the children of his church, he took the theme from a visit he had made to the Holy Land three years earlier. In December, 1865, he rode horseback from Jerusalem to Bethlehem and viewed the town for the first time as he arrived at night. Brooks asked his organist, Lewis H. Redner (1831-1908), to set his words to music. Redner struggled to find the right melody throughout Christmas week, but was unable to solve the problem until he awoke during the night on Christmas Eve with the needed inspiration. Hearing the sound of "an angel strain" he quickly wrote the melody down. Brooks was so pleased with Redner's inspiration he insisted that the tune name (hymn tunes are assigned their own particular names, separate from any particular text with which they are associated at the time) be designated *Saint Louis,* in honor of the organist. Brooks's children's hymn is a favorite of children of all ages for Christmas singing.

If children are present, why not let them sing the first verse by themselves while the rest hum quietly? Then finish with the third verse sung quietly by all.

97

Oh, Dear, What Can the Matter Be?

English Folk Song

Fast
Introd.
Em
A7
D
A7
Chorus
D
Pompously, with humor
Oh,
ten.
A7
Em
dear, what can the mat - ter be? Dear, dear,
A7
D
what can the mat - ter be? Oh, dear, what can the

D Em A7 D Fine
mat - ter be? John - ny's so long at the fair.
Fine
Verse
D A7
He prom - ised to buy me a fair - ing to please me, And then for a
Em A7 D
kiss, oh, he vowed he would tease me. He prom - ised to buy me a
Em A7 D D.C.
bunch of blue rib - bons To tie up my bon - ny brown hair.
D.C.

2. He promised to buy me a pair of sleeve buttons,
   A pair of new garters would cost him but tuppence,
   A pair of red stockings to go with the ribbons
   That tie up my bonny brown hair.

3. He promised he'd bring me a basket of posies,
   A garland of lilies, a garland of roses,
   A little straw hat to set off the blue ribbons
   That tie up my bonny brown hair.

PROGRAM GUIDE: *English folk song, romantic*

The tragedy of it all is too much! How would you feel if you were standing there dressed to the teeth, waiting for Johnny to bring you all those goodies—and Johnnie never showed? You must roll out this old British folk song from the eighteenth century in the *grande* style and encourage your singers to perform with drama and anguish. The tempo should be very lively, one beat to the measure at the pace of a walk. A chorus of whistling also will add a merry sound. You might ask the ladies only to sing the verses.

A *fairing* is an archaic word that means "a gift," especially one bought at a fair, naturally.

The routine *with* accompaniment is introduction, chorus, verse, introduction, chorus, verse, etc., ending with a final chorus. The repetition of the introduction serves as an interlude. Of course you may skip the interlude, if you wish, and go directly from verse to chorus. The routine *without* accompaniment is chorus, verse, chorus, etc.

98

Oh, How Lovely Is the Evening

Traditional English Round

Moderately fast
1
Oh, how love - ly is the eve - ning, is the eve - ning;
2
When the bells are sweet - ly ring - ing, sweet - ly ring - ing;
3
Ding, dong, ding; ding, dong, ding.

Divide the group into three sections. Each section sings the entire round the agreed-upon number of times, beginning at point 1 when the preceding section reaches point 2. Thus the round begins and ends with one section singing alone: Section 1 at the beginning and Section 3 at the end.

PROGRAM GUIDE: *Traditional English round*

This three-part song is one of the most satisfying of all the old traditional rounds to sing with informal singers. Divide your audience into three groups and fill the evening air with the sound of all that lovely singing. I hope you brought some bells along to ring. Use a light, moderately fast tempo.

99

Oh, Mary, Don't You Weep

Additional lyrics by J.F.L.

American Negro Spiritual

Moderately
Chorus
G C G D7 G D7
Oh, Mar - y, don't you weep, don't you mourn; Oh, Mar - y, don't you
G C G
weep, don't you mourn; Phar - aoh's ar - my got drown - ded,
Fine
Verse
G D7 G C G D7 G C G
Oh, Mar - y don't you weep. If I could I
Fine

D7
G
sure - ly would Stand on the rock where Mos - es stood.
C
G
G
D7
G
D.C.
Phar-aoh's ar - my got drown - ded, Oh, Mar-y, don't you weep.
D.C.

2. Wonder what Satan's grumblin' 'bout,
   Chained in Hell an' he can't git out.
   Pharaoh's army got drownded,
   Oh, Mary, don't you weep.

Continue, as above:

3. Ol' Satan's mad an' I am glad,
   He missed that soul he thought he had.

4. Brother, better mind how you walk on the cross,
   Foot might slip and your soul get lost.

5. One of these nights about twelve o'clock,
   This old world's goin' to reel and rock.

6. I went down in the valley to pray,
   My soul got joy and I stayed all day.

7. Now don't you believe the Bible ain't true,
   'Cause you'll be sorry if you do.

8. That primrose path is wide and fair,
   Many a soul's done perished there.

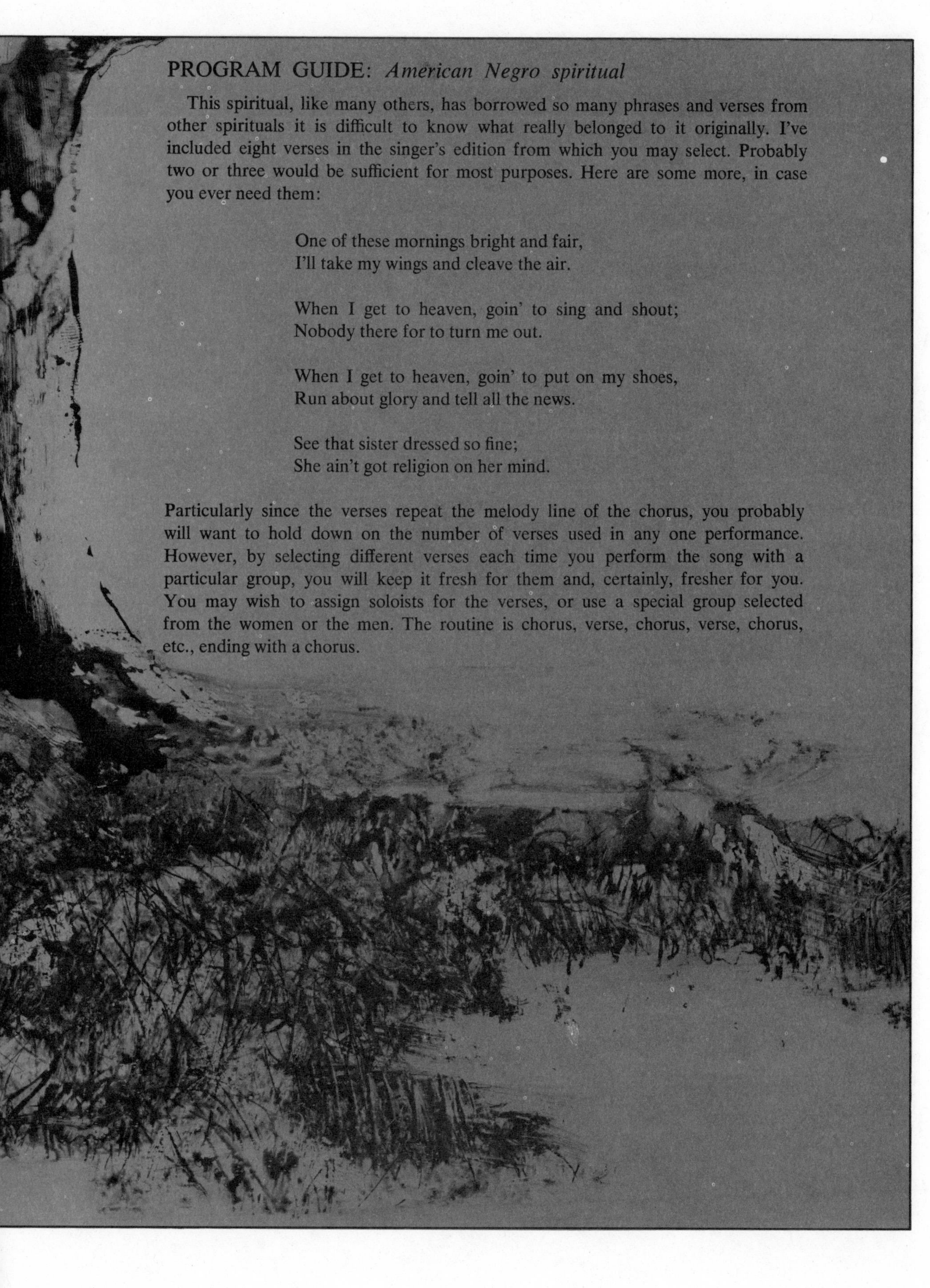

PROGRAM GUIDE: *American Negro spiritual*

This spiritual, like many others, has borrowed so many phrases and verses from other spirituals it is difficult to know what really belonged to it originally. I've included eight verses in the singer's edition from which you may select. Probably two or three would be sufficient for most purposes. Here are some more, in case you ever need them:

One of these mornings bright and fair,
I'll take my wings and cleave the air.

When I get to heaven, goin' to sing and shout;
Nobody there for to turn me out.

When I get to heaven, goin' to put on my shoes,
Run about glory and tell all the news.

See that sister dressed so fine;
She ain't got religion on her mind.

Particularly since the verses repeat the melody line of the chorus, you probably will want to hold down on the number of verses used in any one performance. However, by selecting different verses each time you perform the song with a particular group, you will keep it fresh for them and, certainly, fresher for you. You may wish to assign soloists for the verses, or use a special group selected from the women or the men. The routine is chorus, verse, chorus, verse, chorus, etc., ending with a chorus.

100
Oh, Mister Moon

Traditional, American

Moderately
F F°7 C7 F D7 G7
Oh, Mis - ter Moon, moon, bright and shin - y moon, Won't you
F G7 C7 F G°7 F7 B♭ F°7
please shine down on me? Oh, Mis - ter Moon, moon,
F D7 G7 C7
bright and shin - y moon, Won't you come from be - hind that tree? Oh, my

F6 F°7 Gm7 F°7 F6 F6 F°7
life's in dan-ger but I'm scared to run. There's a man be - hind me with a

Gm7 F°7 C7 F F°7 C7 F D7 G7
big shot-gun, Oh, Mis-ter Moon, moon, bright and shin-y moon, Won't you

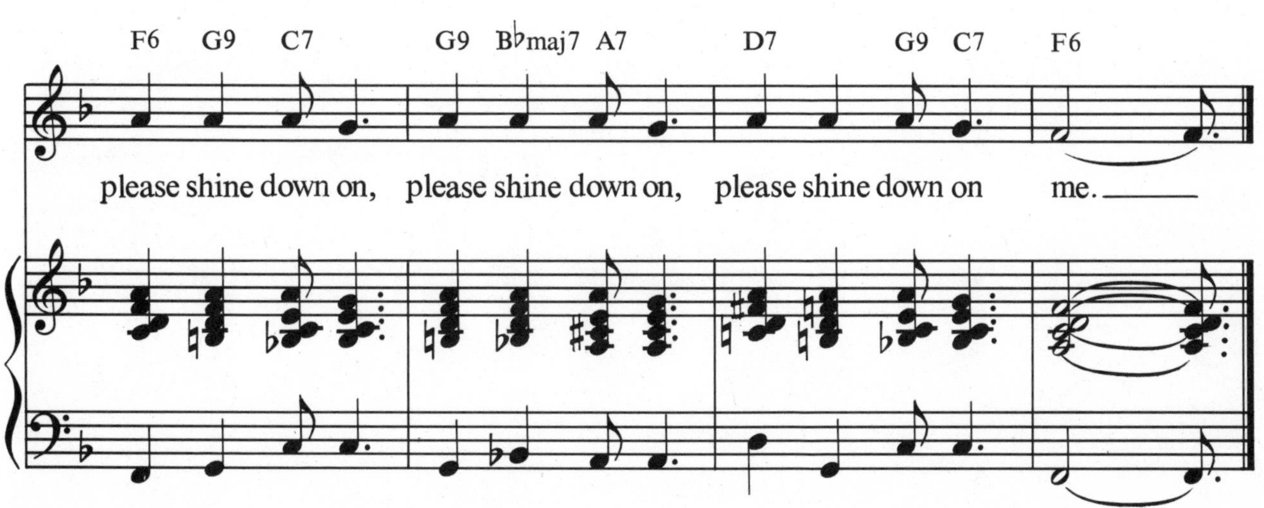
F6 G9 C7 G9 B♭maj7 A7 D7 G9 C7 F6
please shine down on, please shine down on, please shine down on me.

PROGRAM GUIDE: *Traditional American barbershop quartet song*

Why, you might ask, would anyone being sought by a man with a shotgun ask to be exposed by the moon? Maybe he wants to be caught? Does it matter? Not to barbershop quartet addicts. You can make this one easy for your singers by doing it in unison. Of course, you may as well let those who know what to do do it since they will anyway. Barber shops were, for many centuries (going back to the days of Greece and Rome), a favorite sanctuary for men, a place where they could congregate for the exchange of gossip and opinion. The singing entertainment of barbershop quartets was a natural outgrowth. And, although the invention of the safety razor (and subsequent developments) greatly reduced the cultural influence of barbershops, the style of singing that developed still flourishes today. One of the most famous musical signatures is associated with the style:

Shave and a hair - cut, bay - rum!

Or, if you prefer, "six bits" instead of "bay rum." Tack on this old barbershop quartet tag at the end, if you like.

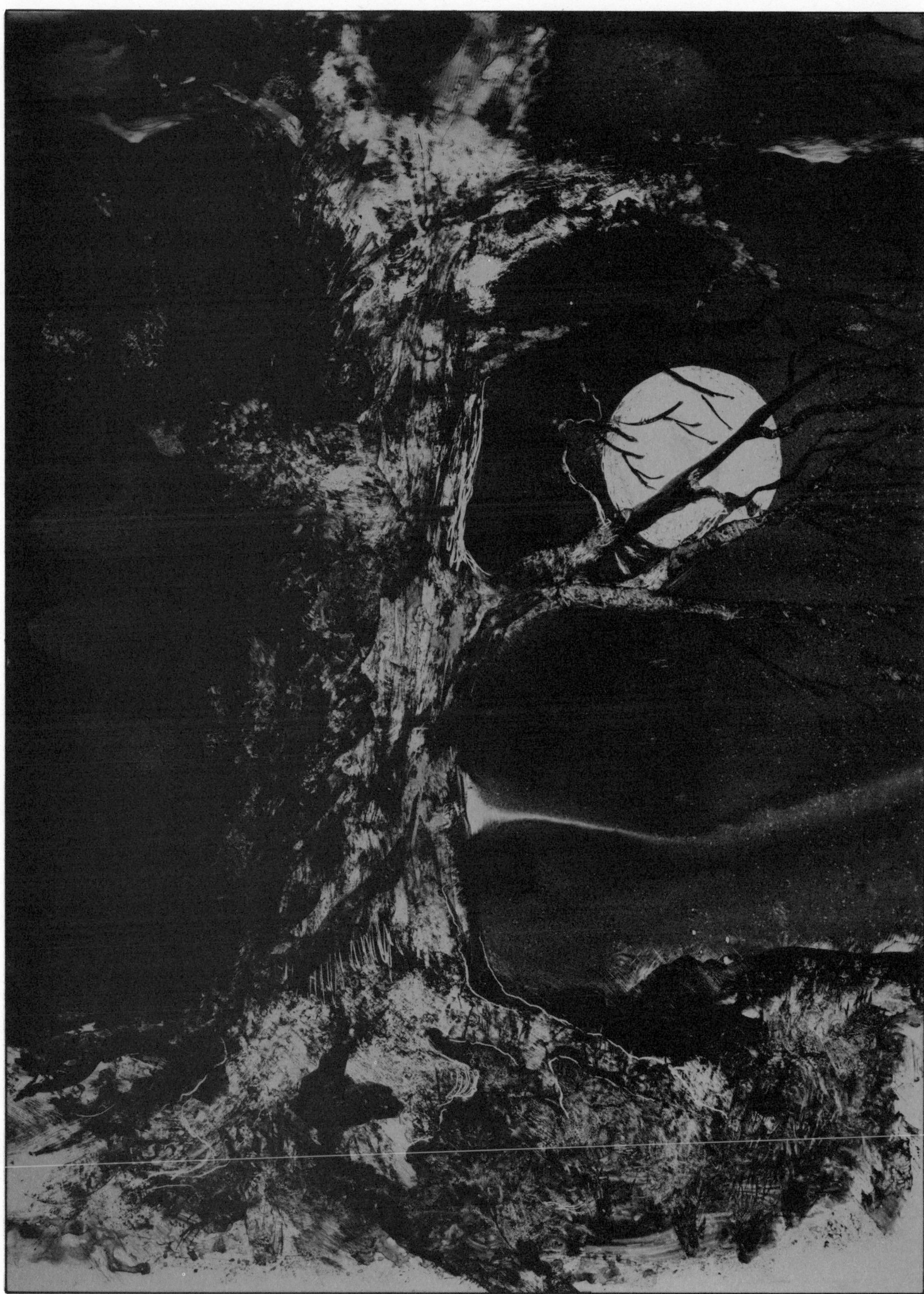

101

Oh, No, John

English Folk Song

Moderately
Verse
F C7 F C7 F C7
(Men) On yon-der hill there stands a — crea-ture, Who she is I
C7 F C7 F B♭
do not know. I'll go and court her for her beau-ty; She must an-swer
Chorus
C7 F C7 F C7 F
yes or no. (Ladies) Oh, no, John, no, John, no, John, no.

Women:

2. My father was a Spanish captain,
Went to sea a month ago;
First he kissed me, then he left me;
Told me always answer no. (*Chorus*)

Men:

3. Oh, madam, in your face is beauty,
On your lips red roses' glow,
Will you take me for your lover?
Madam, answer yes or no. (*Chorus*)

Men:

4. Oh, madam, I will give you jewels,
I will make you rich and free,
I will give you silken dresses;
Madam, will you marry me? (*Chorus*)

Men:

5. Oh, madam, since you are so cruel,
And since you do scorn me so,
If I may not be your lover,
Madam, will you let me go? (*Chorus*)

Men:

6. Then I will stay with you forever,
If you will not be unkind,
Madam, I have vowed to love you,
Would you have me change my mind? (*Chorus*)

Men:

7. Oh, hark, I hear the church bells ringing,
Will you come and be my wife?
Or, dear madam, have you settled
To live single all your life? (*Chorus*)

PROGRAM GUIDE: *Traditional English song; courtship song, humorous*

Singing can be instructional. This courtship song tells you how to turn *no* into *yes,* when you are a clever suitor. Although there are several versions of this song, this particular one has remained popular ever since folk song collector Cecil Sharp cleaned up a bawdier version and took it from the boudoir into the drawing room. The song doesn't make much sense unless you follow the directions: men sing all the verses except the second one; women sing all the choruses and the second verse. Of course, you may use soloists, if you wish, but that pretty well knocks out any group participation. Be careful about the tempo—not too fast.

102

Oh, Won't You Sit Down?

Moderately and rhythmically
American Negro Spiritual
Chorus
Call
Response
Call
G
D7
Oh, won't you sit down? Lord, I can't sit down. Oh, won't you
Response
Call
Response
G
D7
G
sit down? Lord, I can't sit down. Oh, won't you sit down? Lord, I
All
D7
G
D7
Fine
can't sit down, 'Cause I just got to heav-en, Got to look a - round.
Fine

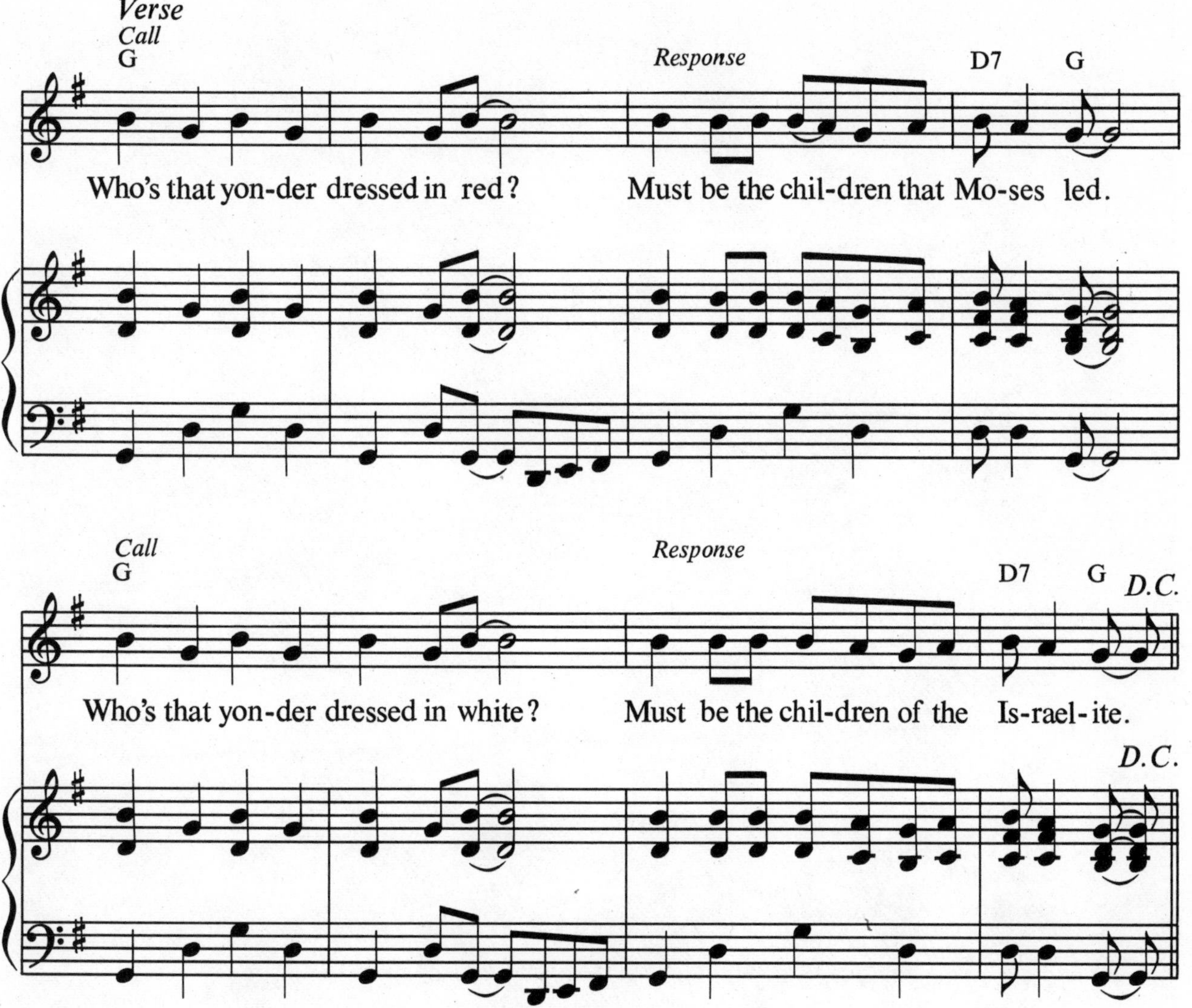
Verse
Call
G
Response
D7
G
Who's that yon-der dressed in red?
Must be the chil-dren that Mo-ses led.
Call
G
Response
D7
G
D.C.
Who's that yon-der dressed in white?
Must be the chil-dren of the Is-rael-ite.
D.C.

2. Who's that yonder dressed in blue?
Must be the children that are comin' through.
Who's that yonder dressed in black?
Must be the hypocrites a-turnin' back.

PROGRAM GUIDE: *American Negro spiritual*

You really should divide your singers into callers and responders to make the performance of this spiritual more effective. You may also wish to use soloists on the verses. You'll know you have the rhythm right if you observe your singers rocking or swaying to the beat as the singing swings from call to response. That's why it's particularly important to divide the singers. The routine is chorus, verse, chorus, verse, chorus. Don't hesitate to make a shouter out of this. That's the idea behind the song. It's the same sentiment that backs up these famous lines from a spiritual:

I really do believe without a doubt,
That the church has a mighty right to shout!

And:

I tell you what I like the best
It is them shoutin' Methodists.

And:

Gon' have a happy meetin'
Gon' shout in heaven,
Gon' shout an never tire.
Oh, slap your hands, children,
Oh, pat your feet, children
I feel the spirit movin',
Oh, now I'm gettin' happy.

Here's a pattern for your clappers and patters:

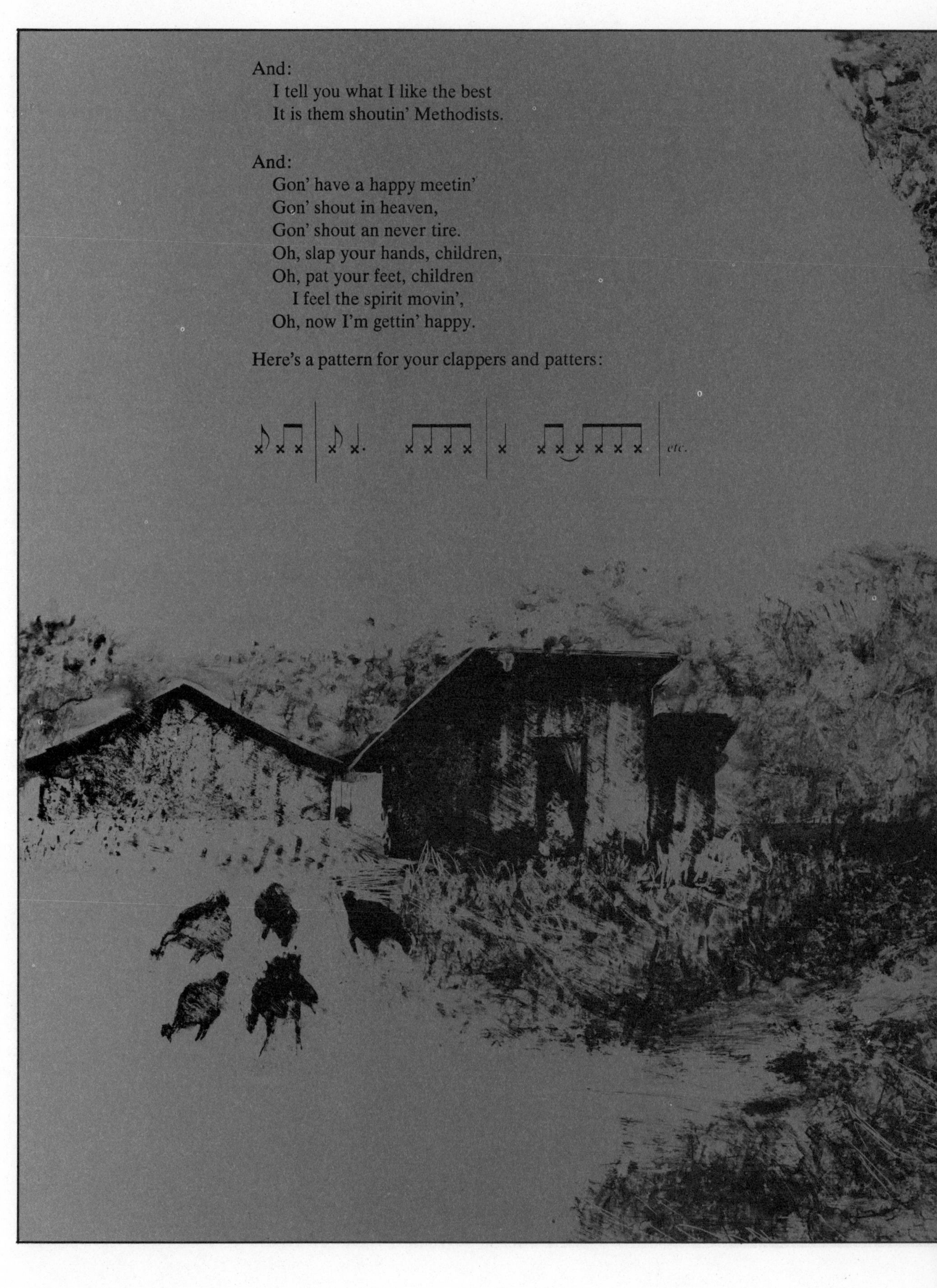
etc.

103
The Old Ark's A-Moverin'

American Negro Spiritual

Moderately brisk and rhythmic
Chorus
F
C7
F
The old ark's a-mov-er-in', a-mov-er-in', a-mov-er-in', The
old ark's a-mov-in' by the Spir-it of God! The old ark's a-mov-er-in', a-
C7
F7
mov-er-in', a-mov-er-in', The old ark's a-mov-in' and I thank God.
Fine
Fine

Verse
Call F
Response
C7
F C7 F
How man - y days did the wa-ter fall? For- ty days and nights in all.
Call
F
Response
C7
F C7 F
D.C.
Old ark she rocked, Old ark she rocked, Old ark she land-ed on the moun-tain top.
D.C.

2. Ham, Shem, and Japheth were settin' one day,
Talkin' on the upper deck and lookin' at the bay;
While they were disputin' 'bout this and that,
The ark done bump on Ararat.

3. See that sister all dressed so fine.
She ain't got Jesus on her mind.
See that brother all dressed so gay?
Death's gonna come and carry him away.

4. See that sister there comin' so slow?
She wants to go to heaven 'fore the heaven door close.
Ain't but one-a thing on my mind,
My sister's gone to heaven an'-a lef'-a me behin'.

PROGRAM GUIDE: *American Negro spiritual*

It is easy to get this spiritual "a-moverin' " the way it should; the marvelously rhythmic words do it for you. Assign soloists or a group to do the calls in the verse and let everyone join in the responses and the choruses. The routine is chorus, verse, chorus, verse, chorus, etc., ending on a chorus. You may also want to set up a rhythm section for clapping. Any of the natural patterns work, but the melodic rhythm itself suggests a very nice pattern:

etc.

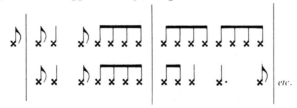

104

On the First Thanksgiving Day

Traditional, American

Moderately slow

C Am C G7 C G7 C Dm7 G7 C

On the first Thanks-giv - ing Day, Pil-grims went to church to pray,

C Am C G7 C G7 C Dm7 G7 C

Thanked the Lord for sun and rain, Thanked him for the fields of grain.

G C Em C D7 G Dm Am Dm E7 Am

Now Thanks-giv - ing comes a - gain: Praise the Lord as they did then.

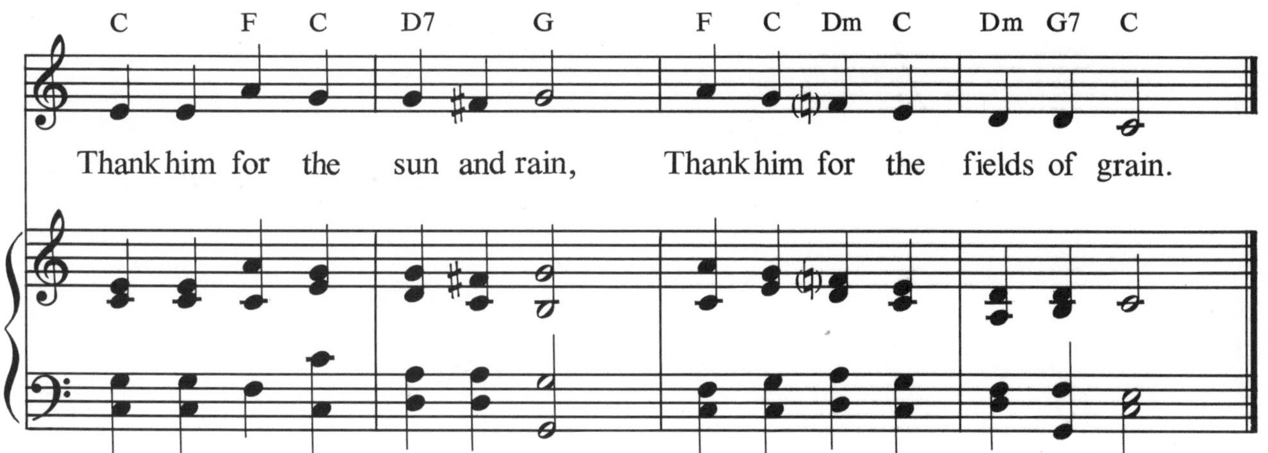
C F C D7 G F C Dm C Dm G7 C
Thank him for the sun and rain, Thank him for the fields of grain.

PROGRAM GUIDE: *Traditional American hymn; Thanksgiving; prayer*

This traditional Thanksgiving hymn, of unknown origin, is appropriate to any program during the Thanksgiving season or any program related to the early days of American history. It may also be used as a grace.

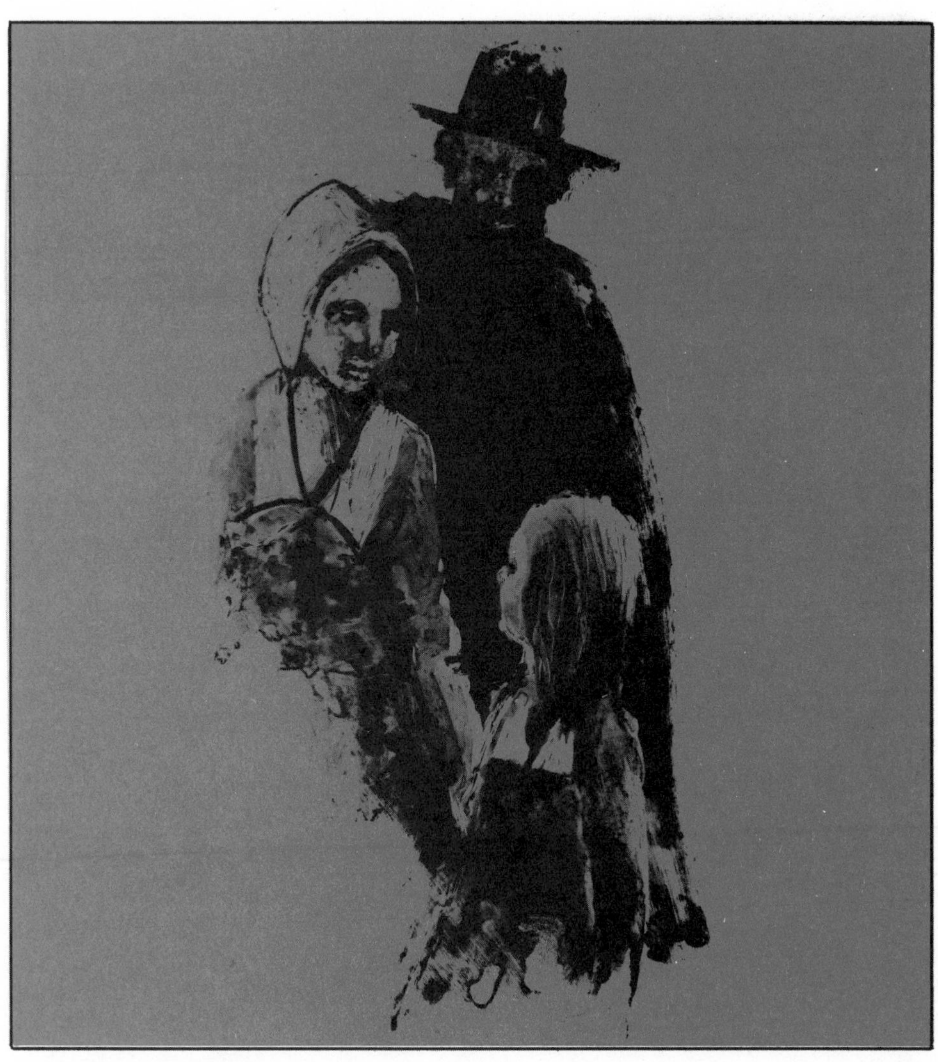

105
On Top of Old Smoky

American Folk Song

Moderately
(Melody in upper notes)
C F C
On top of old Smok - y, All cov- ered with snow,
(Melody in lower notes)
G7 C
I lost my true lov - er By court-in' too slow.

2. Now, courting's a pleasure,
Parting is grief;
But a false-hearted lover
Is worse than a thief.

3. A thief he will rob you
And take all you have;
But a false-hearted lover
Will lead you to the grave.

4. The grave will decay you
And turn you to dust,
There ain't one in a million
A poor girl (boy) can trust.

5. They'll hug you and kiss you
And tell you more lies
Than the crossties on railroads
Or the stars in the skies.

6. They'll tell you they love you
To give your heart ease;
But the minute your back's turned,
They'll court who they please.

7. I'll go back to old Smoky,
Old Smoky so high,
Where the wild birds and turtledoves
Can hear my sad cry.

8. Bury me on old Smoky,
Old Smoky so high,
Where the wild birds in heaven
Can hear my sad cry.

9. On top of old Smoky,
All covered with snow,
I lost my true lover
By courtin' too slow.

PROGRAM GUIDE: *American folk song; romantic*

This evergreen mountain-country lament has been a standby for audience participation for decades. A familiar routine uses a leader who speaks each line before it is sung. It takes a little practice to make sure the lines are spoken without breaking the rhythm or delaying the singing. But it can add to the show, particularly if you use someone with a melodramatic flair. It's also a useful way to perform the song when your singers don't have the words in their hands. Note easy harmony parts on vocal score. In camp situations don't be surprised if someone comes up with this verse:

On top of old Smokey,
All covered with hair.
Of course I'm referring
To Smokey the bear.

106
Once There Were Three Fishermen

American Folk Song

Lively

F C7 F

Once there were three fish - er - men,

F C7 F

Once there were three fish- er - men.

Fish-er, fish-er, men, men, men.

F C7 F

Fish-er, fish-er, men, men, men, Once there were three fish- er - men.

2. The first one's name was Abraham,
The first one's name was Abraham,
Abra, Abra, ham, ham, ham,
Abra, Abra, ham, ham, ham,
The first one's name was Abraham.

Continue, as above:

3. The second one's name was Isaac.
Isey, Isey, ack, ack, ack.

4. The third one's name was Jacob.
Jakey, Jakey, cub, cub, cub.

5. They all sailed up to Jericho.
Jerry, Jerry, cho, cho, cho.

6. Instead of going to Amsterdam.
Amster, Amster, sh, sh, sh.

7. Oh, do not say that naughty word.
Naughty, naughty, word, word, word.

PROGRAM GUIDE: *American folk song; camp song, humorous*

Here is another zany camp song which probably grew out of extracurricular Bible school days. It works well with younger children of any age—but bombs with sophisticates of any age.

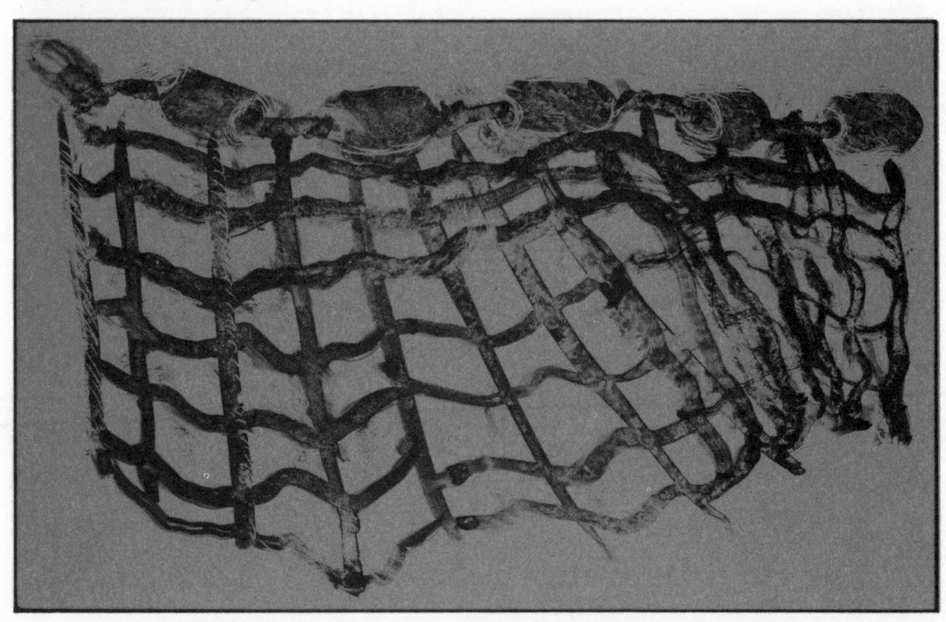

107
One More River to Cross

American Student Song

Lively
F
C7
F
Old No-ah, he built him-self an ark, There's one more riv-er to cross, He
*See note
F
C7
F
Chorus
built it out of hick-o-ry bark, There's one more riv-er to cross. There's
F
B♭
F
C7
F
one more riv-er, And that's the riv-er of Jor-dan: There's

Note: Ends here on last verse

F
B♭
F
C7
F
one more riv - er, Just one more riv-er to cross.

2. He went to work to load his stock,
   There's one more river to cross.
   He anchored the ark with a great big rock,
   There's one more river to cross.

   Chorus.

Continue, as above:

3. The animals went in one by one,
   The elephant with a big bass drum.
4. The animals went in two by two,
   The rhinoceros and the kangaroo.
5. The animals went in three by three,
   The bear, the flea, and the bumblebee.
6. The animals went in four by four,
   Noah got mad and hollered for more.
7. The animals went in five by five,
   Shem, Ham, and Japhet, and their wives.
8. When Noah found he had no sail,
   He just ran up his old shirttail.
9. Now, Mrs. Noah, she got drunk,
   She kicked the old sailor out of his bunk,
10. Now you may think there's another verse,
    Well, there ain't!

PROGRAM GUIDE: *American folk song; camp song, humorous*

Two beats to the measure and set a lively pace for this bit of camp and campus nonsense. See if you can get all the animals in the ark before everybody hates you. Otherwise, cut down on the verses used. Check the sudden ending (warn your accompanist) before you go into your act. The source of the song is not known, but it sounds like it might have come out of a minstrel show. There was an attempt to emulate the spiritual style by the writer, in a phony-baloney sort of way. You may divide the group into callers and responders it you wish. The responders confine their singing to the crossing of the river after each verse line, and to the choruses.

108
Over the River and Through the Woods

Traditional, American

Briskly
C F G7 C
O-ver the riv-er and through the woods To grand-fa-ther's house we go.___ The
G7 C D7 G7
horse knows the way To car-ry the sleigh Thro' the white and drift-ed snow.__
C F G7 C
O-ver the riv-er and through the woods, Oh how the wind does blow!___ It

F
G7
C
F
C
G7
C
stings your nose And bites your toes, As o-ver the ground we go.

2. Over the river and through the woods,
   Trot fast, my dapple gray!
      Spring over the ground
      Like a hunting hound,
   For this is Thanksgiving Day!
   Over the river and through the wood,
   Now grandmother's face I spy!
      Hurrah for the fun!
      Is the pudding done?
   Hurrah for the pumpkin pie!

PROGRAM GUIDE: *Traditional American song; Thanksgiving*

"Over the River" is to the Thanksgiving season what "Jingle Bells" is to the Christmas season. Sing it lightly at a brisk two-beats-to-the-measure pace. The author is Lydia Maria Child, an ardent American abolitionist of the nineteenth century.

109
Paper of Pins

Anglo-American Folk Song

Brightly
G
D7
Boy: I'll give to you a pa-per of pins, And that's the way my
G
C
G
D7
G
love be-gins, If you will mar-ry me, me, me, If you will mar-ry me.

Girl:
2. I'll not accept your paper of pins,
   If that's the way your love begins,
   And I'll not marry you, you, you,
   For I'll not marry you.

Boy:
3. I'll give to you a dress of red
   All bound round with golden thread,
   If you will marry me, me, me,
   If you will marry me.

Girl:
4. I'll not accept your dress of red
   All bound round with golden thread,
   And I'll not marry you, you, you,
   For I'll not marry you.

Boy:
5. I'll give to you a little dog
   To take with you abroad, abroad.
   (*Refrain*)

Girl:

6. I'll not accept your little dog
To take with me abroad, abroad.
(*Refrain*)

Boy:

7. I'll give to you a dappled horse
So you can ride from cross to cross.
(*Refrain*)

Girl:

8. I'll not accept your dappled horse
And I'll not ride from cross to cross.
(*Refrain*)

Boy:

9. I'll give to you the keys to my chest
And all the money that I possess,
If you will marry me, me, me,
If you will marry me.

Girl:

10. Oh, yes, I'll take the keys to your chest
And all the money that you possess,
And I will marry you, you, you,
And I will marry you.

Boy:

11. Oh, now I see that money is all,
And your love is nothing at all,
So I won't marry you, you, you,
No, I won't marry you.

Girl:

12. Then I shall be an old maid,
And take a chair and sit in the shade,
And I will marry none at all,
I'll marry none at all.

If you want the boy to win the girl, use this ending:

Boy:

9A. I'll give to you the gift of my heart,
That we may love and never part,
And I will marry you, you, you,
Oh, I will marry you.

Girl:

10A. Oh, I'll accept the gift of your heart,
And we shall love and never part.
Yes, I will marry you, you, you,
Oh, I will marry you.

Or she can marry someone else:

Boy:

11A. Well, you love coffee and I love tea;
You love money, but you don't love me.
I won't marry you, you, you,
No, I won't marry you.

Girl:

12A. Yes, I love coffee and I hate tea;
Without your money you're not for me;
And I will marry someone else,
I'll marry someone else.

PROGRAM GUIDE: *Anglo-American folk song; courtship song*

For this courtship song you should divide the group into boys and girls (regardless of age, that's what is needed for the purposes of this song). I've provided three different ways of resolving the courtship. Take your pick or, better still, let your singers choose the ending. The tempo should be moderately fast and bright.

110

Pick a Bale of Cotton

American Negro Folk Song

Brightly
G
D7
You got to jump down, turn a-round, pick a bale of cot-ton,
G
D7
G
Chorus
G
C
D7
Jump down, turn a-round, pick a bale a day. Oh, Man-dy,
G
D7
G
C
D7
G
pick a bale of cot-ton. Oh, Man-dy, pick a bale a day.

2. Me and my partner can
Pick a bale of cotton,
Me and my partner can
Pick a bale a day. (*Chorus*)

3. Me and my wife can
Pick a bale of cotton,
Me and my wife can
Pick a bale a day. (*Chorus*)

4. Well, I believe to my soul I can
Pick a bale of cotton,
Believe to my soul I can
Pick a bale a day. (*Chorus*)

Extra verses:

I went down the road to, etc.

Gonna fill my jeans if I, etc.

Knew a little woman could, etc.

You can't go home till you, etc.

PROGRAM GUIDE: *American Negro folk song; work song*

This work song calls for the kind of energy you wouldn't (at least I wouldn't) have if you were doing what the song says. Tear it apart at a fast clip. I've listed enough extra verses to keep everyone busy for about one minute. You may toss the assignments around in a call-and-response fashion (responses: *pick a bale of cotton* and *pick a bale a day*) if you wish. Otherwise, just let it rip!

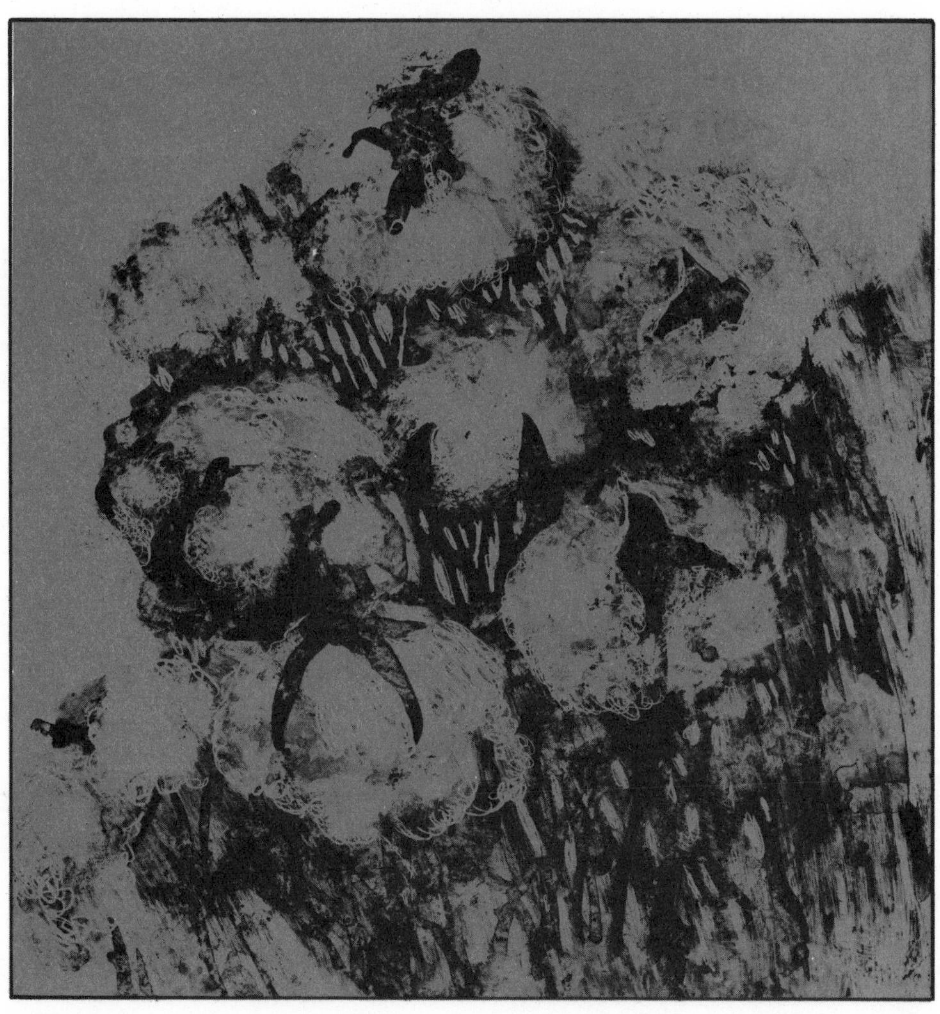

111
A Poor Wayfaring Stranger

American White Spiritual

Moderately
Dm Gm Dm Gm
I'm just a poor way-far-ing stran-ger, A-trav-eling through this world of
A Dm Gm Dm
woe. But there's no sick - ness, toil, or trou-ble In that bright
Gm Am Dm F B♭
world to which I go. I'm go-ing there to see my

Gm Am B♭ F

fa - ther; I'm go - ing there___ no more to roam.___ I'm just a -

Dm Gm Dm Gm Am Dm

go - ing o - ver Jor-dan, I'm just a - go - ing o - ver home.

PROGRAM GUIDE: *American white spiritual*

Very few of the white spirituals from the last century still appeal to singers as the Negro spirituals do. This one, however, does. The melancholy, modal tune is haunting. I've used a musical setting which allows you fairly wide latitude in both phrasing and tempo. Singers today—like those of yesterday also—tend to sing it as they feel it, not bothering to maintain a strict, inflexible beat. Once through should be enough, although you might want to try humming softly through a second chorus, perhaps singing only the last line, "I'm just a-going over home." This can be very effective. If you do wish to sing more than one chorus you may substitute *mother, sister, brother,* etc., for *father.*

112
Putting on the Style

American Popular Song

Lively *
Verse
D
A7
Two wheels 'round a cor - ner, Driv- ing like he's mad;
legato (simulating mouth organ wahwah)
(Melody in lower notes)
A7
D
Young man in an au - to He bor - rowed from his dad; He
D
A7
honks his horn so loud - ly To see his girl friend smile;

*Tempo should be fast enough for piano bass part to sound like a mouth organ (as a result of colliding overtones)

A7
(Melody in lower notes)
D
But she knows he's on - ly Put-ting on the style.
Chorus
D
A7
Put-ting on the ag - o - ny, Put-ting on the style,
A7
(Melody in lower notes)
D
That's what ev - 'ry - bod-y's Do-ing all the while. And
D
A7
as I look a - round me It makes me want to smile, To

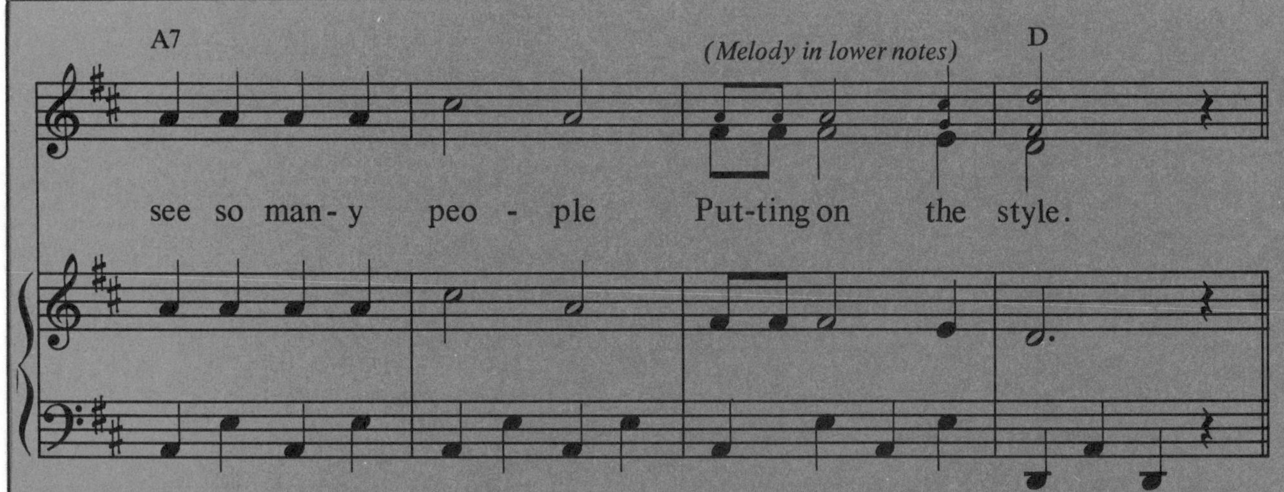
A7
(Melody in lower notes)
D
see so man - y peo - ple Put-ting on the style.

2. Sweet sixteen and goes to church
Just to see the boys;
See her laugh and giggle
At every little noise.
She turns her head a little
And stands that way awhile,
But everybody knows she's only
Putting on the style. (*Chorus*)

3. Young man home from college
Makes a big display
With a giant jawbreaker
That he can hardly say;
It can't be found in Webster
And won't be for awhile,
But everybody knows he's only
Putting on the style. (*Chorus*)

PROGRAM GUIDE: *Traditional American popular song; humorous*

This turn-of-the-century (twentieth) popular song remarks philosophically about the kind of put-on that never seems to go out of style. You can have some fun creating a new verse to fit yourself or your associates. Set a lively pace and sing it so it can be heard a mile away. The harmony notes at the end of each phrase are easy to teach to the women including the division into three parts at the end of the chorus.

113

The Riddle Song

English Folk Song

Slowly
F
B♭
F
I gave my love a cher-ry that has no stone, I
C7
F
C7
F
gave my love a chick-en that has no bone, I gave my love a ring that
F
C7
F
B♭
F
has no end, I gave my love a ba-by that's no cry - in'.

2. How can there be a cherry that has no stone?
How can there be a chicken that has no bone?
How can there be a ring that has no end?
How can there be a baby that's no cryin'?

3. A cherry when it's bloomin', it has no stone;
A chicken when it's pippin', it has no bone;
A ring when it's rollin', it has no end;
A baby when it's sleepin', it's no cryin'.

PROGRAM GUIDE: *English folk song; romantic*

Riddles in courtship situations have been used frequently as a basis for folk songs (see also number 148, "Tumbalalaika"). "The Riddle Song," or "I Gave My Love a Cherry" (sometimes "I Gave My Love an Apple"), is probably the best known of this variety of romantic folk songs in America. It's a beautiful melody with an Irish lilt and should be sung softly and gently. Here's a not-so-gentle parody, substituting for verse 3, that has circulated widely in recent years:

A cherry in a Manhattan, it has no stone;
Chicken á la king, it has no bone;
A story from the Bible, it has no end;
A baby when it's strangled has no cryin'.

Use it, if at all, at your own risk.

114
Rise and Shine

American Negro Folk Song
(Adapted)
Brightly
C
1. Rise and shine, and give God the glo-ry, glo-ry,
(2. The) Lord said, "No-ah, there's gon-na be a flood-y, flood-y,
(3. So) No-ah he went out and he built an ark-y, ark-y,
(4. The) an-i-mals, they came, and went in__ by two-sy, two-sy,
(5. It) rained and rained for for__ ty day-sy, day-sy,
R. H.
L. H.
G7
Rise__ and shine__ and give God__ the glo - ry, glo - ry,
Lord__ said: "No - ah, there's gon - na be a flood - y, flood - y,
No - ah he went out and he built__ an ark - y, ark - y,
An-imals, they came, and went in____ by two - sy, two - sy,
Rained and rained ___ for for - ty day - sy, day - sy,

C
C7
F
C
Rise and shine and give God the glo - ry, glo - ry,
Get your chil - dren out of the mud - dy, mud - dy,
Made it out of hick - o - ry bark - y, bark - y,
El - e - phants and kan - ga - roo - sy, roo - sy,
Drove those an - imals near - ly cra - zy, cra - zy,
C
G7
C
1.2.3.4.
last time
Chil-dren of the Lord.
2. The
3. So
4. The
5. It
1.2.3.4.
last time

PROGRAM GUIDE: *American Negro folk song (adapted); camp song, humorous*

An old spiritual was revamped by a clever folk poet to fashion a delightful song for children of all ages. If you compare this song with "Jacob's Ladder" you will find structural similarities, suggesting that both songs may have been developed from a common ancestor. Though they are related melodically and harmonically, they have nothing in common rhythmically. "Rise and Shine" is a shouter, so feel free to let yourself go. If five verses aren't enough, close with a repeat of the first verse. Also it wouldn't hurt to organize a small rhythm section of clappers and foot-tappers to back up your singers percussively.

115
The Rock Island Line

American Folk Song

Fast
Chorus
G6
I say the Rock Is-land Line is a might-y good road,
R. H.
L. H.
A7
I say the Rock Is-land Line is the road to
D7
G6
ride. Oh, the Rock Is-land Line is a might-y good road,

G6
C6
C7
If you want to ride it, got to ride it, like you're
G6
D7
G6
Fine
fly-in', Buy your tick-et at the sta-tion on the Rock Is - land Line.
Fine
Verse
G6
I may be right and I may be wrong, I
D7
G
D.C.
know you're gon - na miss me when I have gone.
D.C.

2. A, B, C, Double X, Y, Z,
   Cat's in the cupboard, but he can't see me.

3. Jesus died to save our sins,
   Glory be to God, we're gonna need him again.

PROGRAM GUIDE: *American folk song*

Don't hop aboard the Rock Island Line unless you expect to get wherever you're going in a hurry. I've indicated a fast tempo, but lickety-split might be more appropriate. Be sure you have the phrasing, particularly the syncopation, down pat before you attempt to lead the song. Getting everything right and in the right place can be tricky if you are not sure of yourself. The routine is chorus, verse, chorus, verse, chorus, verse, chorus. There are a couple of effects you might want to add if you can round up from two to four good harmonizers among your singers. If you have four, see if they can pick up the train whistle blasts from the piano score in the last measure of the chorus. They should sing:

Hoo hoot!

If that works, you might as well have them throw it in at the beginning of the song, before everybody else gets aboard. Another harmonic effect can be used to back up the chorus like this, using two or more harmonizers:

Harmony
Hoo
Hoo
Melody
I say the Rock Is-land Line is a might-y good road

Your harmonizers follow the chords throughout the chorus, and join on the lyric at the end. For putting both the above together, here is a score of the chorus for your harmonizers:

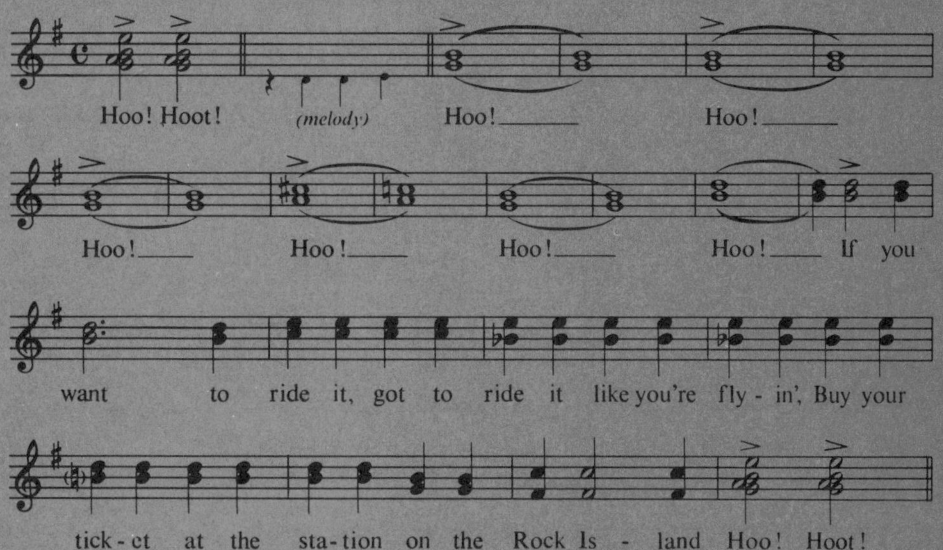
Hoo! Hoot!
(melody)
Hoo!
Hoo!
Hoo!
Hoo!
Hoo!
Hoo! If you
want to ride it, got to ride it like you're fly - in', Buy your
tick - et at the sta - tion on the Rock Is - land Hoo! Hoot!

You may also wish to use soloists, for variety, on the verses. Have a good trip!

116

Roll, Jordan, Roll

American Negro Spiritual

Majestically
Chorus
C F C G7
Roll, Jor-dan, roll, Roll, Jor-dan, roll, I want to go to
Am F C G7 C
Fine
Verse
Call
C
heav-en when I die, To hear Jor-dan roll. Oh, broth-ers, you ought-a been there,
Fine
Response
Call
Response
C G7 C G7 C
D.C.
Yes, my Lord, A sit-tin' in the king-dom, To hear Jor-dan roll.
D.C.

2. Oh, preacher, you oughta been there,
Yes, my Lord,
A-sittin' in the Kingdom
To hear Jordan roll.

Continue, as above:

3. Oh, sinner, you oughta been there.
4. Oh, mourner, you oughta been there.
5. Oh, seekers, you oughta been there.
6. Oh, mothers, you oughta been there.
7. Oh, children, you oughta been there.

PROGRAM GUIDE: *American Negro spiritual*

This magnificent anthem helps to demonstrate the great diversity of Negro spirituals. It should be sung majestically, or, if you prefer, softly, or with a combination of the two, varying the dynamics between verse and choruses. You may wish to assign soloists or a group of voices to the calls, everyone to the responses in the verse, and, of course, everyone on the choruses.

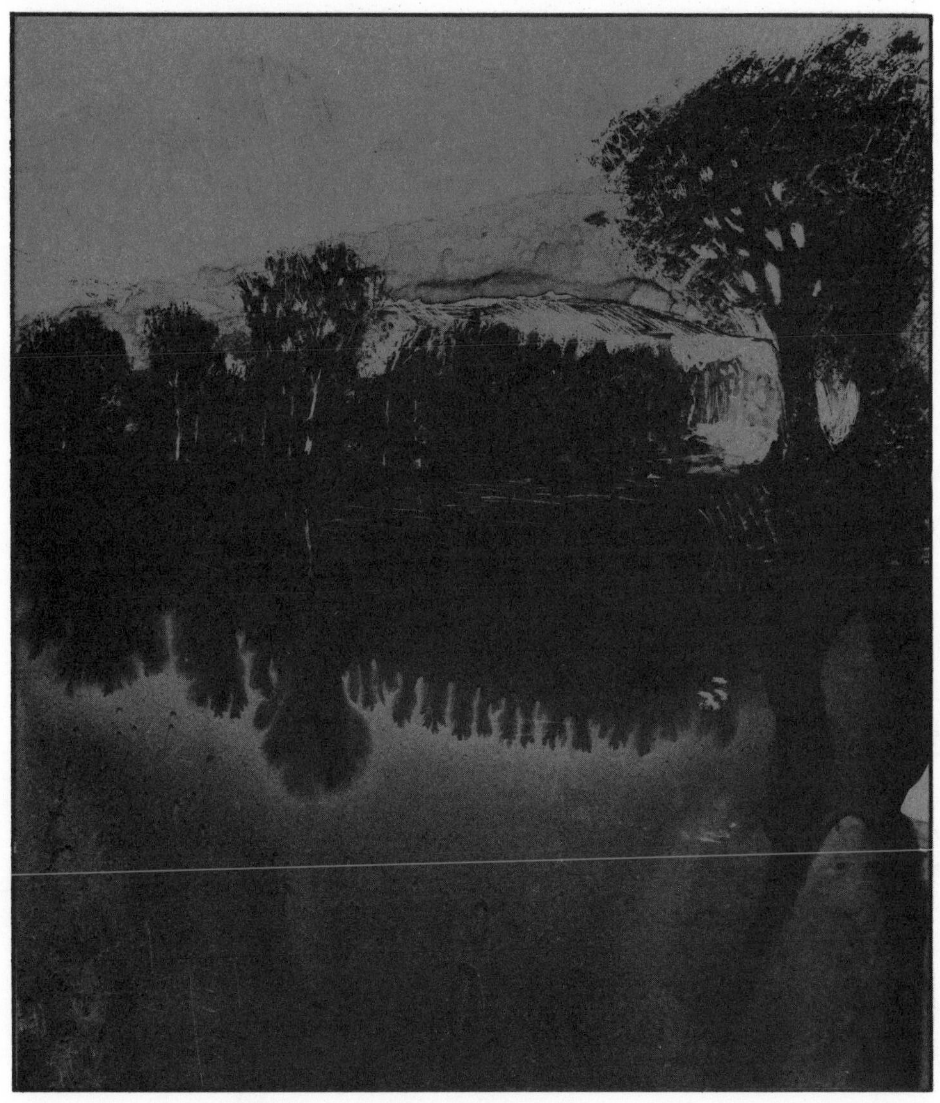

117

Row, Row, Row Your Boat

Traditional American Round

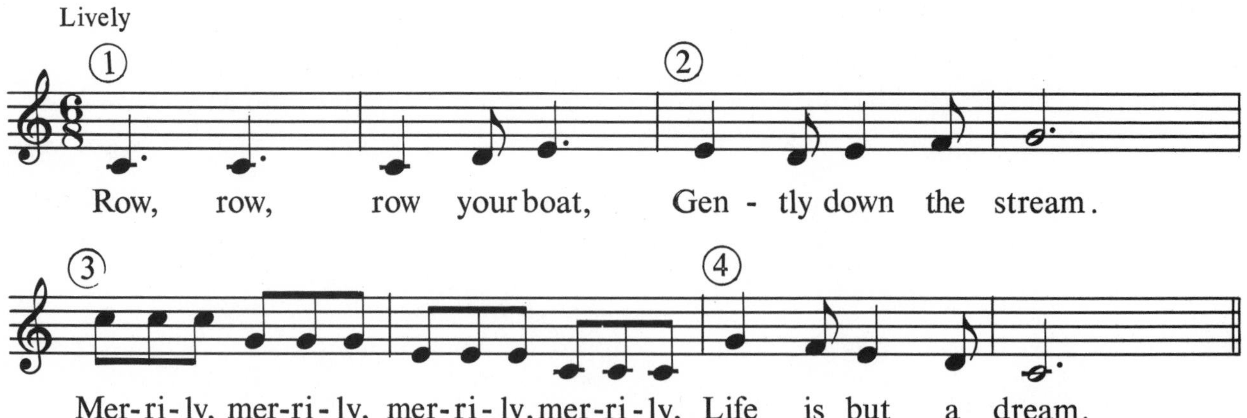
Lively
Row, row, row your boat, Gen - tly down the stream.
Mer-ri-ly, mer-ri-ly, mer-ri-ly, mer-ri-ly, Life is but a dream.

Divide the group into four sections. Each section sings the entire round the agreed-upon number of times, beginning at point 1 when the preceding section reaches point 2. Thus the round begins and ends with one section singing alone: Section 1 at the beginning and Section 4 at the end.

PROGRAM GUIDE: *Traditional American round*

The big advantage in using this familiar four-part round is that, usually, everybody knows it. It is therefore a good warm-up number when you are working with an unfamiliar group. It gives you a chance to see what they can and will do before you tackle more ambitious activities. This American round appears to have had its origin, or at least its original popularity, with minstrel shows, like Christy's minstrels, in the middle part of the nineteenth century.

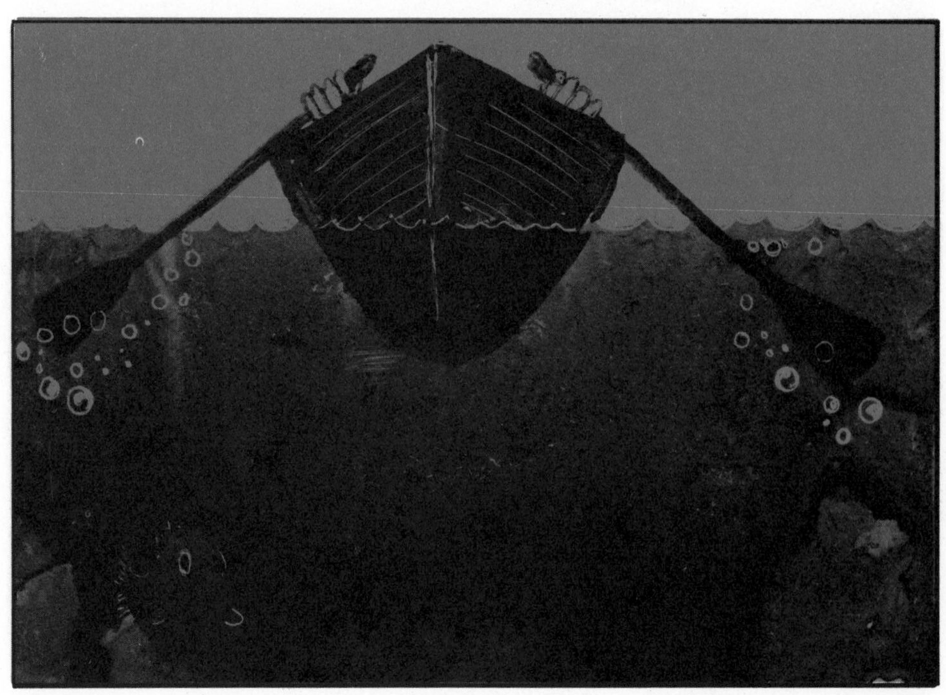

118
Scotland's Burning

Traditional British Round

Brightly
1
2
Scot-land's burn-ing, Scot-land's burn-ing, Look out! Look out!
3
4
Fire! Fire! Fire! Fire! Pour on wa-ter, Pour on wa-ter.

Divide the group into four sections. Each section sings the entire round the agreed-upon number of times, beginning at point 1 when the preceding section reaches point 2. Thus the round begins and ends with one section singing alone: Section 1 at the beginning and Section 4 at the end.

PROGRAM GUIDE: *Traditional British round*

Divide your singers into four groups and try to put out the fire, vigorously!

119

The Seven Joys of Mary

Traditional English Carol
Arr. by John Stainer

Moderately fast
G Em D G D7 Em Am D G
The first good joy that Ma - ry had, It was the joy of one; To
G Em D G D Em Am D G Em
see the bless - ed Je - sus Christ, When he was first her Son, When
D A7 D G C D G D G D
he was first her Son, Good Lord, And hap - py may we be; Praise

G F♯°7 Em C G D7 Em Am D G
Fa - ther, Son, and Ho - ly Ghost To all e - ter - ni - ty.

2. The next good joy that Mary had,
It was the joy of two;
To see her own Son Jesus Christ,
Making the lame to go,
Making the lame to go, Good Lord,
And happy may we be;
Praise Father, Son, and Holy Ghost
To all eternity.

3. The next good joy that Mary had,
It was the joy of three;
To see her own Son Jesus Christ,
Making the blind to see,
Making the blind to see, Good Lord,
And happy may we be;
Praise Father, Son, and Holy Ghost
To all eternity.

4. The next good joy that Mary had,
It was the joy of four;
To see her own Son Jesus Christ,
Reading the Bible o'er.
Reading the Bible o'er, Good Lord,
And happy may we be;
Praise Father, Son, and Holy Ghost
To all eternity.

5. The next good joy that May had,
It was the joy of five;
To see her own Son Jesus Christ,
Raising the dead to life.
Raising the dead to life, Good Lord,
And happy may we be;
Praise Father, Son, and Holy Ghost
To all eternity.

6. The next good joy that Mary had,
It was the joy of six;
To see her own Son Jesus Christ
Upon the Crucifix.
Upon the Crucifix, Good Lord,
And happy may we be;
Praise Father, Son, and Holy Ghost
To all eternity.

7. The next good joy that Mary had,
It was the joy of seven;
To see her own Son Jesus Christ
Ascending into heaven.
Ascending into heaven, Good Lord,
And happy may we be;
Praise Father, Son, and Holy Ghost
To all eternity.

PROGRAM GUIDE: *Traditional English Christmas carol*

This arrangement by John Stainer made in 1871 is one of the more popular versions of a fifteenth-century folk carol that has described as many as twenty-five joys for Mary. Contemporary audiences might not sit still for so much joy, even during the Christmas season. And some will question the credibility of joy number six, in any event. Personally, I prefer singing two or three joys at the most. The tempo indicated is *allegretto,* light, graceful, and relatively fast. You may vary the dynamics, from soft in the verse to loud for the refrain, to add variety.

120

She'll Be Coming 'Round the Mountain

American Folk Song

Brightly
Toot!
G
She'll be com - ing 'round the moun-tain when she comes.
Toot!
D7
Toot!
She'll be com - ing 'round the moun-tain when she comes.
Toot!
G
C
She'll be com-ing 'round the moun-tain, She'll be com - ing 'round the

Toot! Toot!
G D7 G
moun-tain, She'll be com-ing 'round the moun-tain when she comes.

2. She'll be driving six white horses when she comes. (Whoa, back!)
   She'll be driving six white horses when she comes. (Whoa, back!)
   She'll be driving six white horses,
   She'll be driving six white horses,
   She'll be driving six white horses when she comes. (Whoa, back!)

   Continue, as above:
3. Oh, we'll all go out to meet her when she comes. (Hi, babe!)
4. Oh, we'll all have chicken and dumplings when she comes. (Yum! yum!)

PROGRAM GUIDE: *American folk song; camp song, action song*

Audiences are positive in their feelings about "Coming 'Round the Mountain." Some people like to be silly, others don't. And of course there is always the question of the right time, place, and mood. So weigh these matters carefully before you stick your neck out. In any event, the song is *camp* in every sense of the word. If you play it that way you are more likely to get away with it. You can have your singers add, if you and they wish, the action to the spoken (that is, shouted) cues shown on the vocal score, as follows:

1. Toot! Toot! With arm extended upward, yank the train whistle twice.
2. Whoa, back! With both arms extended forward, simulate holding the reins of a skittery horse, and pull back.
3. Hi, babe! You're on your own. I suppose anything from a waved hanky to shaking hands with the ladies in the crowd ought to be okay.
4. Yum! Yum! Rub stomach.

If you want or need to add some more verses, try these (not shown in singer's edition):

5. We will kill the old red rooster when she comes. (Chop, chop!)
6. Tell me, do you know what's coming 'round the mountain?
7. *Then why are we singing this idiotic ditty?*

Don't sing that last line; shout it, once, and duck for cover.

"She'll Be Coming 'Round the Mountain" seems to have originated in the latter part of the nineteenth century as a plantation hymn called "When the Chariot Comes."

121
Shenandoah

Revised by J.F.L.

American Sea Chantey

Slowly
D
G
Oh, Shen-an-doah, I long to see you, A - way, you roll-ing
legato
D
G
riv-er. Oh, Shen-an-doah, I long to see you. A -
D
A7
D
way, we're bound a - way 'Cross the wide Mis - sou - ri.

2. Oh, Shenandoah's my native valley,
Away, you rolling river.
Oh, Shenandoah's my native valley.
Away, we're bound away
'Cross the wide Missouri.

Continue, as above:

3. Oh, Shenandoah, it's far I wander.
4. Oh, Shenandoah has rushing waters.
5. Oh, Shenandoah, I long to hear you.
6. Oh, Shenandoah, I love your daughter.
7. Oh, Shenandoah, I'll never leave you.
8. Oh, Shenandoah, I'll never grieve you.

PROGRAM GUIDE: *American sea chantey*

Shenandoah is a corruption of the name used by the Iroquois Indians for the mountains on both sides of the Shenandoah Valley in Virginia. It means "land of big mountains." In the nineteenth century, "Shenandoah" went to sea as the title of a beautiful chantey used for weighing anchor; and, as "The Wild Missouri," the same song was popular with cavalrymen. The melodic and rhythmic interpretation of the song varies with the performer and the performance. Seamen, according to an old sailor, used "a very peculiar time, or rather no set time at all, and the singer could make his own rendering of it as far as the solo part was concerned, the heaving stresses of the chorus being dictated by the strain on a rope or anchor cable."

Some versions tell the story of a redskin chief, Shenandoah, and his beautiful daughter. A white trader elopes with the maiden after silencing the chief with firewater. I prefer the genuine feeling and simplicity of the version I have used here. My setting is designed for group singing with regular rhythm, but you may feel free to direct it at liberty, if you prefer. Three or four verses should be enough. You may wish to hum the last or next to last chorus. Or you may repeat the first verse at the end, if you like.

122
The Sidewalks of New York

Words and Music by
Charles B. Lawlor and James W. Blake

Brightly
G D7 G7 C
East side, west side, all a-
G G7 C
round the town, The tots sang "Ring-a-
G E7 A7 D7
Ros-ie," "Lon-don bridge is fall-ing down."

G
D7
G
G7
C
Boys and girls to - geth - er,
Me and
G
G7
C
Ma - mie O' - Rourk,
Tripped the light fan -
G
E7
A7
D7
G
tas-tic On the side-walks of New York.

PROGRAM GUIDE: *Traditional American popular song*

"The Sidewalks of New York" was one of the big songs of 1894, a good year for New York songs. Two other hits of the year were "My Pearl's a Bowery Girl" and "Only a Bowery Boy." That same year Congress designated the first Monday in September as Labor Day, and labor unrest was the order (or disorder) of the day, with Coxey's famous "Industrial Army" marching to Washington to present a petition for relief legislation. Things were so bad that year that the U.S. government had to borrow $100,000,000 to deal with political and labor unrest. (It seemed like a lot of money to those concerned at the time.) But these problems were not much on the minds of Charles B. Lawlor and James W. Blake when they sat down to write this carefree, happy-go-lucky song about young life on the sidewalks of New York. Eventually, the song became practically the unofficial anthem of the proud city. If you have a soft-shoe artist or a tap dancer in your group, invite him or her to accompany the singing with a routine. And sing the song as though you are enjoying it. After all, Al Smith used it as his campaign song when he ran for President in 1928, expecting the good times to be just ahead!

123
Silent Night

Joseph Mohr
Trans. by John F. Young and others

Franz Gruber

Moderately slow
B♭
F7
B♭
Si - lent night, ho - ly night, All is calm, All is bright
E♭
B♭
E♭
B♭
Round yon vir - gin moth-er and child. Ho - ly in - fant so ten-der and mild,
F7
B♭
F7
B♭
Sleep in heav-en-ly peace,__ sleep_ in heav-en-ly peace.__

2. Silent night, holy night,
Shepherds quake at the sight,
Glories stream from heaven afar,
Heavenly hosts sing Alleluiah;
Christ the Savior is born!
Christ the Savior is born!

3. Silent night, holy night,
Son of God, love's pure light
Radiant beams from thy holy face,
With the dawn of redeeming grace,
Jesus, Lord, at thy birth,
Jesus, Lord, at thy birth,

German words:

1. Stille nacht, heilige nacht,
Alles schlaft, einsam wacht
Nur das traute hochheilige Paar,
Holder Knabe im lockigen Haar,
Schlaf in himmlischer Ruh,
Schlaf in himmlischer Ruh,

2. Stille Nacht, heilige Nacht!
Hirten erst kundgemacht
Durch der Engel Halleluja
Tönt es laut von fern und nah:
Christ, der Retter, ist da,
Christ, der Retter, ist da!

3. Stille Nacht, heilige Nacht!
Gottes Sohn, o wie lacht
Lieb' aus deinem göttlichen Mund,
Da uns schlagt die rettende Stund',
Christ, in deiner Geburt,
Christ, in deiner Geburt.

PROGRAM GUIDE: *Traditional German Christmas song*

Joseph Mohr (1792-1848), an Austrian Roman Catholic priest, collaborated with Franz Xavier Gruber (1787-1863), his organist, to create "Silent Night" for a Christmas Eve program in 1818, when Mohr was assistant priest of the parish church at Oberndorf, Austria. I've included both the German lyric and the English. You might wish to sing a verse in each language. It's also nice to hum a verse. Guitar accompaniment is particularly appropriate, since the carol was originally written with that accompaniment in mind, the church organ being *kaput*.

124

Sing Your Way Home

Traditional, American

Brightly
F
C7
Sing your way home at the close of the day.
C7
F
Sing your way home, drive the shad - ows a - way.
F
F7
B♭
Smile ev - ery mile for wher - ev - er you roam, It will bright-en your

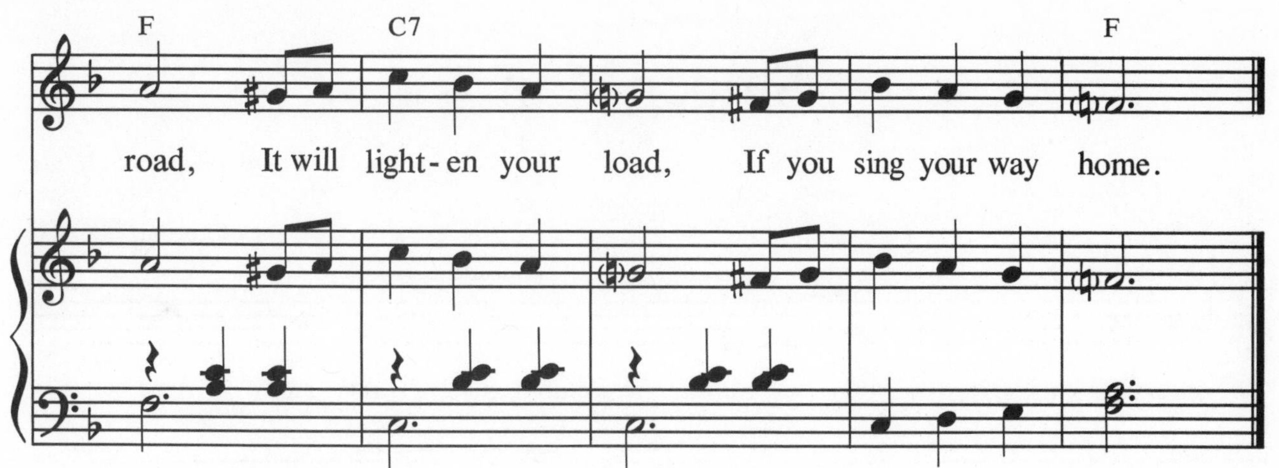
F
C7
F
road, It will light-en your load, If you sing your way home.

PROGRAM GUIDE: *Traditional American camp song*

It's a pretty song, especially for young girls' voices, but that's about all there is to it. After a few too many choruses of this song on a long bus trip home you'll be ready—for home. Once or twice through should be enough.

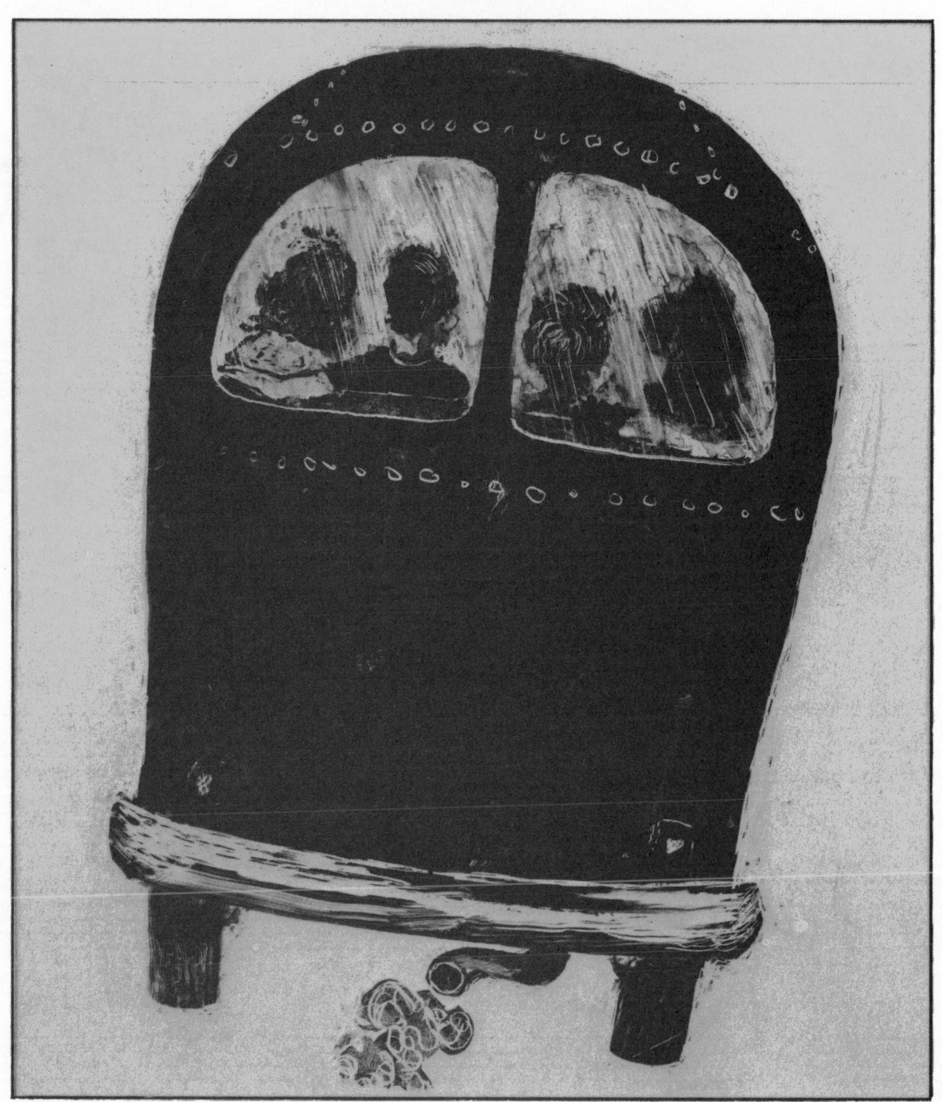

125
Sinner Man

American Folk Hymn

Fast
Dm
Oh sin - ner man, where you gon - na run to?
C
Dm
Oh, sin-ner man, where you gon-na run to? Oh, sin-ner man,
Dm
Am
Dm
where you gon-na run to? All on that day?

2. Run to the rock, the rock was a-melting, (*3 times*)
All on that day.

3. Run to the sea, the sea was a-boiling, (*3 times*)
All on that day.

4. Run to the moon, the moon was a-bleeding, (*3 times*)
All on that day.

5. Run to the Lord, "Lord, won't you hide me?" (*3 times*)
All on that day.

6. Run to the Devil, Devil was a-waiting. (*3 times*)
All on that day.

7. Oh, sinner man, you oughta been a-praying, (*3 times*)
All on that day.

PROGRAM GUIDE: *American folk hymn*

"Sinner Man" is found in both Negro and white religious folk music traditions, and it is not possible to tell where it originated. There are several spirituals that treat the same theme. The Jubilee Singers of Fisk University sing:

Oh, sinner man, oh, sinner man,
Oh, sinner man, oh.
Which way are you going?

Oh, come back, sinner, and don't go there,
Which way are you going?
For hell is deep and dark, despair.
Oh, which way are you going?

It's a good song for unison singing at a fast tempo. A typical routine would be the singing of three selected verses, followed by a repeat of the first verse as a final chorus.

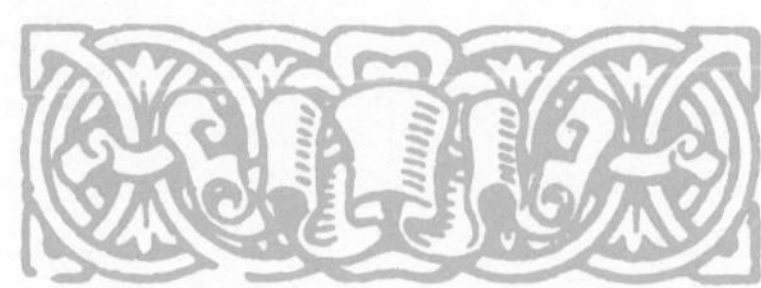

126

Sipping Cider Through a Straw

Traditional American

Brightly

1st Group (lead)

C G7

The pret-ti-est girl I ev - er saw

2nd Group (imitators and harmonizers)

The pret-ti-est girl I ev - er

C

was sip-ping ci - der through a straw, ________

saw was sip-ping ci - der through a

C
C7
F
The pret-ti-est girl I ev - er saw
straw, The pret-ti-est girl I ev - er saw
G7
C
was sip-ping ci - der through a straw.
was sip-ping ci - der through a straw.

2. I told that girl I didn't see how
   She sipped that cider through a straw.
   I told that girl I didn't see how
   She sipped that cider through a straw.

Continue, as above:

3. Then cheek to cheek, and jaw to jaw,
   We sipped that cider through a straw.

4. And now and then the straw would slip,
   And I'd sip cider from her lip.

5. And now I've got a mother-in-law
   From sipping cider through a straw.

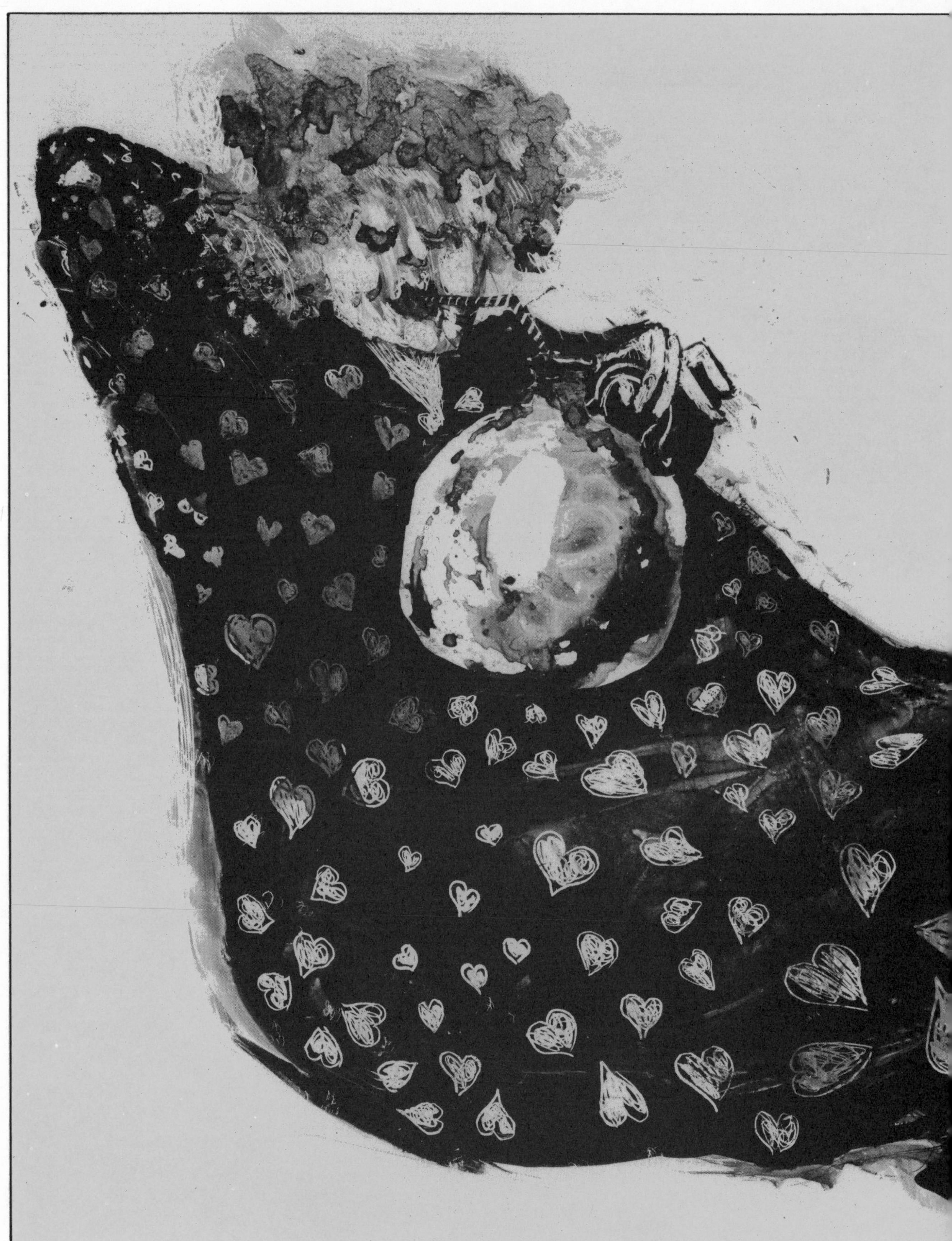

PROGRAM GUIDE: *Traditional American camp song; humorous*

Divide your singers into leaders and imitators. To use this arrangement exactly as it is written you should get some good harmonizers into the imitator group or at least give the imitators a brief rehearsal on their tune. If you want to avoid the fuss, tell the imitators to shift to the top staff of the vocal score for the last eight measures. Unless you sing this one fast, everybody will go to sleep.

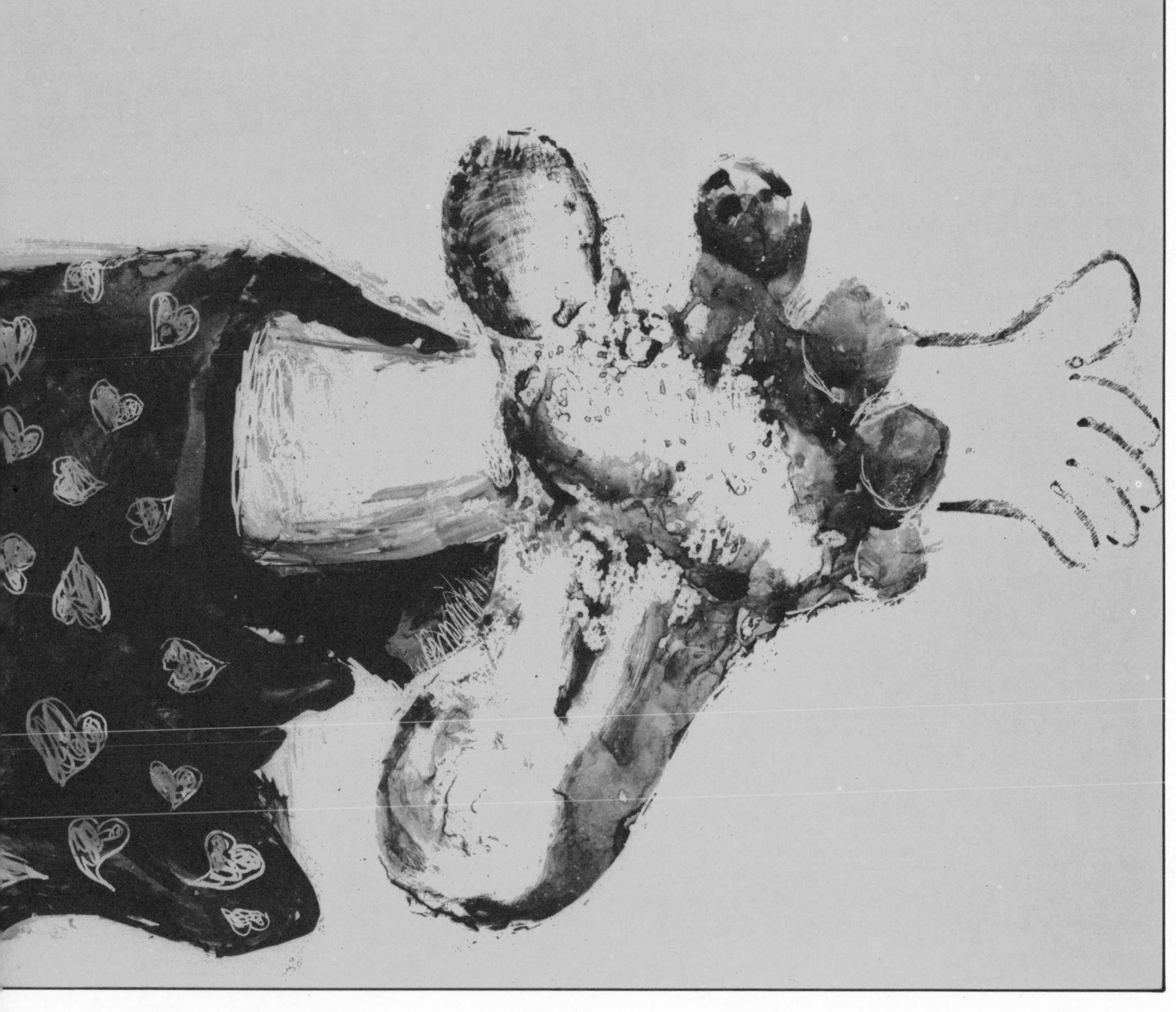

127
Six Little Ducks

Traditional, American

Moderately fast

F C7

Six lit- tle ducks that I once knew, Fat ones, skin- ny ones,

F C7

cute ones, too. But the one lit- tle duck with a feath-er in his back,

C7 F

He ruled the oth-ers with a quack, quack, quack; quack, quack, quack.

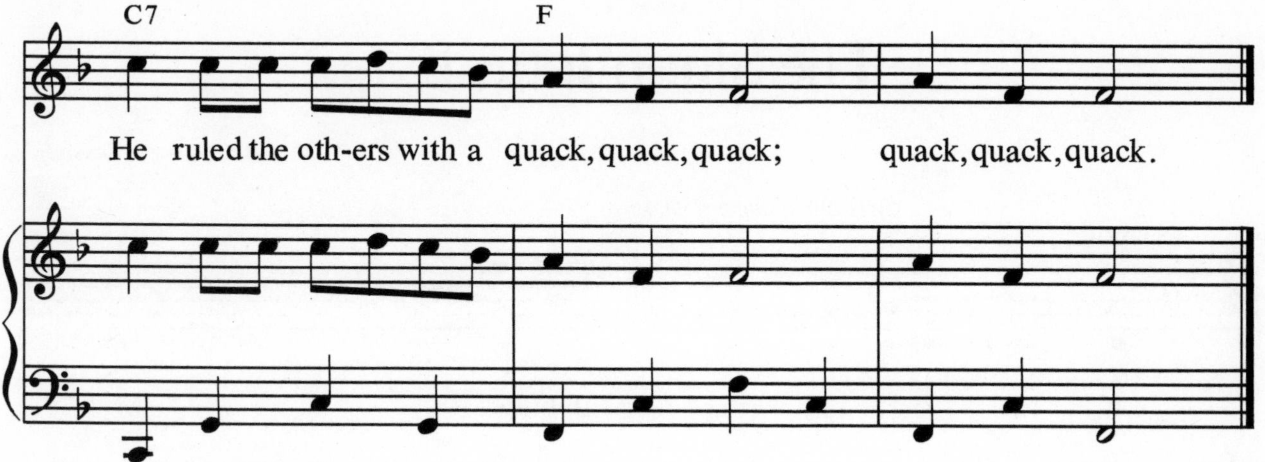
C7
F
He ruled the oth-ers with a quack, quack, quack; quack, quack, quack.

2. Down to the river they would go,
Wibble, wabble, wibble, wabble to and fro.
But the one little duck with a feather in his back,
He ruled the others with a slap, slap, slap.
He ruled the others with a slap, slap, slap.

3. Home from the river they would come,
Wibble, wabble, wibble, wabble, ho-um-hum.
But the one little duck with a feather in his back,
He led the others with a quack, quack, quack.
He led the others with a quack, quack, quack.

PROGRAM GUIDE: *Traditional children's song; action song*

This one is strictly for the little kiddies. So, when you use it, play it to the hilt—get a prize for the best little duck in the group. The actions go with the *quacks* and the *slaps,* slapping hands together in front of the face, the heels of the hands together at the wrists, simulating a duck's bill. And, of course, those quacks should be sung the way a duck would do it.

128

The Sloop John B.

Bahamian Folk Song

(Melody in upper notes)
Calypso
F
Oh, we came on the Sloop John B. My
F
grand - fa-ther and me. 'Round Nas - sau
F
C7
town we_ did roam. Drink-in' all
3
3
3

F7
B♭
night
We got in a fight,
Oh, I
F
C7
F
feel so break-up,
I want-a go home.

Chorus (*same tune as verse*):

So, hoist up the John B. sails, see how the mainsail's set,
Send for the cap'n ashore, lemme go home!
Lemme go home! Lemme go home!
I feel so break-up, I want to go home.

2. The first mate he got drunk, break up the people's trunk,
Constable come aboard and take him away,
Mr. Johnstone, please let me alone,
I feel so break-up, I want to go home.

3. The poor cook he got fits, throw 'way all the grits,
Then he took and eat up all o' my corn,
Lemme go home, I want to go home,
This is the worst trip, since I been born!

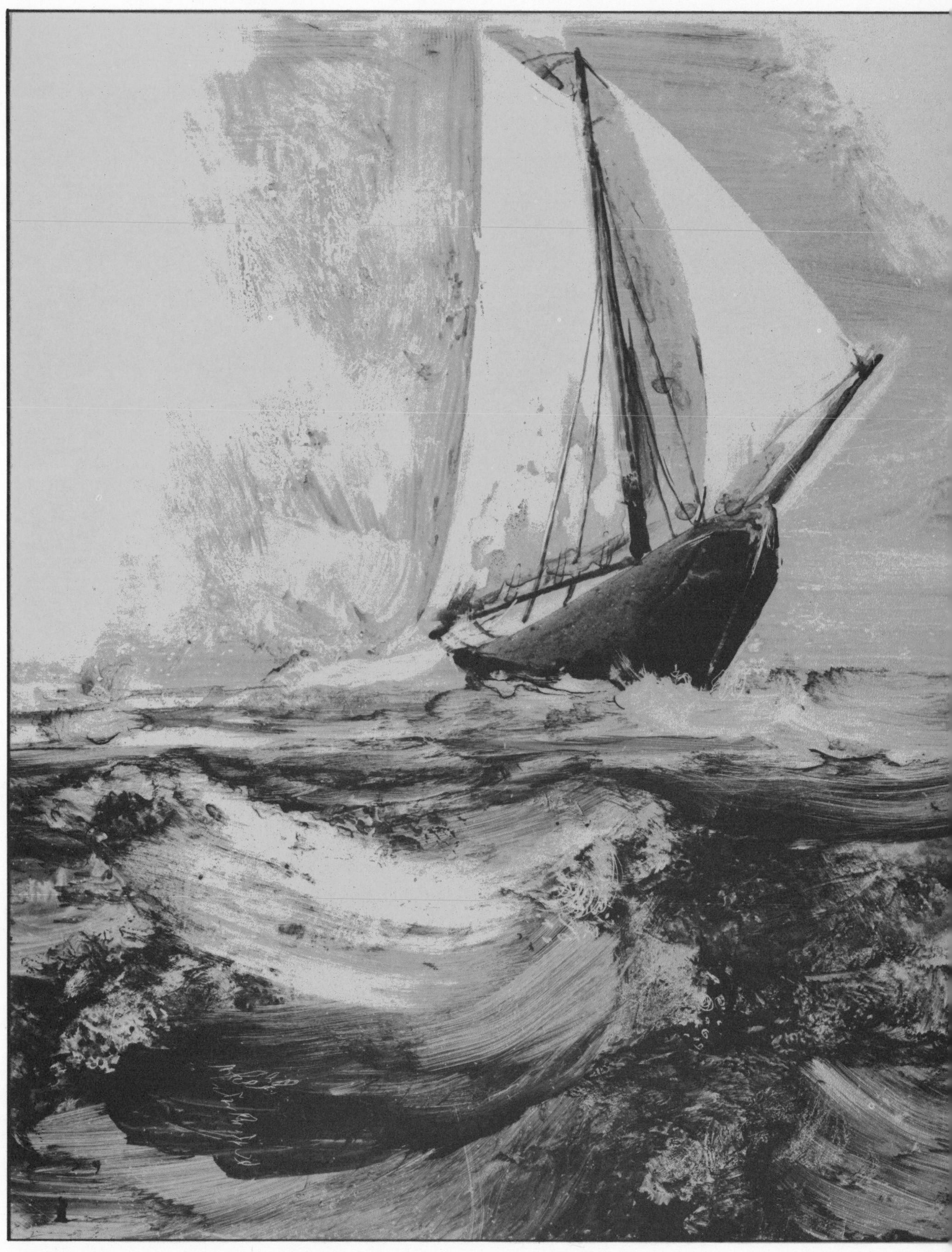

PROGRAM GUIDE: *Bahamian folk song; humorous*

You may know this song as "The Wreck of the John B. Sails" or simply the "John B." It appeared in the *The Island Song Book* (published privately in the 1920s), and later, in Carl Sandburg's famous *American Songbag.* In *The Island Song Book,* John and Evelyn McCutcheon said: "Time and usage have given this song almost the dignity of a national anthem around Nassau. The weathered ribs of the historic craft lie embedded in the sand at Governor's Harbor, whence an expedition, especially set up for the purpose in 1926, extracted a knee of horseflesh and a ring-bolt. These relics are now preserved and built into the Watch Tower."

There is evidence that twentieth-century folk poets have been at work adding new verses. At our Cable Car Hoots in San Francisco in 1964 a girl sang a verse that began: "The stewardess she got stewed, ran around the deck in the nude; we sent the captain ashore and—" She stopped at that point, overcome by modesty, and we never found out what happened after that. I've supplied a calypso-style accompaniment for the piano. Sing it at a relaxed pace, and enjoy. I've added an easy harmony part, mostly in sixths below the melody, for your harmonizers.

129
Soldier, Soldier, Will You Marry Me?

Anglo-American Folk Song

Moderately
Ladies
Men
F
B♭
F
C7
"Oh, sol-dier, sol-dier, will you mar-ry me with your fife and drum?" "Oh,
F
B♭
F
C7
F
no, oh no," the sol-dier re-plied, "I have no shoes to put on."

2. Away she flew to the cobbler's shop.
Bought him the very best pair.
Came right back and he put them on,
And she said, "Now there you are. So . . .

3. "Soldier, soldier, will you marry me
With your fife and drum?"
"Oh no, oh no," the soldier replied,
"I have no hat to put on."

4. Away she flew to the hatter's shop,
Got him the very best hat.
Came right back and he put it on,
And she said, "Now look at that. So . . .

5. "Soldier, soldier, will you marry me
With your fife and drum?"
"Oh no, oh no," the soldier replied,
"I have no suit to put on."

6. Away she flew to the tailor's shop,
Got him the very best suit.
Came right back and he put it on,
And she said, "Now that's to boot. So . . .

7. "Soldier, soldier, will you marry me
With your fife and drum?"
"Oh no, oh no," the soldier replied,
"I've a wife and children at home!"

PROGRAM GUIDE: *Anglo/American folk song; courting song, humorous*

Many years ago, before the liberation of women, men often did all they could to avoid marriage and its responsibilities, and eager young ladies were often the victims of deceiving males. This is no longer true, of course, but if you can get your singers to turn the clock back to an earlier, more sinister era, they might have some fun with this male chauvinist's courtship song. In the odd-numbered verses the men sing the first two lines, the ladies sing the last two. Everybody sings the even-numbered verses. This humorous song usually works out best with mature audiences of any age. It usually fails with immature audiences of any age.

130

Standing in the Need of Prayer

Moderately
Verse
Call
American Negro Spiritual
F
C7
F
Ain't my broth-er or my sis - ter, but it's me, oh Lord,
Response (Melody in upper notes)
Call
C7
F
stand-ing in the need of prayer.
Ain't my broth-er or my sis-ter, but it's
Response (Melody in upper notes)
C7
F
C7
F
Fine
me, oh Lord,
stand-ing in the need of prayer.
Fine

Chorus
Call
F
Response
Call
C7
F
It's me (it's me), it's me, oh Lord,
Response
C7
F
Call
Response
Call
Stand-ing in the need of prayer. It's me (it's me), it's
C7
F
Response
C7
F
D.C.
me, oh Lord, Stand-ing in the need of prayer.
D.C.

2. Ain't my father or my mother, but it's me, oh Lord,
Standing in the need of prayer.
Ain't my father or my mother, but it's me, oh Lord,
Standing in the need of prayer.

Chorus

Continue, as above:

3. Ain't the preacher or the deacon, but it's me, oh Lord.

4. Ain't my neighbor or a stranger, but it's me, oh Lord.

PROGRAM GUIDE: *American Negro spiritual*

Singers are accustomed to singing this spiritual straight through without regard for call and response divisions. If you can restrain your singers and make assignments (either for solos, or by dividing the group into callers and responders), they may find it even more enjoyable. There is also an easy harmony part in the score you can teach for the responses. A rhythm section, formed by a few members of your group, can add to the performance by clapping more-or-less, the rhythm of the melody:

131
The Star-Spangled Banner

Francis Scott Key *John Stafford Smith (?)*

Majestically
A♭ Fm7 C7 Fm7 B♭7
1. O___ say, can you see, by the dawn's ear - ly
Whose broad stripes and bright stars, through the per - il - ous
E♭ A♭ E♭ E♭7 A♭
light, What so proud - ly we hailed at the twi-light's last gleam - ing?
fight, O'er the ram - parts we watched were so gal - lant - ly stream - ing.
(Melody in upper notes)
A♭ E♭7
And the rock - ets' red glare, the bombs burst - ing in air, Gave

A♭
E♭
E♭7
Fm7
B♭7
E♭
E♭7
proof through the night that our flag was still there. O
A♭
D♭
F7
B♭m
E♭
E♭ E♭7
rit.
say, does that Star-Span-gled Ban-ner yet wave O'er the
rit.
A♭
(Melody in upper notes)
Fm B♭7
A♭
E♭7
A♭
land of the free, and the home of the brave?

PROGRAM GUIDE: *The United States National Anthem; patriotic*

Congress saw fit to proclaim "The Star-Spangled Banner" as our National Anthem in 1931. I assume our duly elected representatives at the time were not required to sing the anthem during their deliberations, since doing so might have influenced their decision otherwise. I am using the service version, pitched in the most singable key available. The ladies, particularly, will have trouble getting

way

down

here

at the beginning. But at least the men won't be screeching during the last half. Though it is difficult to sing, when the national Anthem is used, stand and sing with spirit and pride. Some easy harmony parts are indicated on the vocal score in the last half of the song.

As almost everybody knows by now, Francis Scott Key (1779-1843) wrote the lyric as a poem while he was held aboard a British warship during a battle in the War of 1812. His lines were inspired by the sight of the American flag flying proudly over Fort McHenry in Baltimore, Maryland. The tune is based on an old drinking song attributed to John Stafford Smith (1750-1836). Here is more of Key's poem (two stanzas which are not included in the singer's edition).

2. On the shore, dimly seen through the mists of the deep,
   Where the foe's haughty host in dread silence reposes,
   What is that which the breeze, o'er the towering steep,
   As it fitfully blows, half conceals, half discloses?
   Now it catches the gleam of the morning's first beam,
   In full glory reflected now shines on the stream;
   'Tis the Star-Spangled Banner, Oh long may it wave
   O'er the land of the free and the home of the brave.

3. O thus be it ever when free men shall stand
   Between their loved homes and the war's desolation!
   Blest with vict'ry and peace, may the heav'n-rescued land
   Praise the Pow'r that hath made and preserved us a nation.
   Then conquer we must, for our cause it is just,
   And this be our motto: "In God is our trust."
   And the Star-Spangled Banner in triumph shall wave
   O'er the land of the free and the home of the brave!

132

Steal Away

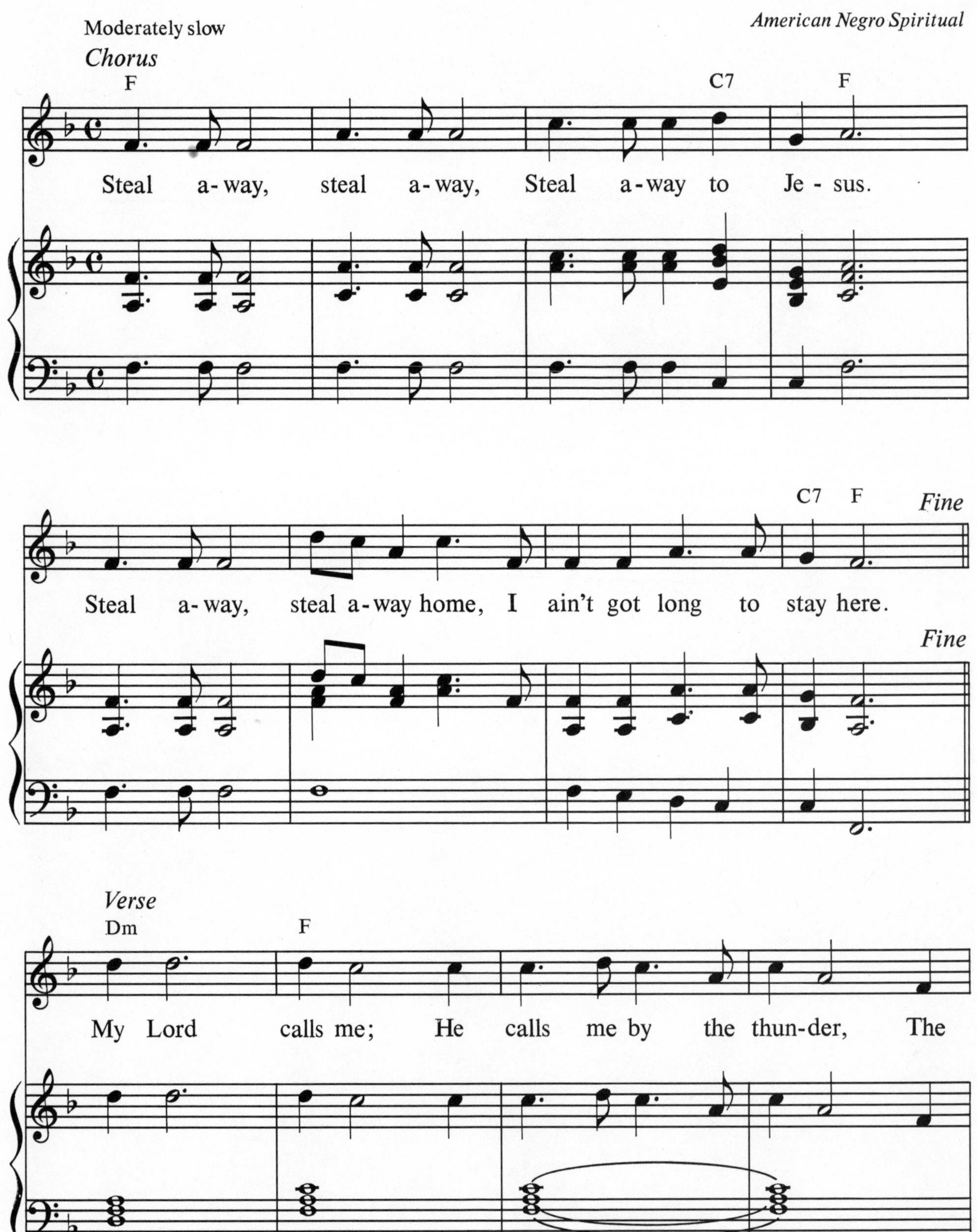

Moderately slow
American Negro Spiritual
Chorus
F
C7
F
Steal a-way, steal a-way, Steal a-way to Je-sus.
C7 F
Fine
Steal a-way, steal a-way home, I ain't got long to stay here.
Fine
Verse
Dm
F
My Lord calls me; He calls me by the thun-der, The

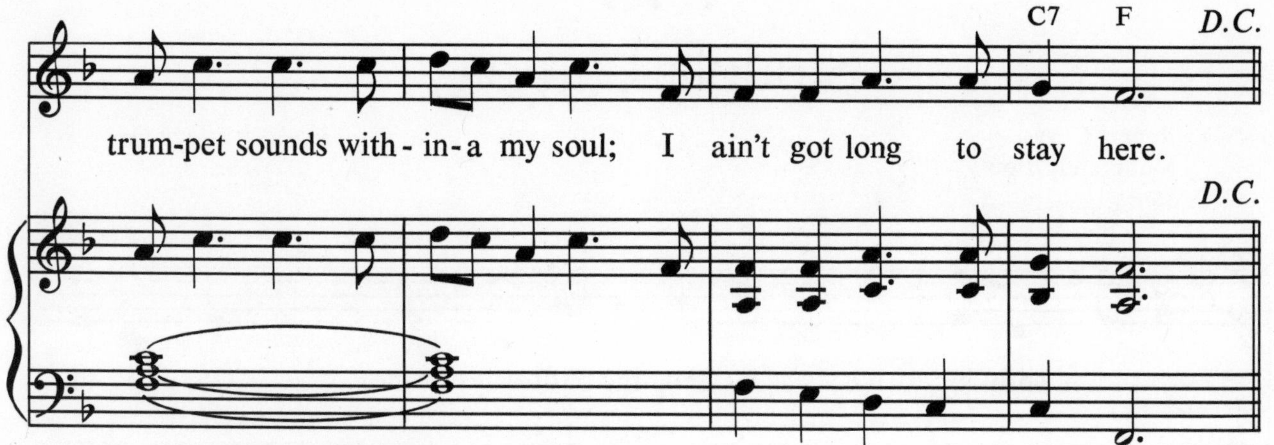
C7
F
D.C.
trum-pet sounds with - in - a my soul; I ain't got long to stay here.
D.C.

2. Green trees a-bending,
   Poor sinner stands a-trembling.
   The trumpet sounds with-in-a my soul,
   I ain't got long to stay here.

Continue, as above:

3. My Lord calls me,
   He calls me by the lightning.

4. Tombstones are bursting,
   Poor sinners stand trembling.

PROGRAM GUIDE: *American Negro spiritual*

Sing this slowly and softly, and you will hear one of the prettiest hymn-like spirituals extant. If you have a trained soprano in your group available for a solo on the verse, use her backed by humming. The routine is chorus, verse, chorus, verse, chorus. One or two verses should be sufficient, especially without the soloist.

133

Stodola Pumpa

Verse by Robert E. Nye — *Czechoslovakian Folk Song*

Moderately slow
Verse
B♭ E♭ Cm F7
Moon shin-ing bright a - long the path-way home, Un - der the
B♭ E°7 B♭ D7
trees, we walk there all a - lone. Moon shin-ing bright a -
E♭ B♭ F7 B♭
long the path-way home, Un - der the trees we walk there all a - lone. Hey!

Fast

Chorus

B♭ F7 B♭ F7 B♭

Sto-do-la, sto-do-la, sto-do-la, pum-pa, Sto-do-la pum-pa, Sto-do-la pum-pa.

B♭ F7 B♭ F7 B♭

Sto-do-la, sto-do-la, sto-do-la, pum-pa, Sto-do-la, pum-pa, pum, pum, pum!

PROGRAM GUIDE: *Czechoslovakian folk song*

The English words for the verse were provided by Robert E. Nye. Start out moderately slow for the verse (not too slow) and then tear into the chorus. Or, if you prefer, start the chorus at the same pace as the verse, but rapidly or gradually accelerate the tempo. In any event, everyone should end up breathless. The chorus should be repeated at least once. If you want to keep going after that, turn it into a marathon race with an award for the survivor. If you want to repeat the verse, whistle it. Here is an easy harmony part for the chorus, if you want to take the time to teach it:

(Harmony in lower notes)
Sto-do-la, sto-do-la, sto-do-la, pum-pa, Sto-do-la, pum-pa, Sto-do-la, pum-pa.
Sto-do-la, sto-do-la, sto-do-la, pum-pa, Sto-do-la, pum-pa pum, pum, pum!

134
The Streets of Laredo

Anglo-American Ballad

Moderately slow
F C7 F C7 F
As I ___ walked out in the streets of La - re - do, As I walked
C7 F C7 F C7
out in La - re - do one day, I spied a young cow - boy wrapped
(Melody in lower notes)
F C7 F Gm C7 F
up in white lin - en, Wrapped in white lin - en as cold as the clay.

2. "I see by your outfit that you are a cowboy"—
These words he did say as I boldly stepped by,
"Come sit down beside me and hear my sad story;
I was shot in the breast and I know I must die.

3. "It was once in the saddle I used to go dashing,
It was once in the saddle I used to go gay;
First to the dram-house and then to the card-house;
Got shot in the breast; I am dying today.

4. "Get six jolly cowboys to carry my coffin;
Get six pretty maidens to carry my pall;
Put bunches of roses all over my coffin,
Roses to deaden the clods as they fall.

5. "Oh, beat the drum slowly and play the fife lowly.
Play the dead march as you carry me along;
Take me to the green valley and lay the sod o'er me.
For I'm a young cowboy and I know I've done wrong.

6. "Go gather around you a crowd of young cowboys
And tell them the story of this, my sad fate,
Tell one and the other before they go further
To stop their wild roving before it's too late.

7. "Go fetch me a cup, a cup of cold water,
To cool my parched lips," the cowboy then said;
Before I returned, the spirit had left him
And gone to its Maker—the cowboy was dead.

PROGRAM GUIDE: *American folk ballad; cowboy ballad*

Though the trail-driving Amercian cowboy has vanished from the scene, his songs still live on. The cowboy, like the seaman, sang as he worked—and his songs have become a part of our folk-song tradition. "Streets of Laredo," or "The Cowboy's Lament" is typical of the sentimental ballads that were popular with the cowboys. It is based on an old British ballad, "The Unfortunate Rake," which was also the ancestor of "The Saint James Infirmary Blues." A nice, easy, loping tempo goes well with "Laredo." If the singers start going to sleep, toss in:

I see by your outfit that you are a cowboy.
You see by my outfit I'm a cowboy, too.
We see by our outfits that we are all cowboys.
If you get an outfit you can be a cowboy, too.

Better still, cut out verses 3, 4, 5, and 6. Laredo is a natural for outdoor programs.

135
Sur le Pont d'Avignon

French Folk Song

Moderately fast and light
G D7 G D7
French: Sur le pont d'A-vi-gnon, L'on y dan-se, L'on y dan-se,
English: On the bridge, A-vi-gnon, See them danc-ing, See them danc-ing,
G D7 G D7 G Fine
Sur le pont d'A-vi-gnon, L'on y dan-se tout en rond.
On the bridge, A-vi-gnon, See them danc-ing all a-round.
Fine
G D7 G D7 G D.C.
Les mes-sieurs font comme ci, Et puis en-core comme ça.
Gen-tle-men go this way, And a-gain go this way.
D.C.

French:

2. Les mesdames font comme ci,
   Et puis encore comme ça.

English:

2. Ladies then go this way,
   And again go this way.

PROGRAM GUIDE: *French folk song*

You came back for another French lesson. This one is much easier than "Au Clair de la Lune." It's a children's dancing-game song. I've provided English words as well as French, so you may skip the French, if you prefer (but what's the point in that?). Here is David Earle's handy pronunciation guide:

Sur luh(r) pon da-vi-nyo(n),
Lo(n) ee dah(n)-suh, lo(n) ee dah(n)-suh.
Sur luh(r) pon da-vi-nyo(n),
Lo(n) ee dah(n)-suh too tah(n) ro(n).

Lay mess-sieu fah(n) kum-see,
Ay pooey ah(n)-core kum-sah.

Lay may-dam fah(n) kum-see,
Ay pooey ah(n)-core kum-sah.

The *Ay* is pronounced with a long *A* as in hay. There still is no equivalent in English for the French nasal sound. So come as close to it as you can. If you want to dance, it's up to you. Any step is fine with me, as long as it goes this way, and again like this.

The song was originally composed as a round dance to celebrate the dancing under a bridge over the Rhone River, Pont St. Bénézet. The bridge was built in 1185 and, though part of it still stands, is no longer in use. The song is supposed to have originated in the early 1800s in a tavern on the island of Barthelesse which was located under one of the arches of the bridge. The song was a hit in Adolphe Adam's *opéra comique, Le Sourd,* in 1853.

136

Sweetly Sings the Donkey

Traditional American Round

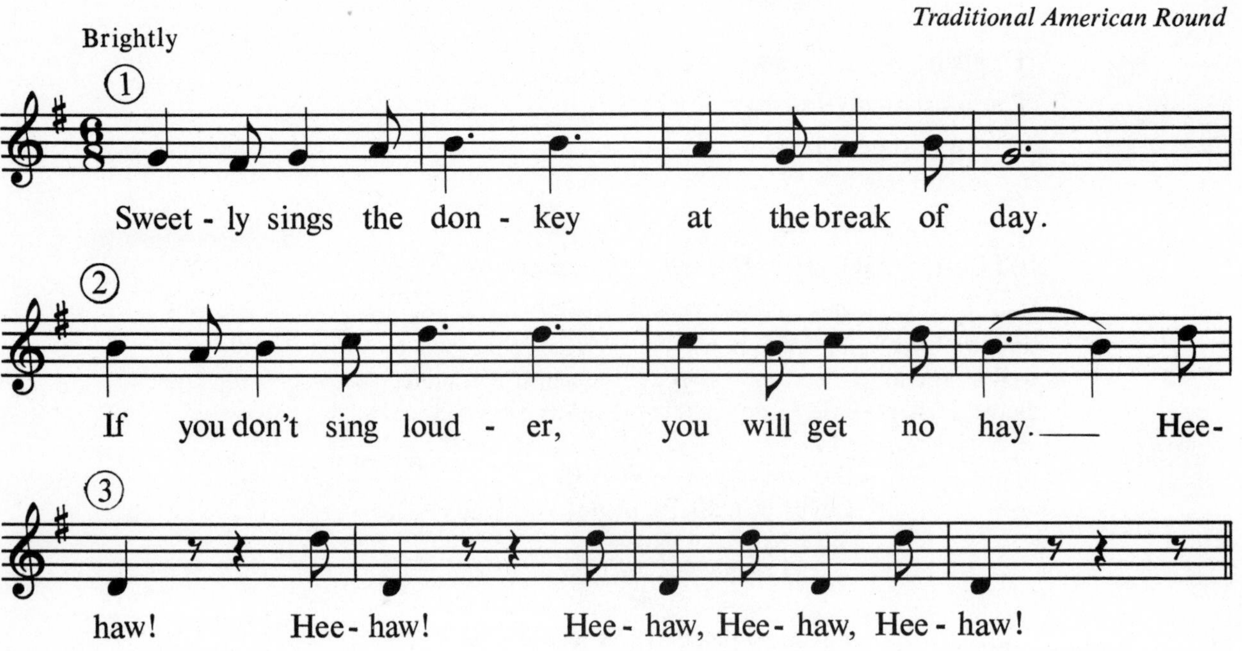
Brightly
1
Sweet - ly sings the don - key at the break of day.
2
If you don't sing loud - er, you will get no hay.___ Hee-
3
haw! Hee - haw! Hee - haw, Hee - haw, Hee - haw!

Divide the group into three sections. Each section sings the entire round the agreed-upon number of times, beginning at point 1 when the preceding section reaches point 2. Thus the round begins and ends with one section singing alone: Section 1 at the beginning and Section 3 at the end.

PROGRAM GUIDE: *Traditional American round; humorous*

Juxtapose this bucolic American round with one of the English drawing room rounds and you may prove something—I'm not sure what. Divide the singers into three groups and conquer.

137
Swing Low, Sweet Chariot

American Negro Spiritual

Moderately slow
Chorus
F Bb F C7
Swing low, sweet char - i - ot,
Com-in' for to car-ry me home!
(Melody in lower notes)
Fine
F Bb F C7 F Bb F
Swing low, sweet char - i - ot,
Com-in' for to car-ry me home.
Fine
Verse
Call
F Bb C7
I looked o - ver Jor-dan and what did I see,

Response
C7
Call
F
Com-in' for to car-ry me
home?
A
band of
an - gels,
B♭
C7
Response
(Melody in lower notes)
F
C7
F
D.C.
com-in' af- ter me,_
Com-in' for to car- ry me
home!
D.C.

2. If you get there before I do,
   Comin' for to carry me home!
   Tell all my friends I'm coming, too,
   Comin' for to carry me home!

Continue, as above:

3. The brightest day that ever I saw,
   When Jesus washed my sins away.

4. I'm sometimes up an' sometimes down,
   But still my soul feels heavenly boun'.

5. I never went to heaven, but I been told
   The streets in heaven are paved with gold.

PROGRAM GUIDE: *American Negro spiritual*

This stately spiritual hymn should be sung in that fashion. Don't rush it. Use a soloist, or divide your group into callers and responders for the verse. The routine is chorus, verse, chorus, verse, chorus. Two verses selected from those shown normally should be sufficient. A humming chorus can provide a nice interlude. You can, if you wish, add some nice harmony parts for the responses by borrowing the tones used in the piano score.

138
Taps

Traditional, American

Slowly, quietly
Day is done; gone the sun, From the lakes, from the hills, from the
sky. All is well, safe - ly rest; God is nigh.

2. Fading light dims the sight,
   And a star lights the sky, gleaming bright;
   From afar, drawing nigh,
   Falls the night.

3. Thanks and praise for our days
   'Neath the sun, 'neath the stars, 'neath the sky;
   As we go, this we know:
   God is nigh.

PROGRAM GUIDE: *U.S. Army bugle call; camp song*

"Taps" provides a nice closer for any evening program. Campers often use "Taps" at sunset or at the close of a campfire program. Sing it slowly and quietly, pausing on the hold notes as indicated on the score. Usually only one verse is sung, but I've provided three from which to make your selection. Sing them all, of course, if you wish.

"Taps" is supposed to have been composed, or commissioned, in 1862 by General Daniel Butterfield, commander of a brigade in the Army of the Potomac. Butterfield asked his bugler Oliver Wilcox Norton, to play a more subdued call for "extinguish lights."

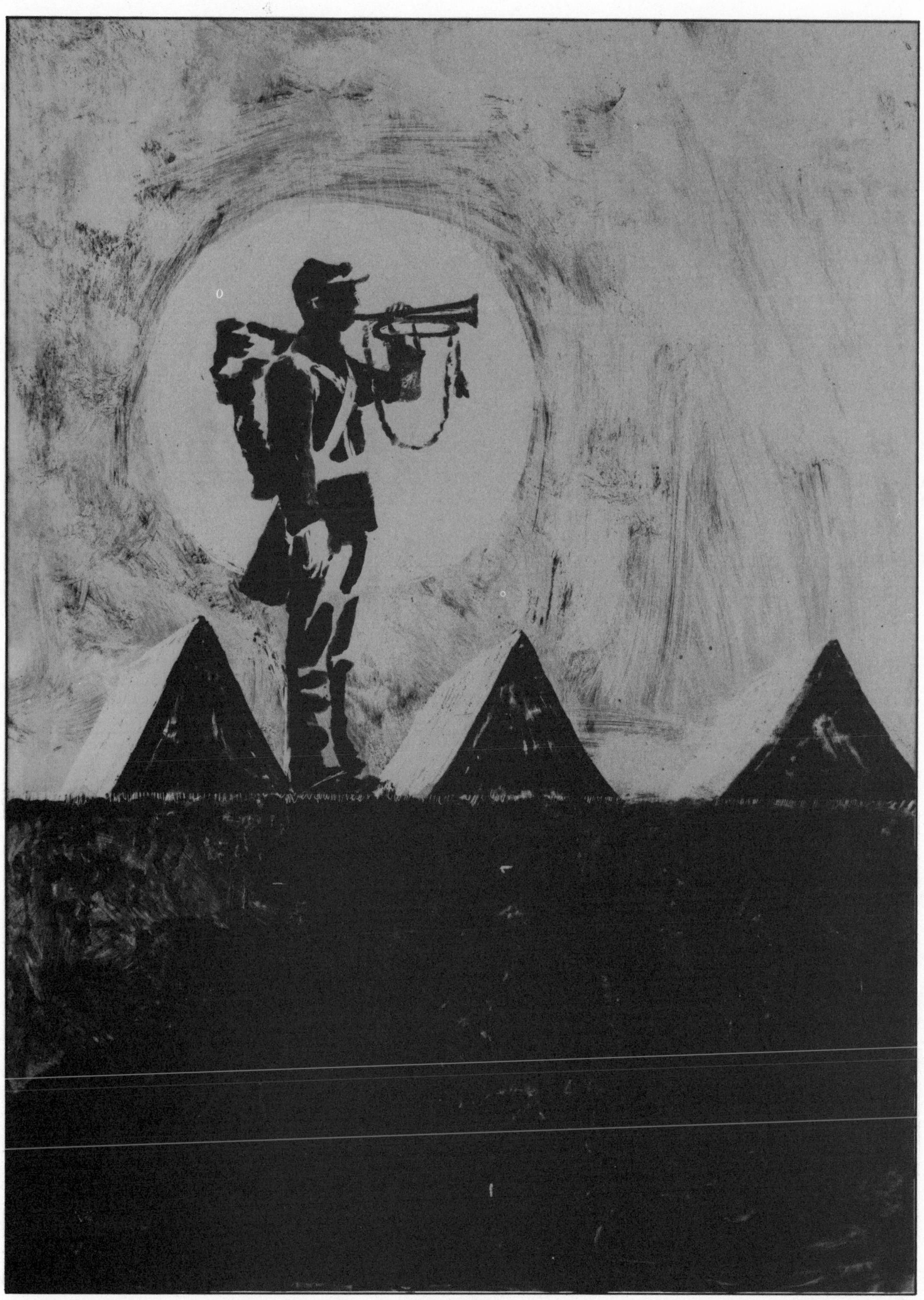

139

Tell Me Why

Adapted by J.F.L.

Traditional, American
Adapted by J.F.L.

Slowly
Melody
G E°7 D7 G B7 C G
Please tell__ me why__ the stars do shine.
Harmony
legato
G E°7 D7 G A7 D7
Tell__ me why__ the i - vy twines, Then

G E°7 D7 G B7 C B7
tell ___ me why ___ the sky is blue,
E7 A7 D7 G
And I will tell you why I ___ love you.

2. Because God made the stars to shine,
   Because God made the ivy twine,
   Because God made the sky so blue,
   Because God made you so sweet and true.

3. I know it's true that God above,
   He wanted someone for me to love.
   And he chose you from all the rest,
   Because he knew, dear, I'd love you the best.

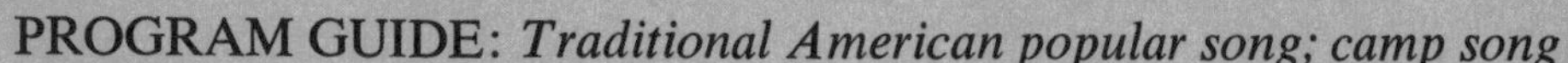

PROGRAM GUIDE: *Traditional American popular song; camp song*

You can get a very nice sound by using the ladies for the melody and the male voices for the harmony. This is the way we arranged it for Betty Johnson's successful recording a few years ago. The harmony part has a melody of its own so that it *can* be learned with a little effort. I've scored it this way in the hope that you will use it. You can take the idea a step further by having the male voices sing the melody line on the first chorus, hum the harmony line on the second chorus, and sing the harmony line on the third chorus. The ladies meanwhile, hum the first chorus, and then sing the last two. To me, all this is well worth the effort, but you and your singers may prefer singing the whole song in unison. The harmony part may also be sung by girls' voices above or below the melody.

140
Ten Green Bottles

American Folk Song

Lively

F C7 F

Ten green bot-tles hang - ing on the wall,

C7 F B♭ F

Ten green bot-tles hang-ing on the wall. If one green bot-tle should

C7 B♭ C7 F (Melody in lower notes) F C7 F

ac - ci-dent-'ly fall, There'd be nine green bot-tles hang-ing on the wall.

2. Nine green bottles hanging on the wall,
   Nine green bottles hanging on the wall.
   If one green bottle should accidentally fall,
   There'd be eight green bottles hanging on the wall.

   Continue with eight, then seven, and so on, until there are no green bottles left on the wall.

PROGRAM GUIDE: *American folk song; camp song, counting song*

When you've worn out "Nine Men Slept in a Boardinghouse Bed," you can always turn to "bottles" to while away the time with song. You count down from ten by substituting nine, then eight, and so on, until there are no bottles left.

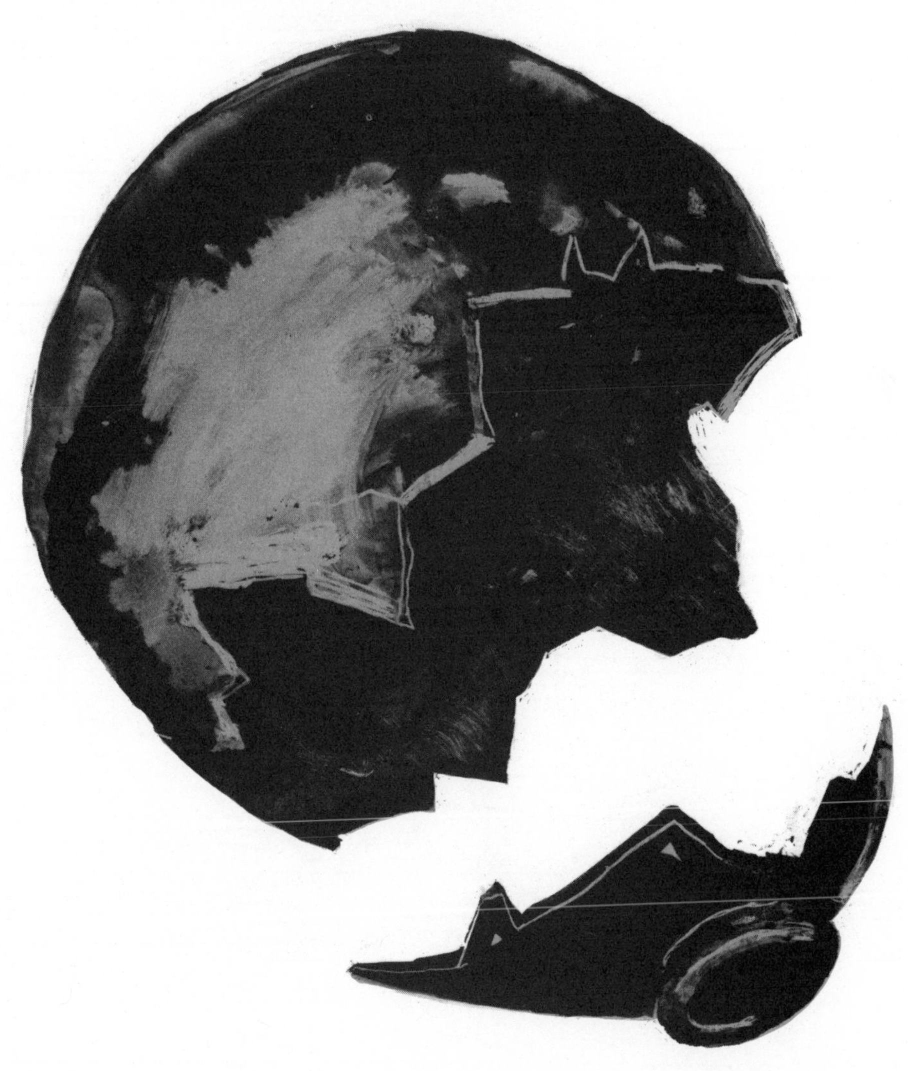

141
There Was an Old Woman

American Folk Song

Moderately
G
1. There was an old wo - man who swal - lowed a fly.
Am
D7
G
I don't know why she swal - lowed a fly, Per - haps she'll die.
G
Am
2. There was an old wo - man who swal - lowed a spi - der, who wrig - gled and jig - gled and
D7
G
tic - kled in - side her. She swal - lowed the spi - der to catch the fly. And

Am
D7
G
I don't know why she swal-lowed a fly. Per - haps she'll die.
G
Guitar tacet
3. There was an old wo-man who swal-lowed a bird. (Spoken) How ab-surd! To
D7
G
swal-low a bird. She swal-lowed the bird to catch the spi-der that
Am
D7
G
wrig-gled and jig-gled and tic-kled in-side her. She swal-lowed the spi-der to

G
Am
D7
G
catch the fly, And I don't know why she swal- lowed a fly. Per- haps she'll die.
G
Am
There was an old wo-man who swal-lowed a
(4) cat, I - mag - ine that! She
(5) dog. What a hog To
(6) goat, Just o-pened her throat And
(7) cow I don't know how She
(Repeat as need to complete accumulation)
D7
G
swal- lowed a cat. She swal- lowed the cat to catch the bird,
swal- low a dog. She swal- lowed the dog to catch the cat,
swal - lowed a goat. She swal- lowed the goat to catch the dog,
swal - lowed a cow. She swal- lowed the cow to catch the goat,
She
(Note: Don't repeat first time)

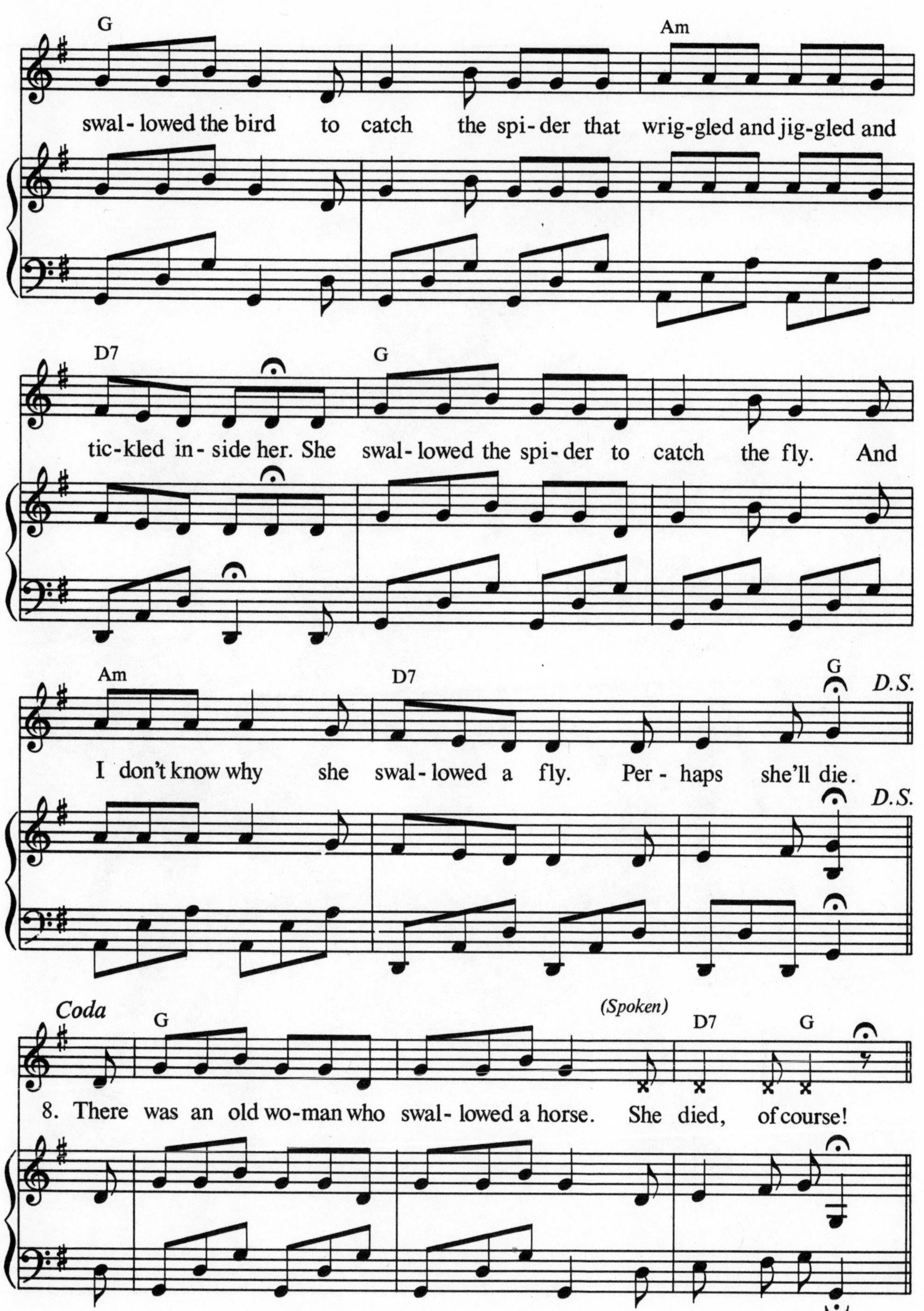
G
Am
swal - lowed the bird to catch the spi - der that wrig-gled and jig-gled and
D7
G
tic-kled in - side her. She swal - lowed the spi - der to catch the fly. And
Am
D7
G
D.S.
I don't know why she swal - lowed a fly. Per - haps she'll die.
D.S.
Coda
G
(Spoken)
D7
G
8. There was an old wo-man who swal - lowed a horse. She died, of course!

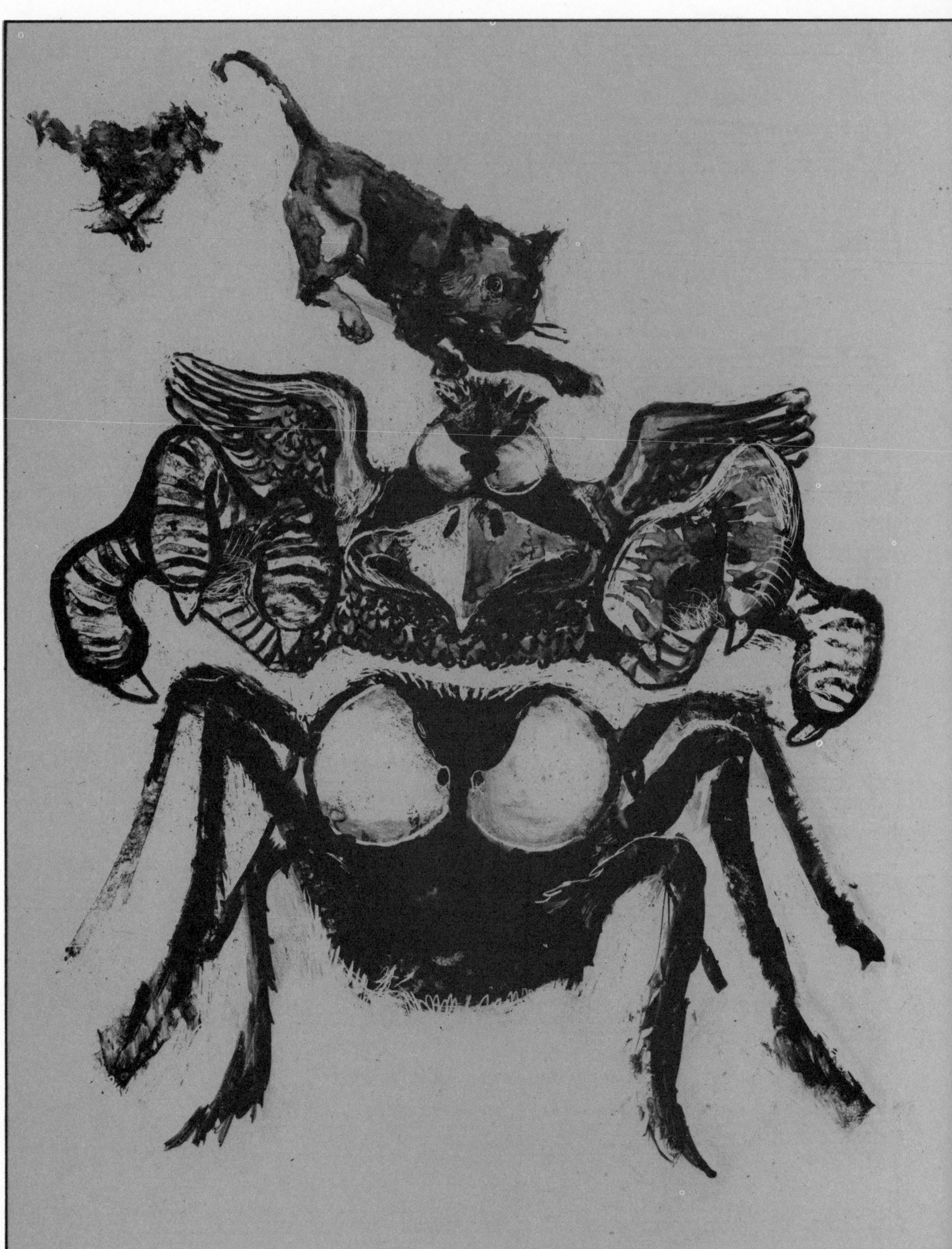

PROGRAM GUIDE: *American folk song; cumulative, humorous*

The all-time honors for the best cumulative song ought to go to this old American folk song. It was first recorded in the Journal of the American Folklore Society in the nineteenth century, and has changed very little since. This is understandable since the animal life gets swallowed in what is reasonable pecking (or should I say hunting?) order. And it's difficult to imagine how the woman could handle anything larger. A cow, yes, but not a horse, and certainly not a whale! Still:

> There was an old woman who swallowed a whale
> Upended its tail and swallowed a whale.

No, better forget it. To keep the score from filling up the rest of the book I made a strategic accumulation beginning with the fourth verse. The repeat signs in the fourth and sixth measures should be ignored for the fourth verse. Thereafter you accumulate by repeating the phrase and working your way up to the top line, like this:

> 5. She swallowed the dog to catch the cat,
> She swallowed the cat to catch the bird,
> (*Move on to*) She swallowed the bird, etc.
>
> 6. She swallowed the goat to catch the dog,
> She swallowed the dog to catch the cat,
> She swallowed the cat to catch the bird,
> (*Move on to*) She swallowed the bird, etc.

Be sure to observe the spoken lines and held notes as indicated in the vocal score. The song is long, but that is what it is all about. You can speed up as you go along if you feel the need to.

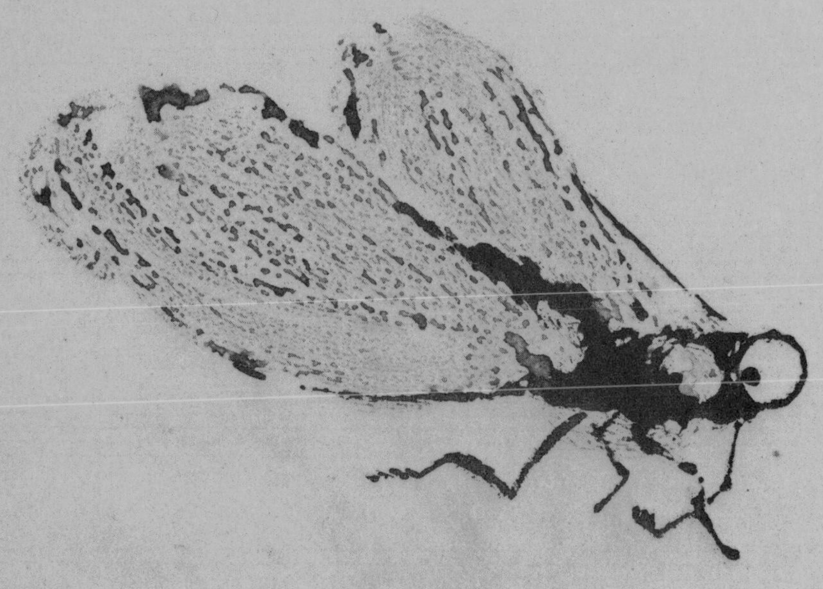

142

There's a Song in the Air

Josiah G. Holland
Karl P. Harrington
Moderately
F C7 F C7
There's a song in the air! There's a star in the sky! There's a
F Fm6 C C7 G7 C C7
moth - er's deep prayer, And a ba - by's low cry! And the
F C7 C
star rains its fire while the beau - ti - ful sing, For the

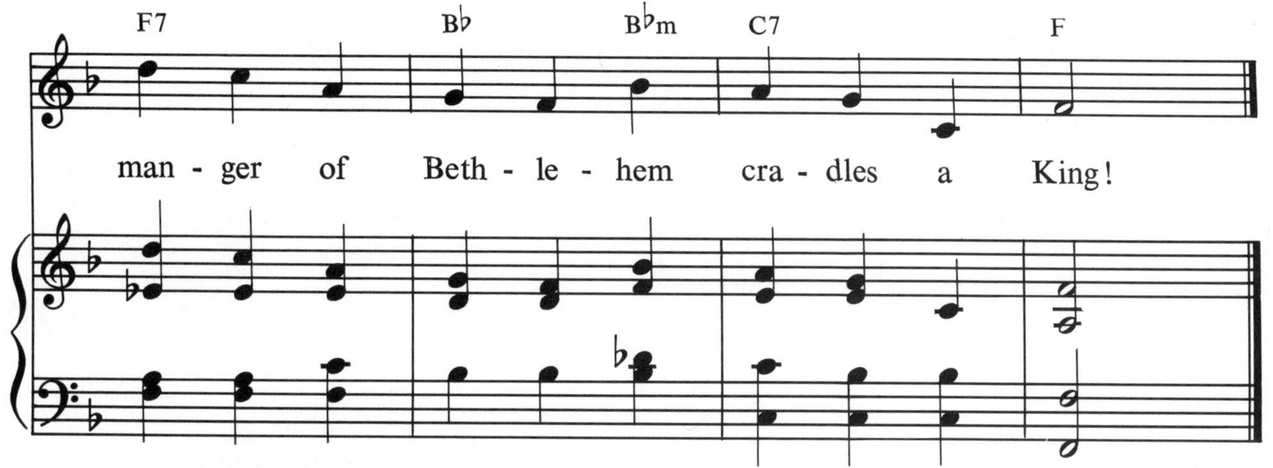
F7
B♭
B♭m
C7
F
man - ger of Beth - le - hem cra - dles a King!

2. There's a tumult of joy
O'er the wonderful birth,
For the virgin's sweet boy
Is the Lord of the earth.
Ay! the star rains its fire while the beautiful sing,
For the manger of Bethlehem cradles a King!

3. In the light of that star
Lie the ages impearled,
And that song from afar
Has swept over the world.
Every hearth is aflame, and the beautiful sing
In the homes of the nations that Jesus is King!

4. We rejoice in the light,
And we echo the song
That comes down through the night
From the heavenly throng.
Ay! we shout to the lovely evangel they bring,
And we greet in his cradle our Savior and King!

PROGRAM GUIDE: *Traditional American Christmas song*

The words of this favorite Christmas song were written as a poem by Josiah G. Holland (1819-1881), a founder (in 1869) and the editor of *Scribner's Magazine.* He was also a newspaper editor and the author of several books. The music was composed by Karl Harrington (1861-1953), a professor of classical languages. The song has a nice lilt to it and should be sung gently and joyfully.

143
This Old Man

Traditional, English

Lively
F
B♭
C7
This old man, he played one, He played knick knack on my thumb;
(lightly)
F
C7
F C7 F
knick knack pad-dy whack, Give a dog a bone, This old man came roll - ing home.

2. This old man, he played two,
He played knick knack on my shoe.
Knick knack, paddy whack, give a dog a bone,
This old man came rolling home.

Continue, as above:

3. This old man, he played three,
He played knick knack on my knee.

4. This old man, he played four,
He played knick knack on my door;

5. This old man, he played five,
He played knick knack on my hive;

6. This old man, he played six,
He played knick knack on my sticks;

7. This old man, he played seven
He played knick knack up in heaven;

8. This old man, he played eight,
He played knick knack on my pate;

9. This old man, he played nine,
He played knick knack on my spine,

10. This old man, he played ten,
He played knick knack once again;
Knick knack, paddy whack, give a dog a bone,
Now we'll all go running home.

PROGRAM GUIDE: *Traditional English singing game; counting song*

Here is another song for the children. Although some adults enjoy it, I would hesitate to use it except in mixed company, the mix being with children. It should be sung in a brisk and lively manner. There is really no point in counting past ten.

144
This Train

American Negro Spiritual

Lively (in Two)
E♭
Fm Cm A♭ B♭7
E♭
Ladies This train is bound for glo - ry, this train.
Men This train,
This train is bound for glo - ry.
E♭
Cm
E♭
B♭7
This train is bound for glo - ry, this train.
This train,
this train is bound for glo - ry,

Eb
Eb7
Fm
Ab
Eb
This train is bound for glo-ry, Don't ride noth-in' but the righ-teous and the ho - ly.
This train is bound for glo-ry, Don't ride noth-in' but the righ-teous and the ho - ly.
Eb
Fm
Cm
Ab
Bb7
Eb
This train is bound for glo - ry, this train.
This train is bound for glo - ry, this train.
(omit last time)

2. This train don't carry no gamblers, this train,
This train don't carry no gamblers, this train,
This train don't carry no gamblers,
No hypocrites, no midnight ramblers,
This train is bound for glory, this train.

Continue, as above:

3. This train is built for speed now, *etc.*
   Fastest train you ever did see,
   This train is bound for glory, this train.

4. This train don't carry no liars, *etc.*
   No hypocrites and no high flyers,
   This train is bound for glory, this train.

5. This train don't carry no rustlers, *etc.*
   Sidestreet walkers, two-bit hustlers.
   This train is bound for glory, this train.

PROGRAM GUIDE: *American Negro spiritual*

Chariots, ships, and trains have all served as symbols of escape to freedom, or redemption, in Negro religious music. "This Train" is a good song for straight, spirited unison singing. It has only one problem—the range. I've used the best key for the average voice, but you will still find the high voices scratching for the low notes, and the low voices stretching for the high ones. So remember the old adage: if you can't sing it good, sing it loud. I've set the men up for some easy imitations in the first half of each verse. If you don't want to tackle them, just advise everybody to sing the top line.

145
Three Blind Mice

Traditional English Round

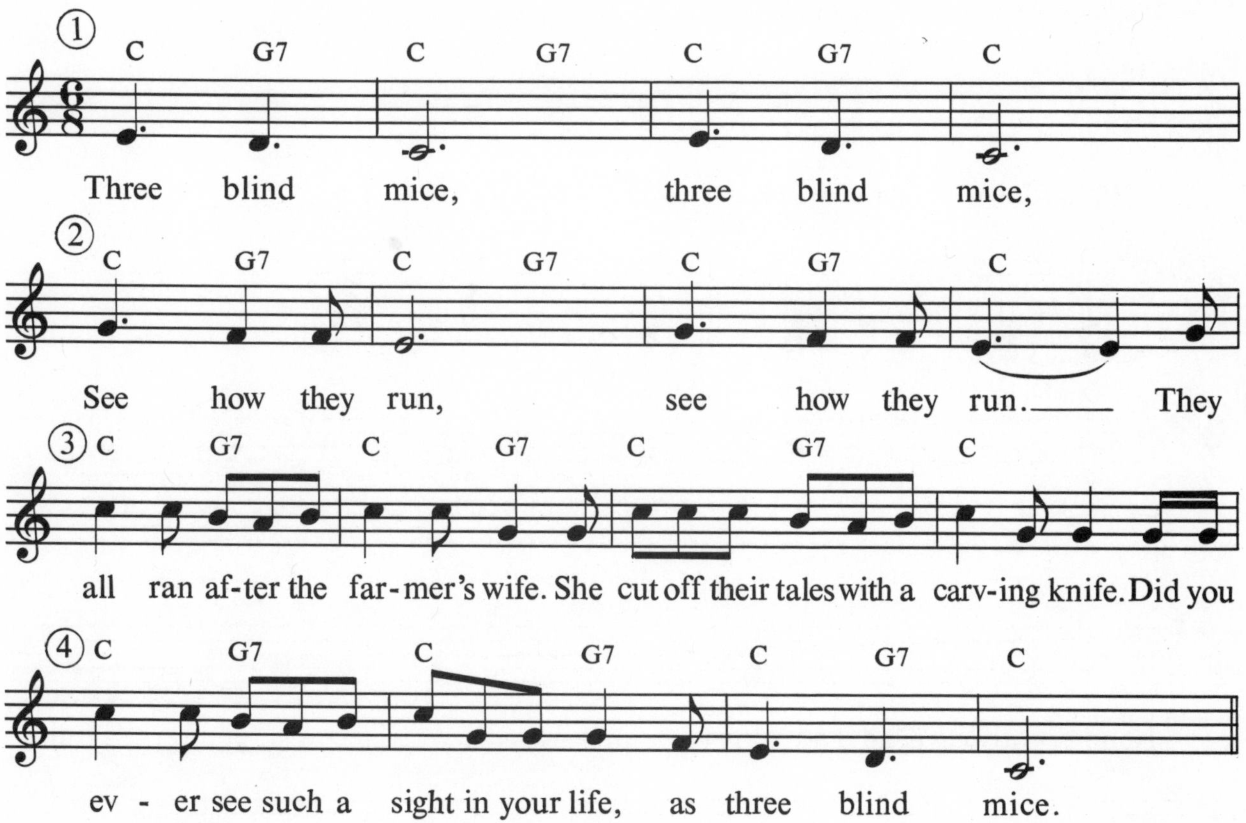

①
C G7 C G7 C G7 C
Three blind mice, three blind mice,
②
C G7 C G7 C G7 C
See how they run, see how they run.___ They
③
C G7 C G7 C G7 C
all ran af-ter the far-mer's wife. She cut off their tales with a carv-ing knife. Did you
④
C G7 C G7 C G7 C
ev - er see such a sight in your life, as three blind mice.

Divide the group into four sections. Each section sings the entire round the agreed-upon number of times, beginning at point 1 when the preceding section reaches point 2. Thus the round begins and ends with one section singing alone: Section 1 at the beginning and Section 4 at the end.

PROGRAM GUIDE: *Traditional English round*

This grisly four-part round is so familiar it makes a good starter for any round-singing, because the singers usually know what to do without being told. Sing it in a lively manner, and go on quickly to better things. "Three Blinde Mice" dates back at least to 1609, when it appeared as one of several "pleasant rondelaies" in *Deuteromelia,* a collection of "melodius musicke" published in London, with variations in both words and melody from its present form:

> Three blinde Mice, three blinde Mice,
> Dame Julian, Dame Julian,
> The Miller and his merry olde wife,
> fhee fcrapte her tripe licke thou the knife.

146
Tom Dooley

American Ballad

Moderately
Chorus
G
Hang down your head, Tom Doo - ley,
legato
D7
Hang down your head and cry,
Hang down your head, Tom
Doo - ley,
Poor boy, you're bound to
G
die.
(Omit last time)

1. I met her on the hilltop.
There I took her life.
I met her on the hilltop,
And stabbed her with my knife.

2. Tonight I'll pick my banjo,
I'll pick it on my knee.
Tomorrow I'll be hangin'
From a white oak tree.

3. This time tomorrow,
Reckon where I'll be.
This time tomorrow,
I'll be in eternity.

4. Had my trial in Wilkesboro.
What do you think they done?
Bound me over to Statesville,
And that's where I'll be hung.

5. Daddy, oh my Daddy,
What shall I do?
I've lost all my money,
And killed poor Laury, too.

6. Mother, oh dear Mother,
Don't you weep and cry.
I've killed poor Laury Foster,
You know I'm bound to die.

7. Now, what my Mother told me
Is about to come to pass:
That drinkin' and the women
Would be my ruin at last.

8. This time tomorrow,
Reckon where I'll be?
In some lonesome valley,
Hangin' on a white oak tree.

PROGRAM GUIDE: *American murder ballad*

On May 1, 1868, after various trials and appeals and a last-minute confession, Thomas C. Dula was hanged for the murder of Laura Foster. Later that year Ann Melton, charged as his accomplice, was acquitted. The evidence showed that Dula was running around with both girls and, in the process, had picked up a disease from Laura and passed it on to Ann. According to a newspaper description, "a state of immorality unexampled in the history of any country exists among these people, and such a general system of free loveism prevails that it is 'a wise child that knows its father.' " Whether or not this was sensational or biased journalism, the community did draw the line at murder. Sing "Tom Dooley" at the easy, relaxed strolling tempo suggested by the accompaniment. The verses are sung to the same tune as the chorus.

147
Trampin'

American Negro Spiritual

Brightly
C
G7
I'm a - tramp - in', tramp - in', Try-in' to make heav-en my
(Leader in upper notes)
home. (Glo-ry hal-le-lu-jah) Tramp-in', tramp - in', Try-in' to make heav-en my
Verse
Leader
Fine
home. I've nev-er been to heav-en but I've been told,
(Omit last time)

Response
Leader
C
G7
C
Try-in' to make heav-en my home, The streets up there are
paved with gold, Try-in' to make heav-en my home.
D.C.

2. Sometimes I'm up, sometimes I'm down,
   Tryin' to make heaven my home.
   Sometimes my soul feels heavenly bound,
   Tryin' to make heaven my home.

   Continue, as above:

3. See that sister dressed so fine,
   She ain't got religon on her mind.

4. Who's that yonder dressed in blue?
   Must be the children that are comin' through.

5. Who's that yonder dressed in black?
   Must be the hypocrites a-turnin' back.

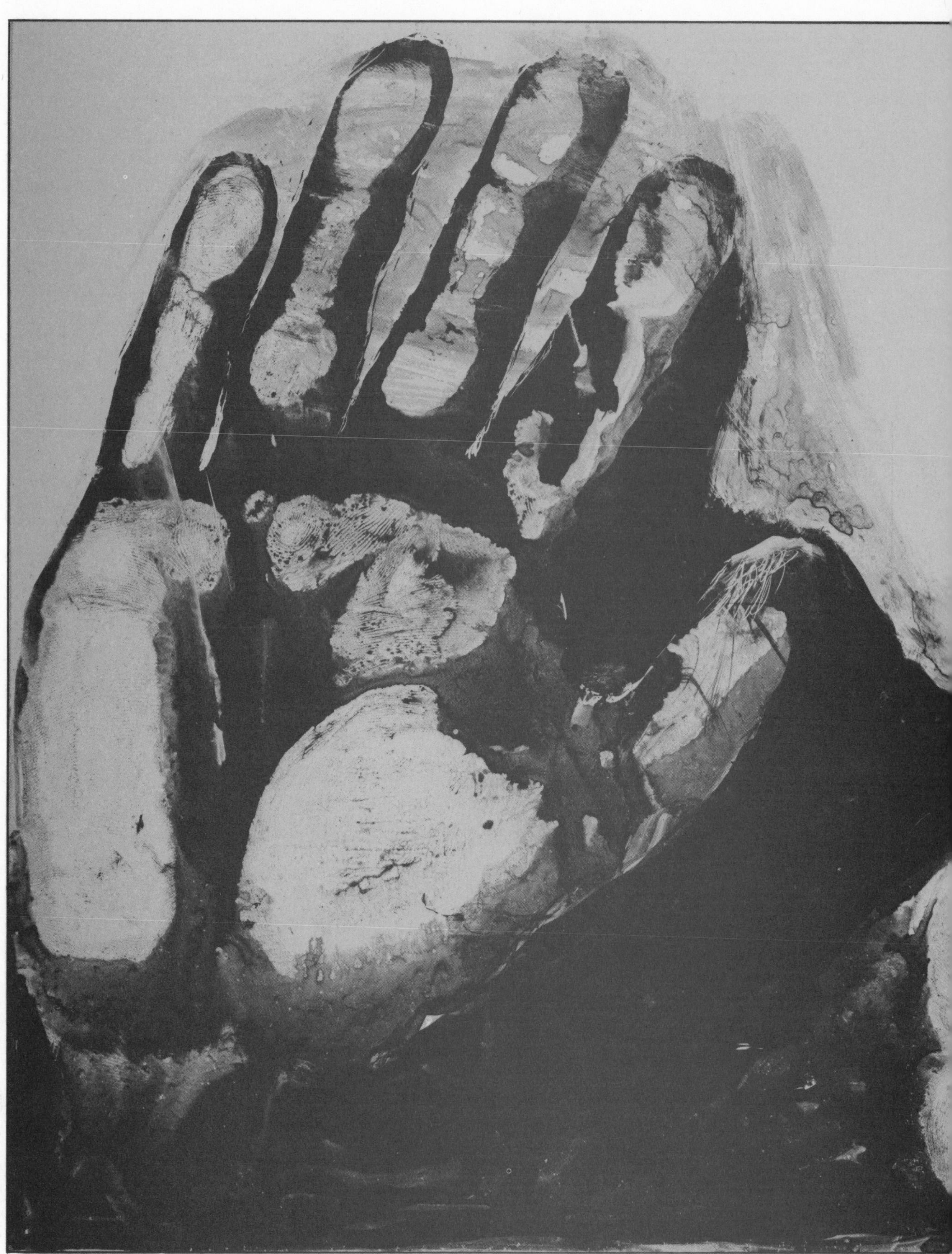

PROGRAM GUIDE: *American Negro spiritual*

Dancing was forbidden by the church, but the church recognized that a substitute was needed. Marching Services resulted. Here is how they were described by Odum and Johnson in *The Negro and His Songs:*

> The benches were piled up together and marching room left for the worshippers. They had various orders for this service and many forms of it have been known to exist. Sometimes they marched two by two, a "sister and brother in the Lord," sometimes they marched singly, and at other times they marched in a general "mix-up." At first they followed a leader to a simple melody, keeping step and working into a rhythmic swing. Then as they became more excited they became more expressive, and with the elaboration of the march into a dance their songs became marching songs.*

And that's what we have here: one of the best. It's a challenge to see if you can do it justice. You need a leader for those calls. And, I don't know about you, but I think marching is a whale of an idea. Why not? You won't have to set up a rhythm section. You'll have one built in. And, if you don't have room to move about, you can always march in place.

* Howard W. Odum and Guy B. Johnson, *The Negro and His Songs* (Chapel Hill: The University of North Carolina Press, 1925).

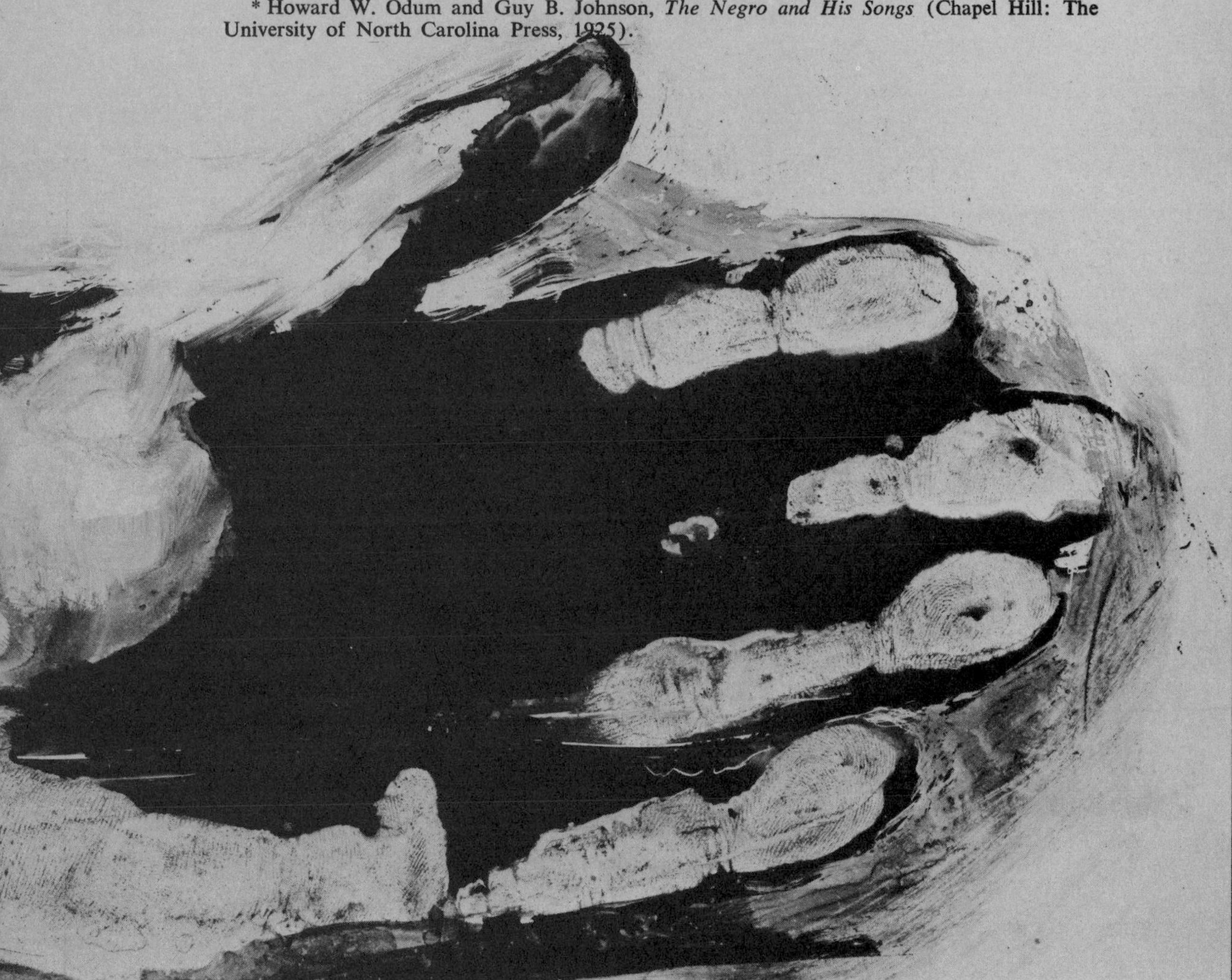

148

Tumbalalaika

Jewish Folk Song

Moderately fast
Cm
G7
1. Shtet a boch - er und er tracht, Tracht und
Chorus: Tum-ba-la, tum-ba - la, tum-ba - la - lai - ka, tum-ba - la,
Cm
tracht die gan - tze nacht. Vem-men zu neh - men
tum-ba - la, tum-ba - la - lai - ka. Tum-ba - la - lai - ka,
Fm
Cm
G7
Cm
ohn nit far-schem - men. Vem-men zu neh - men ohn nit far-schem - men.
Shpiel ba - la - lai - ka, Tum-ba - la - lai - ka, Shpiel ba - la - lai - ka.

2. Medel, Medel, 'chvell ba dir fregen,
Vos ken vaksen, vaksen on regen,
Vos ken brennen on nit oifherren,
Vos ken benken, vehnen on trerren.

Chorus

3. Narishe Bocher vos darfst du fregen,
A shtehn ken vaksen, vaksen on regen,
Liebe ken brennen on nit oifherren,
A hartz ken benken, vehnen on trerren.

Chorus

PROGRAM GUIDE: *Jewish folk song; romantic*

A shy boy is worried about finding a girl. He asks her what can grow without rain, what can burn without burning out, and what can cry without tears. The girl tells him a stone can grow without rain, love can burn without burning out, and a heart can cry without tears. This riddle song has a beautiful melody, and it's more fun to sing it in Jewish than in ersatz English. Try it and compare with another fine companion piece, "The Riddle Song" (number 113). Pronounce *ch* as k, *o* as *oh, a* as *ah u* as *ou, i* as *ee, e* as in *eh.*

149

The Twelve Days of Christmas

Traditional, English

Moderately

I

F C7 F

1. On the first day of Christ - mas my true love gave to me A

F B♭ F C7 F

par - tridge in a pear tree.

II

F

2. On the sec-ond
3. On the third
4. On the fourth
day of Christ-mas my

(Repeat as needed)
C7 F C7 F B♭ F C7 F
D.S.
true love gave to me
two tur-tle doves,
three French hens,
four cal-ling birds,
And a par-tridge in a pear tree.
D.S.
III
C7 F
5. On the fifth day of Christ - mas my true love gave to me
F G7 C C7 F Gm
five gold rings, four cal-ling birds, three French hens,
C7 F B♭ F C7 F
two tur-tle doves, And a par - tridge in a pear tree.

IV
F
C7
F
6. On the sixth
7. On the sev-enth
8. On the eighth
9. On the ninth
10. On the tenth
11. On the 'lev-enth
12. On the twelfth
day of Christ-mas my true love gave to me:
C7
F
G7
C
C7
F
Six geese a - lay - ing,
Sev-en swans a - swim - ming,
Eight maids a - milk - ing,
Nine la - dies danc - ing,
Ten lords a - leap - ing,
'Lev-en pip - ers pip - ing,
Twelve drum - mers drum - ming,
five gold rings, four cal - ling birds,
Gm
C7
F
B♭
F
C7
F
D.S.
three French hens, two tur - tle doves, And a par - tridge in a pear tree.
D.S.

PROGRAM GUIDE: *Traditional English Christmas song; cumulative*

Back to the drawing room for this durable and delightful English Christmas game song. You really must be familiar with the territory to handle the twists and turns of this complex cumulative song. Scoring the song is a problem because it would take reams of paper to write all the verses out in full from beginning to end. To make it easier to follow a condensed score I've set the action up in four basic groups and used Roman numerals in boxes to identify the groups on the score. If you will simply move from group to group as you reach the appropriately numbered verse you should have no trouble with the score. A further advantage for group singing these days is that the song has become very popular in recent years and is now generally well known by singers. The song extends the Christmas season, and Christmas giving, from Christmas Day to the Feast of the Epiphany, twelve days later, and thus preserves the memory of a time when this custom prevailed in England. In earlier days the singers would start with twelve gifts, count down to one, and then back up to twelve. Today most singers are satisfied to work their way up from one through twelve. In recent years there has been a trend toward inventing twelve gifts appropriate to contemporary Christmas giving (transistor radios, color television sets, and so on). You might want to work up such a list for a special program purpose. Otherwise, stick to the original, which most audiences seem to prefer anyhow.

150
Wanderin'

American Folk Song

Slowly and expressively
C Am E E7
My dad-dy is an en-gi-neer, My broth-er drives a hack; My
legato
Play parenthetic notes after 1st verse only.
A A7 Dm Am G7
sis-ter takes in wash-ing, And the ba-by balls the jack, And it
C C7 Fmaj7 F6 Dm G7(add E) C
looks like I'm nev-er gon-na cease my wan - der - in'.

2. I've been a-wanderin'
Early and late,
New York City
To the Golden Gate,
An' it looks like
I'm never gonna cease my wanderin'.

3. Been a-workin' in the army,
Workin' on a farm,
All I got to show for it
Is the muscle in my arm.
An' it looks like
I'm never gonna cease my wanderin'.

4. Snakes in the ocean,
Eels in the sea,
Red-headed woman
Made a fool out of me.
An' it looks like
I'm never gonna cease my wanderin'.

PROGRAM GUIDE: *American folk song; blues-style philosophy*

The unknown folk composer of this autobiographical, blues-style song was a genius. The powerful lyric tells the very personal story of a tragic, wasted, undirected life and its consequences for the individual himself. He provides no answers, but simply states the facts. And he does so with a simple melodic strain that moves with its subtle harmonies interestingly and inevitably to its powerful concluding strains, and the final, simple resolution of the music. I've tried to emphasize all this in the arrangement of the accompaniment which is designed for unison singing. The first verse, which describes the folk composer's family, uses a "swinger's" phrase, "ballin' the jack," from the era in which the song was written (1930s). The composer is referring to himself, the baby of the family, "ballin' the jack" (i.e. living it up, seeking the "good times," going where the action is), instead of settling down as the rest of the family has. The rest of the song is self-explanatory, with the possible exception of the first two lines of the last verse. These two lines (and the next two) are borrowed from fiddle-dance music calls. I hope you will sing "Wanderin' " slowly, quietly, and expressively, in unison, for a very moving performance.

151

The Water Is Wide

British Folk Song

Moderately

G D7 G D7 C G D7

1. Oh, the wa - ter is wide, I can - not cross o - ver, And nei - ther
2. A ship there is and it sails the sea, It's load - ed

G D7 Cmaj7 D7 G

have I wings to fly. But give me a boat that
deep as deep can be. But not so deep as this

G7 Em G D7 G

will car - ry two, And both shall row, my love and I.
love I am in, I know not how to sink or swim.

3. I put my hand into the bush
To pluck a rose of fairest kind.
The thorns they pierced me at the touch,
And so I left that rose behind.

4. I leaned my back against an oak.
I thought it was a trusty tree.
But first it bended, and then it broke,
As did my false, false lord to me.

5. Oh, love is sweet and love is fair,
Fresh as the dew when first it is new,
But love grows old and waxeth cold,
And fades away like morning dew.

PROGRAM GUIDE: *British folk song (Anglo/American version); romantic*

If you are not familiar with this beautiful, haunting love song, head for the woodshed and bone up on it. At first the rhythms seem peculiar, but with familiarity you realize the rhythm is natural and strong, fitted to the song like a glove. The song has many widely differing versions and is probably based on the old British love song "Waly Waly." But there are so many similar songs around, it is difficult to tell which borrowed from which and what came first. The wisdom and imagery of the poetic lines make the song immortal. If you don't know this song, you owe it to yourself to learn it.

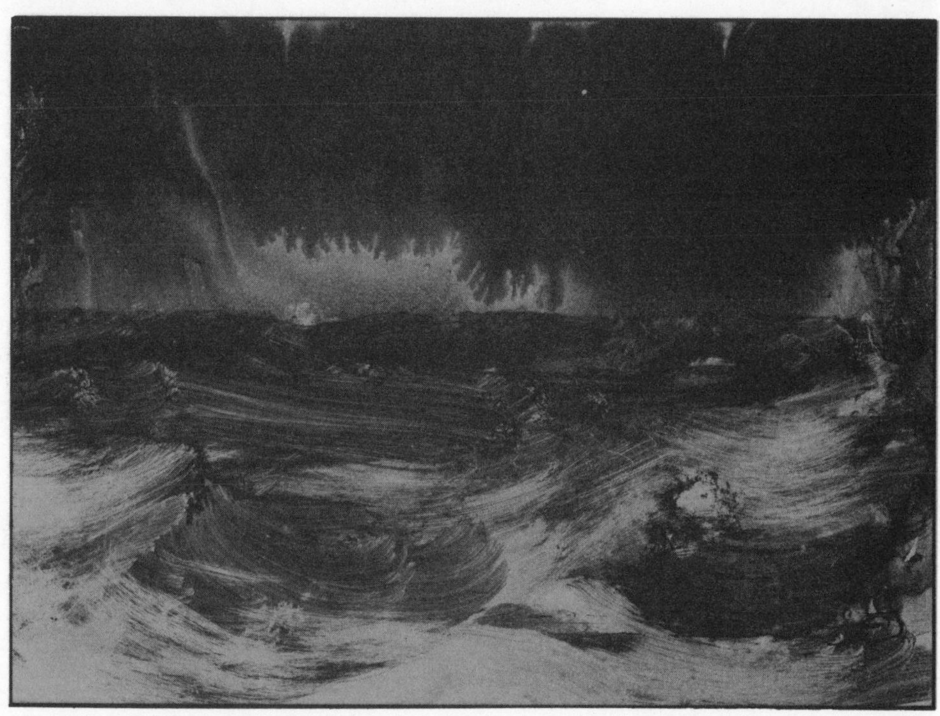

152

We Three Kings of Orient Are

John H. Hopkins, Jr.

John H. Hopkins, Jr.

Moderately
Verse
Em B7 Em
We three kings of O-ri-ent are; Bear-ing gifts we
B7 Em D G
tra-verse a-far, Field and foun-tain, moor and moun-tain,
Chorus
D7 Em B Em D D7 G
Fol-low-ing yon-der star. O star of won-der,

Em C G Em C G Em
star of night, Star with roy - al beau - ty bright, West - ward
D C G D G C G
lead - ing, still pro - ceed - ing, Guide us to thy per - fect light.

Gaspar:

2. Born a King on Bethlehem's plain,
Gold I bring to crown him again,
King forever, ceasing never
Over us all to reign. (*Chorus*)

Melchior:

3. Frankincense to offer have I,
Incense owns a Deity nigh;
Prayer and praising, all men raising,
Worship Him, God on high. (*Chorus*)

Balthasar:

4. Myrrh is mine: its bitter perfume
Breathes a life of gathering gloom:
Sorrowing, sighing, bleeding, dying,
Sealed in the stone-cold tomb. (*Chorus*)

5. Glorious now behold him arise,
King and God and sacrifice;
Alleluia, Alleluia!
Earth to the heavens replies. (*Chorus*)

PROGRAM GUIDE: *Traditional American hymn; Christmas*

The fine poetic quality of the words and the interesting mixture of major and minor modes in a folk-style melody have caused many authorities to hail this Christmas hymn as the very best one to come from America. The words and music were written by Dr. John H. Hopkins in 1857, when he served as rector of Christ Church in Williamsport, Pennsylvania. Technically "Kings" is not a Christmas hymn, but an Epiphany hymn, Epiphany being the Christian festival, observed on January 6, commemorating the manifestation of Christ to the gentiles in the persons of the Magi. You might add a little dramatic touch by assigning individuals or specific groups to sing the roles of the three Magi in verses 2, 3, and 4 as indicated. Everyone sings the first and last verses and the choruses.

153

We Wish You a Merry Christmas

Traditional English Carol

Brightly
(Melody in upper notes)
G C A7 D7
We wish you a mer-ry Christ-mas, We wish you a mer-ry Christ-mas, We
B Em G C Am D7 G
Fine
wish you a mer-ry Christ-mas And a hap - py New Year!
Fine
Refrain
G D7 A7 D7
Good tid - ings to you, Wher - ev - er you are; Good

G
C
Am
D7
G
D.C.
tid - ings for Christ-mas And a hap - py New Year! (We)
D.C.

2. Oh, bring us some figgy pudding,
Oh, bring us some figgy pudding,
Oh, bring us some figgy pudding,
With a cup of good cheer.

Continue, as above:

3. We won't go until we get it, (*3 times*)
So bring it out here.

4. We all love our figgy pudding (*3 times*)
With a cup of good cheer.

5. We wish you a merry Christmas (*3 times*)
And a happy New Year.

PROGRAM GUIDE: *Traditional English Christmas carol*

The observance of Christmas dates back to about A.D. 220, and it became the great popular festival of Western Europe during the Middle Ages. The singing of carols at Christmastime is a typically English custom. But the carol is not exclusively a Christmas song, nor is it in any way related to the hymn.

The *carole* was a French round-dance which was accompanied by leader-chorus singing in the same manner as other familiar folk music presented in this book. It was most closely associated with the festive celebrations occasioned by the incidence of holy days. Despite the religious impulse and theme of the *caroles,* they were essentially a carry-over of pagan practices and were associated with immorality in general.

From its origin in France, carol singing spread throughout all of Europe during the fifteenth century. The church opposed the practice for a long time. The carols spoke in the common language of the people, whereas the hymns of the church were austere and written in a foreign tongue. Ultimately, the carol—without dancing—worked its way into the good graces of the church, and soon carols were being written, both inside and outside the church, for ceremonial occasions.

The sixteenth century brought the Reformation, and the carol was swept out of the sanctuary along with everything else that smacked of "idolatry and superstition." It was then that the practice of singing carols on festive occasions from house to house in minstrel bands grew and flourished. "We Wish You a Merry Christmas" is probably more closely associated with this custom (particularly because of its text) than any other carol we sing at Christmas.

A very simple, easily learned harmonization is indicated by the small lower notes in the first eight measures. Since the harmony can be taught as an easy countermelody, your group might enjoy finding out what hidden talents they have.

154

What Child Is This?

William Chatterton Dix
Traditional, English
Arr. by John Stainer
Moderately
Em G D Em Am B
1. What Child is this, Who, laid to rest_On Ma-ry's lap,_ is sleep - ing? Whom
2. Why lies he in_ such mean es-tate,_Where ox and ass_ are feed - ing? Good
Em G D Em B7 Em
an - gels greet with an-thems sweet, While shep - herds watch_ are keep - ing?
Chris-tian fear: for sin-ners here_ The si - lent Word_ is plead - ing.
Bm G * D Em Am B
This, this_ is Christ the King, Whom shep-herds guard_ and an - gels sing:
Nails, spear, shall pierce him thru,_ The Cross be borne,_ for me, for you:
*

*See program guide

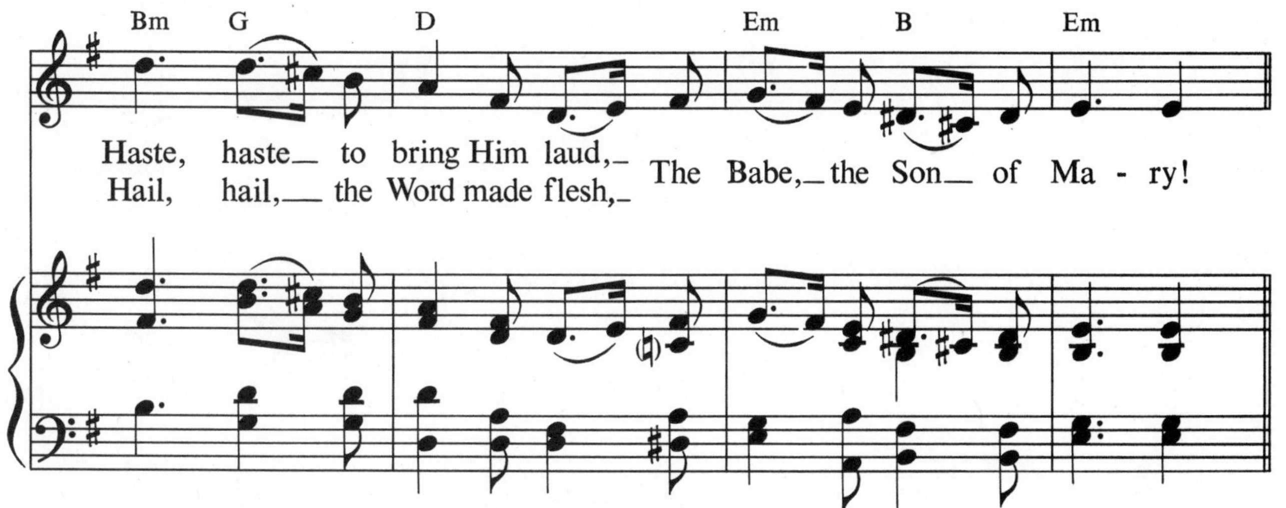
Bm
G
D
Em
B
Em
Haste, haste to bring Him laud, The Babe, the Son of Ma - ry!
Hail, hail, the Word made flesh,

3. So bring him incense, gold, and myrrh,
   Come, peasant, king, to own him;
The King of kings salvation brings,
   Let loving hearts enthrone him.
Raise, raise the song on high,
   The virgin sings her lullaby:
Joy, joy for Christ is born,
   The babe, the son of Mary!

PROGRAM GUIDE: *Traditional British Christmas carol*

The text for "What Child Is This?" was written by William Chatterton Dix (1837-1898), the manager of a marine insurance company in Glasgow. He had a talent for writing devotional poetry, of which he published several volumes. He contributed texts for many hymns and wrote *The Life of Chatterton the Poet.* These particular stanzas were taken from Dix's poem "The Manger Throne." The melody is the familiar Greensleeves (see number 46) tune, harmonized and arranged by Sir John Stainer (1840-1901), a distinguished composer and organist in England. Stainer was organist at St. Paul's and at Oxford. Many of his arrangements of carols are the standard arrangements still in use today. (I took the liberty, however, of sharping the C's in the ninth and thirteenth measures for the passing tone within the G major chord. This reflects my preference. If you prefer the minor sound of the c natural, change it back.)

155
When Johnny Comes Marching Home

Patrick S. Gilmore *Traditional, Irish*

Brightly
Gm Cm7 Gm B♭ Dm
When John-ny comes march-ing home a-gain, Hur - rah, hur - rah! We'll
Gm Cm7 Gm B♭ D7
give him a heart - y wel - come then, Hur - rah, hur - rah! The
Gm D7 Gm D7
men will cheer, the boys will shout, The la - dies they will all turn out, And we'll

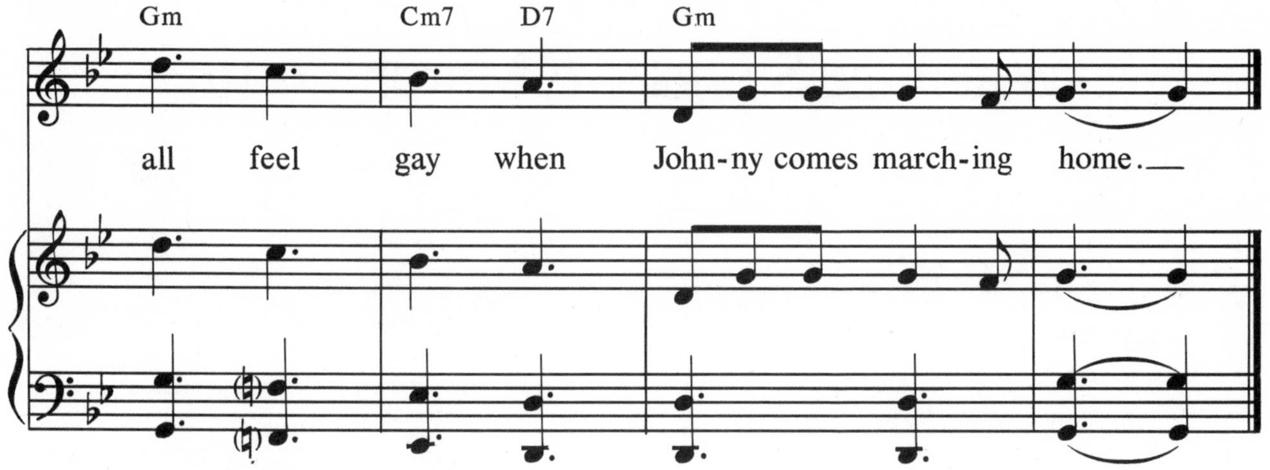
Gm
Cm7
D7
Gm
all feel gay when John-ny comes march-ing home.

2. The old church bell will peal with joy,
   Hurrah, hurrah!
   To welcome home our darling boy,
   Hurrah, hurrah!
   The village lads and lassies say,
   With roses they will strew the way,
   And we'll all feel gay when Johnny comes marching home.

3. Get ready for the Jubilee,
   Hurrah, hurrah!
   We'll give the hero three times three,
   Hurrah, hurrah!
   The laurel wreath is ready now
   To place upon his loyal brow,
   And we'll all feel gay when Johnny comes marching home.

4. Let love and friendship on that day,
   Hurrah, hurrah!
   Their choicest treasures then display,
   Hurrah, hurrah!
   And let each one perform some part,
   To fill with joy the warrior's heart,
   And we'll all feel gay when Johnny comes marching home.

PROGRAM GUIDE: *Traditional American patriotic song*

"When Johnny Comes Marching Home" was probably the most popular song to come out of the Civil War (which produced several great songs). The words were written by Patrick S. Gilmore (using the pseudonym Louis Lambert), and set to an old tune, possibly of Irish origin. Gilmore was the bandmaster attached to General Butler's command in New Orleans during the war. The martial mood of this "Johnny" contrasts sharply with the funeral-procession mood of "Johnny, I Hardly Knew You" (see number 70). Use a march tempo with two strong beats to the measure. And sing out!

156
When the Saints Go Marching In

American Negro Spiritual

Moderately fast

Lead Voices

C

Oh, when the saints ___ go march-ing in, ___

Harmony Voices

Oh, when the saints go march-ing

R.H.

L. H.

___ Oh, when the saints go march - ing in. ___

G7

in. saints go march - ing, go march-ing

C
C7
F
Lord, how I want to be in that num - ber,
in.
Oh, let me be in that num-ber, pre-cious
C
G7
C
When the saints go march - ing in.
num-ber, when the saints go march - ing, go march-ing in.

2. And when the revelation comes,
And when the revelation comes,
Lord, how I want to be in that number,
When the revelation comes.

Continue, as above:

3. And when the new world is revealed.
4. Oh, when they gather 'round the throne.
5. And when they crown him King of kings.
6. And when the sun no more will shine.
7. And when the moon has turned to blood.
8. And on that hallelujah day.
9. And when the earth has turned to fire.
10. Oh, when the saints go marching in.

PROGRAM GUIDE: *American Negro spiritual*

"The Saints," perhaps as much as any song of Negro origin, represents the transition from the spiritual to jazz. It was a favorite of Dixieland groups and remains popular with jazz musicians, whether cool or hot. It's a staple item for audience participation in singing, whether you simply repeat the first verse over and over again or run through all the verses. I've set you up for the kind of informal singing that goes on with a Dixie band or gospel group. The lead (melody) is the top line of the vocal score. Two syncopated harmony parts (very easy to learn) are in the second line. Find out who your harmony enthusiasts are, assign them to the second line, give everybody a brief rehearsal, and then have some fun with the saints. If you want to play it straight, and miss all the fun, just sing the top line.

157
White Coral Bells

Traditional Round

Moderately
1
White cor - al bells up - on a slen-der stalk,
2
Lil - ies of the val - ley deck my gar - den walk.
3
Oh, don't you wish that you could hear them ring?
4
That will on - ly hap-pen when the fair - ies sing.

Divide the group into four sections. Each section sings the entire round the agreed-upon number of times, beginning at point 1 when the preceding section reaches point 2. Thus the round begins and ends with one section singing alone: Section 1 at the beginning and Section 4 at the end.

PROGRAM GUIDE: *Traditional round*

I don't know where this round came from, but I suspect it's an English or American product. It's really a two-part round disguised as a four-part round. The tune in the last half is the same as the tune in the first half, but the words are different. It has one of the prettier round tunes around and makes a nice sound with young voices.

158
Why Shouldn't My Goose?

Traditional English Round

Brightly
1
2
Why should-n't my goose Sing as well as thy goose,
3
4
When I paid for my goose Twice as much as thine?

Divide the group into four sections. Each section sings the entire round the agreed-upon number of times, beginning at point 1 when the preceding section reaches point 2. Thus the round begins and ends with one section singing alone: Section 1 at the beginning and Section 4 at the end.

PROGRAM GUIDE: *Traditional English round*

It's silly, but fun, and very easy to sing. It makes a good warm-up round when you have bigger things in mind for part singing. As a four-part round, everything happens in a hurry, so be prepared.

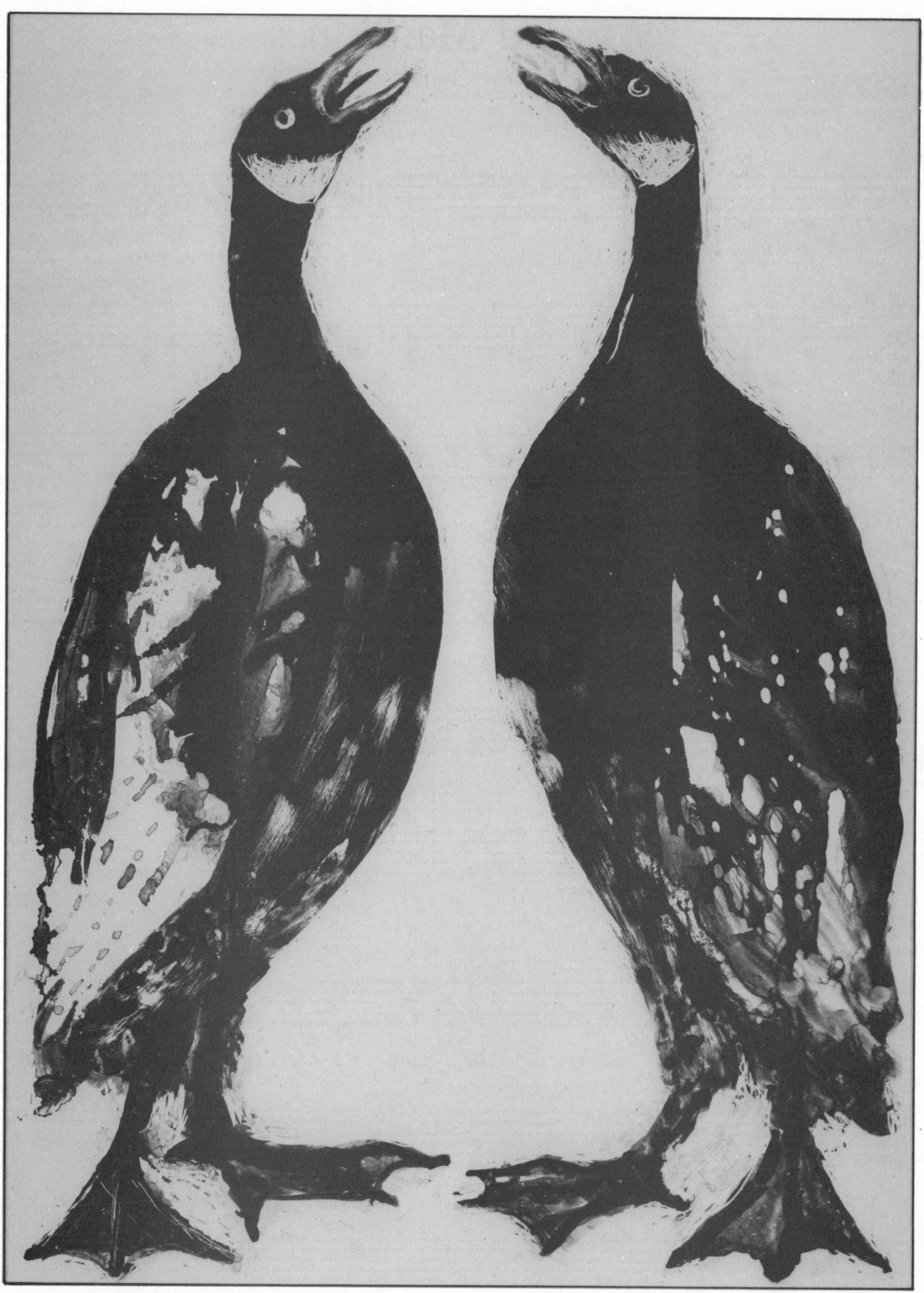

159
Worried Man Blues

American Folk Song

Moderately fast
G
G7
It takes a wor-ried man to sing a wor-ried song, It
C
G
takes a wor-ried man to sing a wor-ried song. It
B7
Em
takes a wor-ried man to sing a wor-ried song, I'm wor-ried

(Melody in lower notes)
D7
G
now,
But I won't be wor-ried long.
(omit after last time)

2. I went across the river and I lay down to sleep,
I went across the river and I lay down to sleep,
I went across the river and I lay down to sleep,
And I woke up with shackles on my feet.

Continue, as above:

3. Twenty-one links of chain wrapped around my leg,
And on each link, an initial of my name.

4. I asked the judge what might be my fine,
Twenty-one years on the R.C. Mountain Line.

5. Twenty-one long years to pay my awful crime,
Twenty-one years—but I got ninety-nine.

6. When the train arrived, it was sixteen coaches long,
The girl I love is on that train and gone.

7. I looked down the track as far as I could see,
Little bitty hand was waving after me.

8. If anyone should ask you who composed this song,
Tell them it was I, and I sing it all day long.

PROGRAM GUIDE: *American folk song*

When hillbilly singers came into contact with Negro blues styles, songs like this one began to emerge. The song probably did originate with Negro singers. But once the famous Carter Family of singers got hold of it, the country music fans made it one of their own. Later on, the folk revivalists picked it up, and now it's a favorite of informal singers everywhere. There's an extra measure thrown in near the end to accommodate that sustained tone (with "now" in the first verse). It shouldn't bother you, particularly when you've been warned in advance. Many singers like to repeat the first verse a time or two as a chorus.

160

Zum Gali Gali

Moderately
Melody
Israeli Folk Song
Fm
Ab
1. He-cha-lutz le - 'man a - vo - dah;
Ostinato
Zum ga - li, ga - li, ga - li, zum ga - li ga - li,
Fm
Ab
A - vo - dah le - 'man he - cha - lutz.
Zum ga - li ga - li, ga - li, zum ga - li ga - li,
Coda (after verse 4)
Fm
Ab
Fm Ab
Fm
Zum ga-li ga-li, ga-li, zum ga-li ga - li, zum.
Zum ga-li ga-li, ga-li, zum ga-li ga - li, zum.

2. A-vo-dah le'man he-cha-lutz;
He-cha-lutz le'man a-vo-dah.

3. He-cha-lutz le'man ha-b'tulah;
Ha-b'tulah le'man he-cha-lutz.

4. Ha-shalom le'man ha'-amin;
Ha'-amin le'man ha-shalom.

PROGRAM GUIDE: *Israeli folk song*

This exciting linguistic exercise is brought to you by the same folk who produced "Hallelujah" (see number 48). The message is: "For the Israeli pioneer, work is purpose, purpose is work. He works for the girl he loves, and wishes peace for all nations." Pronounce *ch* as *k, o* as *oh, a* as *ah, u* as *oo, i* as *ee, e* as in *he*. Divide your group and assign the melody to the stronger group and the *ostinato* (a phrase or motive that is repeated persistently throughout the music) to the weaker group —it's easier. Everybody sings the *ostinato* on the coda. If you make it with this one, go on to "Hallelujah," another great, moving Israeli song.

Program Guide Index

Because the songs appear alphabetically there is no alphabetical index; the book itself serves as one. This index is provided as an aid to song leaders for planning programs. Although I have tried to anticipate most of your needs for quick and ready reference, the categories are not exhaustive or definitive. Browsing remains the popular way to plan a program. This index, however, should help you when you have a specific need and are in a hurry. (References are to the song numbers—not page numbers.)

GUITAR CHORDS

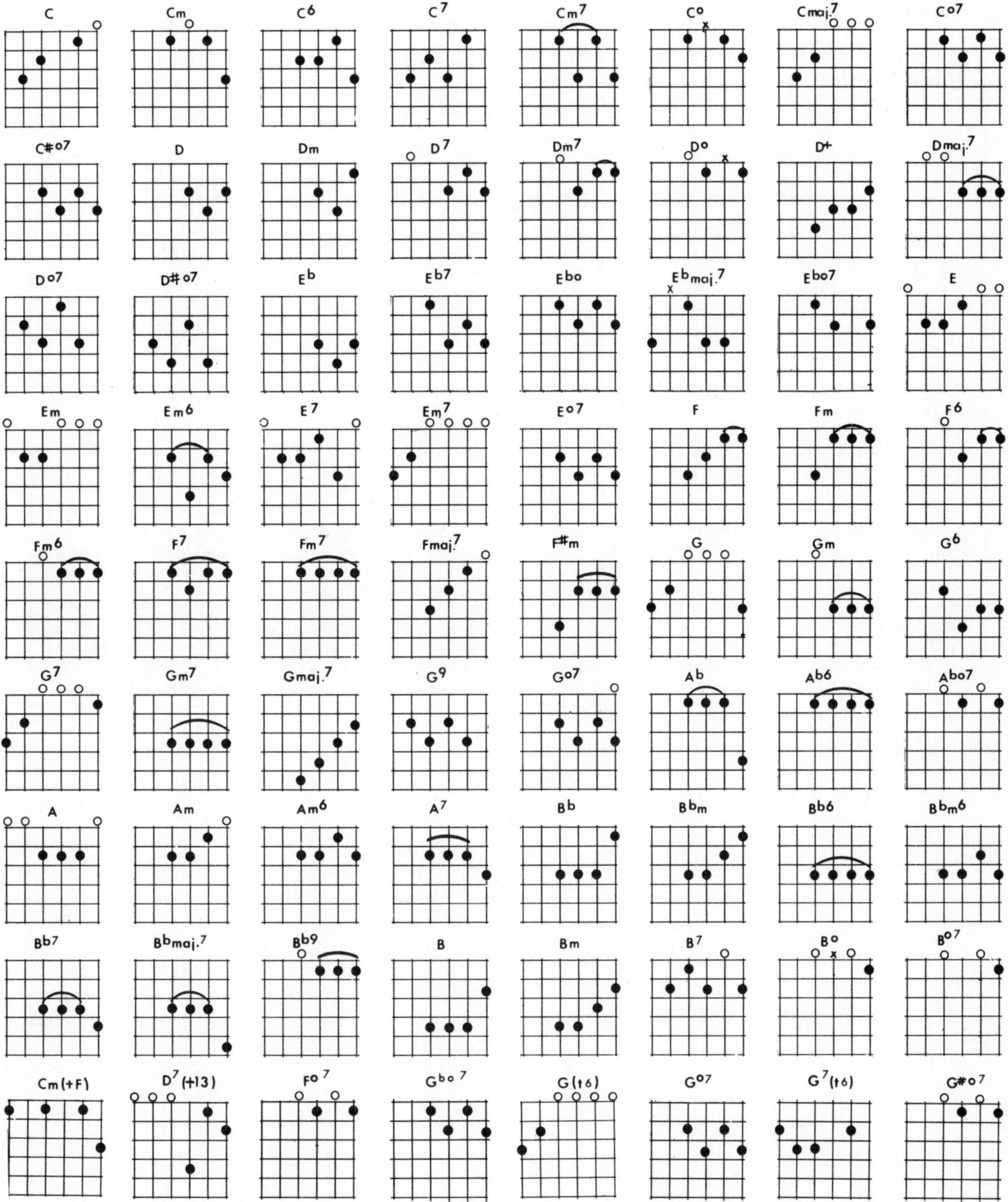
C
Cm
C6
C7
Cm7
C°
Cmaj.7
C°7
C#°7
D
Dm
D7
Dm7
D°
D+
Dmaj.7
D°7
D#°7
Eb
Eb7
Eb°
Ebmaj.7
Eb°7
E
Em
Em6
E7
Em7
E°7
F
Fm
F6
Fm6
F7
Fm7
Fmaj.7
F#m
G
Gm
G6
G7
Gm7
Gmaj.7
G9
G°7
Ab
Ab6
Ab°7
A
Am
Am6
A7
Bb
Bbm
Bb6
Bbm6
Bb7
Bbmaj.7
Bb9
B
Bm
B7
B°
B°7
Cm(+F)
D7(+13)
F°7
Gb°7
G(+6)
G°7
G7(+6)
G#°7

CHORD TRANSPOSITION CHART

Key Names	Key Signatures	CHORD NAMES							
		Tonic I	Super-tonic II	Mediant III	Subdominant IV	Dominant V	Submediant VI	Leading Tone VII	Octave VIII-I
C	No sharps or flats	C	D	E	F	G	A	B	C
G	One sharp	G	A	B	C	D	E	F#	G
D	Two sharps	D	E	F#	G	A	B	C#	D
A	Three sharps	A	B	C#	D	E	F#	G#	A
E	Four sharps	E	F#	G#	A	B	C#	D#	E
F	One flat	F	G	A	Bb	C	D	E	F
Bb	Two flats	Bb	C	D	Eb	F	G	A	Bb
Eb	Three flats	Eb	F	G	Ab	Bb	C	D	Eb
Ab	Four flats	Ab	Bb	C	Db	Eb	F	G	Ab
Db	Five flats	Db	Eb	F	Gb	Ab	Bb	C	Db

If; for example, you would prefer to play the first song in this book ("Ain't It a Shame?") in the key of G (one sharp) instead of the key of F (one flat) in which it is written, you may locate the appropriate chords for the key of G above the chords shown for the key of F on the chart.

If a 7th, 6th, minor, augmented, or diminished is added to the chord you are transposing from, it is also added to the chord you are transposing to. For example, see the second song in this book ("All God's Children Got Shoes"). If you transpose from the key of G (in which it is written) to the key of F, the first chord is changed from G to F, the next chord is changed from G7 to F7, the next chord is changed from C to Bb, the next chord is changed from G to F, and the next one from D7 to C7, and so on. Try transposing the chords of the third song in the book ("Alouette") from the key of G to the key of F before consulting this solution: G becomes F; D7 becomes C7, C becomes Bb.